This book offers a novel account of key features of modern representative democracy. Working from the rational actor tradition, it builts a middle ground between orthodox political theory and the economic analysis of politics. Standard economic models of politics emphasise the design of the institutional devices of democracy as operated by essentially self-interested individuals. This book departs from that model by focusing on democratic desires alongside democratic devices, stressing that important aspects of democracy depend on the motivation of democrats and the interplay between devices and desires. Individuals are taken to be not only rational, but also somewhat moral. The authors argue that this approach provides access to aspects of the debate on democratic institutions that are beyond the narrowly economic model. They apply their analysis to voting, elections, representation, political parties and the separation and division of powers, providing a wide-ranging discussion of the design of democratic institutions.

Geoffrey Brennan is a Research Professor in the Research School of the Social Sciences at the Australian National University, where he was Director between 1991 and 1996. He is author of *The Power to Tax* (with James Buchanan, 1980), *The Reason of Rules* (with James Buchanan, 1985) and *Democracy and Decision* (with Loren Lomasky, 1993).

Alan Hamlin is Professor of Economics at the University of Southampton. He is the author of *Ethics, Economics and the State* (1986), Editor of *Ethics and Economics (1996)*, and co-editor of *The Good Polity* (with Philip Pettit, 1989) and of *Market Capitalism and Moral Values* (with Sam Brittan, 1995).

Series Editor
Robert E. Goodin
Research School of Social Sciences
Australian National University

Advisory Editors
Brian Barry, Russell Hardin, Carole Pateman, Barry Weingast,
Stephen Elkin, Claus Offe, Susan Rose-Ackerman

Social scientists have rediscovered institutions. They have been increasingly concerned with the myriad ways in which social and political institutions shape the patterns of individual interactions which produce social phenomena. They are equally concerned with the ways in which those institutions emerge from such interactions.

This series is devoted to the exploration of the more normative aspects of these issues. What makes one set of institutions better than another? How, if at all, might we move from the less desirable set of institutions to a more desirable set? Alongside the questions of what institutions we would design, if we were designing them afresh, are pragmatic questions of how we can best get from here to there: from our present institutions to new revitalised ones.

Theories of institutional design is insistently multidisciplinary and interdisciplinary, both in the institutions on which it focuses, and in the methodologies used to study them. There are interesting sociological questions to be asked about legal institutions, interesting legal questions to be asked about economic institutions, and interesting social, economic and legal questions to be asked about political institutions. By juxtaposing these approaches in print, this series aims to enrich normative discourse surrounding important issues of designing and redesigning, shaping and reshaping the social, political and economic institutions of contemporary society.

Other books in this series
Brent Fisse and John Braithwaite, *Corporations, Crime, and Accountability*
Robert E. Goodin (ed.), *The Theory of Institutional Design*
Itai Sened, *The Political Institution of Private Property*
Bo Rothstein, *Just Institutions Matter: The Moral and Political Logic of the Universal Welfare State*
Jon Elster, Claus Offe and Ulrich Preuss, *Institutional Design in Post-Communist Societies: Rebuilding the Ship at Sea*
Mark Bovens, *The Quest for Responsibility: Accountability and Citizenship in Complex Organisations*
Adrienne Héritier, *Policy-Making and Diversity in Europe: Escape from Deadlock*

Democratic Devices and Desires

GEOFFREY BRENNAN

and

ALAN HAMLIN

CAMBRIDGE
UNIVERSITY PRESS

PUBLISHED BY THE PRESS SYNDICATE OF THE UNIVERSITY OF CAMBRIDGE
The Pitt Building, Trumpington Street, Cambridge, United Kingdom

CAMBRIDGE UNIVERSITY PRESS
The Edinburgh Building, Cambridge, CB2 2RU, UK   www.cup.cam.ac.uk
40 West 20th Street, New York, NY 10011–4211, USA   www.cup.org
10 Stamford Road, Oakleigh, Melbourne 3166, Australia
Ruiz de Alarcón 13, 28014 Madrid, Spain

© Geoffrey Brennan and Alan Hamlin 2000

First published 2000

Printed in the United Kingdom at the University Press, Cambridge

Typeset in Minion 10.5/12pt   [CE]

A catalogue record for this book is available from the British Library

Library of Congress Cataloguing in Publication Data

Brennan, Geoffrey, 1944–
Democratic devices and desires / by Geoffrey Brennan and Alan Hamlin.
     p.   cm. – (Theories of institutional design)
Includes bibliographical references (p.   ).
ISBN 0 521 63020 7 (hb). – ISBN 0 521 63977 8 (pb)
1. Democracy – Economic aspects.
2. Political science – Economic aspects.
I. Hamlin, Alan P., 1951–. II. Title. III. Series.
JC423.B783   2000
321.8 – dc21   99–36185   CIP

ISBN 0 521 63020 7 hardback
ISBN 0 521 63977 8 paperback

This book is dedicated to Margaret and Jan,
and Robyn, Philip and Beth

Contents

Figures

Preface and acknowledgements

This book has its origins in a number of joint papers written over an extensive period. The first of the relevant papers to appear was published in 1992, and since then there have been around eight further papers, all connected in one way or another to the questions of institutional design with which this book is also concerned. Traces of this earlier work can be found in various places in the text that follows, but the current book is much more than a refiguring of the earlier papers. Indeed, it is much *less* a refiguring than we had originally imagined it would be. Books often have a way of taking on a life of their own and this was certainly so in the present case. As we indicate in the initial chapter, the basic intention of the book changed shape as the enterprise developed. The intellectual scheme laid out originally in the paper 'Economising on virtue' (*Constitutional Political Economy*, 1995) took on a larger and larger place in our thinking and rendered much of our earlier treatment of topics like the separation of powers (*Journal of Theoretical Politics*, 1994) and bicameralism (*Public Choice*, 1992) seriously incomplete. Thus, what was to have been a book on 'devices' became much more a book on 'desires' and on the connection between devices and desires.

Accordingly, much of the book is entirely new material. Some chapters are reasonably close to the articles to which they most closely correspond – most notably, chapters 8 and 9 are clearly based on the 1998 paper in *Public Choice* and the 1999 paper in the *British Journal of Political Science* respectively. Otherwise, however, with due acknowledgement of Miss Manners's sensible dictum that anything worth publishing is worth publishing twice, this book represents substantially new work.

The enterprise in its current form was started in earnest in early 1997 when Brennan began a six-month Visiting Fellowship at All Souls College, Oxford followed by a spell as Visiting Professor in the Public Choice Center at George Mason University. Brennan expresses gratitude to both institutions for their support and more particularly for providing a congenial means to reconnect to full-time scholarship after a reasonably extended brush with the rigours of academic administration. Some of the ideas which shaped the earlier papers and which reappear in this book in modified form were originally formulated while Hamlin was a Visiting Fellow in the Research School of Social Sciences at ANU, and with the support of his ESRC Research Grant R000233782 in 1993–4. Over the period in which this book was written, Hamlin enjoyed the support of a Nuffield Foundation Social Science Fellowship, and the hospitality of Public Choice Center at George Mason University. All of this assistance is gratefully acknowledged. Our primary gratitude, however, must go to our own institutions; the Australian National University (and the Research School of Social Sciences in its Institute of Advanced Studies, more specifically) and the University of Southampton respectively. Both these institutions provide encouragement and support for scholarly activity in an age in which such encouragement and support can no longer be presumed.

In a collaboration as long-standing as this one, academics are bound to accumulate many more personal obligations. On the academic side, a very considerable number of individuals, seminar audiences, editors and referees have contributed their support, criticism and interest and it would be invidious to name only a few. But most notable among our obligations are those that are close to home – to Margaret and Jan, and Robyn and Philip and Beth – who not only had to tolerate the usual distracted husband/father, but also often enough the source of the distraction. There have been many occasions on which Alan and Geoff have spent time in one another's houses monopolising each other's attentions and sweeping aside rival, family claims. This book, such as it is, is the fruit of the families' generosity and understanding. Hence the dedication.

1

Introduction

This book is an exercise in rational actor political theory or 'public choice' theory. (We shall use the two terms without discriminating.) However, the discussion is unusual in two respects.[1] First, it focuses attention on a range of institutional *devices* that, although common enough in democratic practice and in constitutional analysis in other traditions, have been somewhat under-analysed within the rational actor tradition. Second, it adopts a more moralised conception of agent *desires* than rational actor analysis normally assumes. In this initial chapter, we want to say something about what the devices in question are, and speculate as to why they have been relatively ignored within the rational actor tradition. We shall then briefly discuss our picture of desires and agent motivation, and indicate how that picture differs from the standard, more determinedly egoistic one. Because devices and desires are not independent, we also want to direct attention to some aspects of their interconnectedness. Finally, we will offer some guidance to the reader on the organisation and structure of the remainder of the book.

But before any of this, a preliminary comment on our title, and on our use of 'devices' and 'desires' is in order. In the daily office of the Anglican Book of Common Prayer, 1662, the general confession states: 'We have followed too much the devices and desires of our own hearts; we have

---

[1] We offer no real attempt at defining the 'usual' approach to public choice or rational actor political theory, but we have in mind the literature that would recognise Arrow (1963), Black (1958), Buchanan and Tullock (1962) and Downs (1957) amongst its list of modern classics. Mueller (1989) provides a standard text. Brennan and Buchanan (1985) provide a clear statement of the constitutional aspect of the approach.

offended against thy holy laws ...'. In that context, 'devices and desires' are conceived as inventions of 'our own hearts' which we, miserable sinners that we are, have 'followed too much'. Those particular devices and desires are things for which repentance is properly due and absolution rightly sought.

Perhaps there is much in this book for which repentance is appropriate. But the devices and desires of our title are not chosen for their penitential overtones. Nor do we wish to direct attention to an evil or corrupting aspect of democracy. Rather, the terms come to mind because they combine descriptiveness of our purpose with a certain euphony. We use the distinction between devices and desires to mark a rough division between the external and internal aspects of politics. Devices are seen as external political and constitutional artefacts operating across individuals and characterising the institutional and legal framework of society. Desires are seen as internal and more personal matters, formative of individual character; they are the basic motivational triggers that provide a starting point for any explanation of intentional behaviour. But we should emphasise that the distinction between an internal world of desires and an external world of devices is only a rough and ready point of departure. One of the objects of our discussion is to explore the possible interactions between these worlds.

Democratic devices

Traditional political theory – from Aristotle to Locke, from Hobbes to Hume and up to the present day – has focused on democratic institutions, to the extent that it was concerned with them at all, in the context of the question 'how can politics be made to work better?' Public choice theory has, by contrast, been primarily focused on the question 'what should government do?' The former question suggests as its implicit point of comparison a range of alternative ways in which political life might be organised, each with its own distinctive operating characteristics. The latter question takes as its starting point a comparison of political processes with non-political or market processes – a comparison of explicitly collective decision-making procedures with the decentralised, individualistic processes characteristic of market arrangements. It should be clear that these questions and the points of comparison with which they are associated are very different. These differences are part of what distinguishes public choice theory from traditional political theory. Yet some of the differences are arbitrary and entirely historically contingent. In particular, the reason why the comparison of market and political processes came to predominate in the formative years of modern public choice theory is largely a matter of historical accident. And though the relevant history is fairly familiar, at least to public choice theorists, it may bear brief repetition here.

When the economic theory of the state came to be written, it was against the background of standard propositions in welfare economics about the 'success' of markets, derived variously from Adam Smith and David Ricardo and elaborated throughout the ensuing literature. Accordingly, when Paul Samuelson attempted to lay out a systematic account of the role of the state in economic activity in his influential series of papers on 'public goods',[2] his point of departure was to raise the question of what considerations the student of the public economy can set against the well-established economic tradition of *laissez-faire*. The obvious answer was a systematic treatment of market 'failure'. And it was just such a systematic treatment that Samuelson's theory of public goods sought to provide. Armed with the resultant array of market failure theorems, enthusiastic public economists began to discover instances of market failure everywhere and develop an accordingly extensive agenda for the 'properly theorised' state.[3] It was precisely in reaction to this enthusiasm that public choice theory first appeared.[4] The central element in the public choice project, as it was then conceived, was to challenge what public choice scholars saw as a misplaced onus of proof. Market failure could, so the public choice school insisted, only ever constitute a *necessary* condition for government action – not a *sufficient* condition. One would have to supplement charges of market failure with demonstration of relative political success before a coherent case for government action to correct market failure could properly be made. More generally, any satisfactory answer to the question of what government should do would require an analysis of political failure/success on an equal footing with the analysis of market failure/success; and any such analysis would require a treatment of political processes that adopted the same methods and techniques, and the same assumptions about agent motivation, as the economists' theory of markets. Furthermore, evaluation of political and market performance would have to appeal to the same normative criteria. Otherwise, as the public choice theorists of the time insisted, there was simply too much scope for *ad hoc* stipulation and ideological bias.

In other words, what was needed, as public choice theory saw it, was a model of political process that captured the central features of

---

[2] See Samuelson (1954), (1955) and (1958).
[3] Stiglitz (1989) provides a clear overview and discussion of this approach to the state.
[4] See for example, Buchanan (1954, 1964).

contemporary democracy – majority rule, electoral competition and so on – and that could be used to generate predicted equilibrium outcomes which could in turn be directly compared with competitive market analogues. For this purpose, analysts pretty much took as given the political institutions they saw around them, and exploited the most obvious analogies with familiar economic phenomena. The comparative analysis of alternative specifications of democratic political process was, in this setting, a much lower priority than the comparison of political and market equilibria.

It is hardly surprising, therefore, that public choice analysis immediately took on a rather (US) American cast. That is to say, it tended to take as given institutional arrangements that reflected American democratic experience. Since these early days, a wider range of institutional forms has gradually been added to the standard array, as public choice scholarship has become an increasingly significant presence in Europe (mainly over the last few decades). But American scholarship provided the initial impulse, and remains the predominant force and influence within rational actor political theory; subsequent work has inevitably been coloured by that fact. Moreover, there are many features that most Western political systems happen to share. These systems involve representative rather than direct democracy (Switzerland is an important partial exception); they are all dominated by relatively small numbers of political parties; most have bicameral structures of one kind or another; and all exhibit some form of a 'separation of powers'. In this sense, the implicit US orientation has mattered much less than it otherwise might have. But one effect is that these common features – representation; bicameralism; strong parties; separation of powers, etc. – have largely been taken for granted. Certainly, the rational actor tradition has accorded them rather less in the way of detailed analytic scrutiny than one might have thought appropriate.

Against this background, one major objective of this book is to pose what we see as the traditional political theory question – how can politics be made to work better? – in the context of the rational actor theory approach (somewhat modified along lines that we shall shortly describe). That is, we shall set on one side the admittedly important question of the domain of public activity: we shall simply take it as given that the government has scope to act in the policy arena across a specified range. On this basis, we shall examine a set of institutional devices – representation, political parties, bicameralism, the separation of powers – which, it seems to us, deserves more critical attention within the rational actor tradition. To some extent, our thoughts on these devices are coloured by the institutional arrangements with which we ourselves are most familiar

– those associated with the (quasi) Westminster systems of Britain and Australia, with their quite tightly disciplined two-party systems and with their interpretation of the separation of powers doctrine which focuses on the judiciary/parliamentary divide rather than the legislative/executive one. We should make it clear that we have not set out specifically to provide a rational actor analysis of Westminster institutions; nor do we think that that is what we have delivered. But the institutional array we have chosen to study accommodates more of that tradition in political practice than is probably typical in public choice circles.

We should also make it clear that, although the 'domain question' (What should government do?) has been the predominant focus in public choice scholarship, it has not been an exclusive one. Buchanan and Tullock's 1962 classic *The Calculus of Consent*, for example, is explicitly directed at the issue of the appropriate decision-rule for collective action – whether simple majority rule or some more inclusive decision requirement. Although Buchanan and Tullock note the implications of their discussion for the question of how extensive the role of collective decision making should be, this question is a secondary and derivative one. Similarly, Buchanan's most recent book, with Congleton, on 'the generality principle'[5] is addressed to the question of how politics might be made to 'work better' in contexts where the use of more inclusive decision-rules is infeasible. The particular mechanism that Buchanan and Congleton look to is expanded use of a 'generality requirement'. Equally, the 'structure-induced equilibrium' literature[6] is addressed to such questions as how the US committee system might serve to suppress global cycling and impose political stability in settings where global cycling would otherwise be a problem. Finally, we might mention Mueller's recent volume,[7] which shares our general concern with the analysis of a range of constitutional devices, although it offers rather different analysis.

In what follows, we have not sought to discuss at any length the specific decision-rule for collective decisions – nor, with one or two minor exceptions, do we enter the debate on electoral reform. This is in part because these areas have received very considerable attention from public choice theorists following Buchanan and Tullock's lead, and from social choice theorists following Arrow's lead, as well as from scholars using a wide range of other styles of analysis.[8] Accordingly in what follows, we assume simple majority voting – without any external legal

[5] Buchanan and Congleton (1998).
[6] For example, Shepsle and Weingast (1981).
[7] Mueller (1996).
[8] For an introduction see, for example, the papers collected in the Winter 1995 issue of the *Journal of Economic Perspectives*, or Dummett (1997).

constraints beyond those we shall from time to time specify. The same general grounds for exclusion apply to the issue of specifically federal structures of governance. Federalism has been extensively examined in the public economics literature (though not always with an adequate appreciation of the public choice nuances), and it seemed to us better to address constitutional devices that had been less extensively treated. Moreover, even those institutional arrangements that we do address have been subject to some discussion in the recent rational actor literature, a discussion which we cite in the relevant chapters. We do not, nevertheless, resile from our claims that the predominant focus in public choice scholarship has been on the domain issue, and that the democratic devices we examine in this book have so far received rather less attention than they deserve.

When this book was first conceived we intended that the rational actor analysis of the selected devices would be the predominant task. In particular, we had intended that the mode of rational actor analysis used would be standard. As the book has taken shape, however, we have become increasingly convinced that more attention should be given to the nature of rational actor analysis itself. Specifically, as the text has emerged, the discussion of democratic desires has occupied a larger and larger share of the territory and the discussion of particular devices a smaller and smaller share. Relatedly, we have come to see our discussion of the institutional devices less as an attempt to provide a full treatment of them, and more as an opportunity to put our modified rational actor approach through its paces – as a way of illustrating the novelty and power of the modified rational actor model we now endorse. Whether we have succeeded in that ambition, the reader will have to judge. But we can indicate here in this initial chapter something of what is at stake in these 'modifications' and why increasingly they have seemed to us to be necessary.

Democratic desires

For many observers, the most characteristic feature – and for some, the most objectionable feature – of public choice scholarship lies in the particular motivations that are ascribed to political actors. Voters, politicians, bureaucrats, policy advisers are all assumed '... to be knaves, and to have no other purpose in all their action but self-interest'.[9] At one level, this assumption represents no more than the extension of the motivational apparatus standardly assumed in the ordinary economic

---

[9] As Hume (1985) pp. 42–3, puts it.

analysis of markets to the study of politics. But this assumption was justified by first-generation public choice scholars, quite explicitly, on grounds that were much more self-conscious than mere analytic familiarity: public choice analysts were insistent that, if proper institutional comparisons between markets and political process were to be secured, ideological neutrality would require identical motivational assumptions across the two arenas. For example, to diagnose market failure on the basis of an assumption that all individuals are rationally egoistic, as economists routinely do, and then to presume political success on the basis of an assumption that all political agents are intrinsically benevolent seemed to public choice scholars to constitute flagrant bias. As Buchanan puts the point in one of the milder formulations, 'the onus of proof would seem to lie with those who assume different motives in the two arenas'.[10]

Clearly, however, motivational symmetry could be achieved with any particular (common) motivational model – ranging anywhere from complete egoism to complete benevolence (or indeed, malevolence) and covering the huge range of possibilities in between. Conceivably, within that range, the motivational assumption made might turn out to favour some institutional arrangements over others. For example, it seems likely that choosing a pure self-interest model will prove relatively more hospitable to markets (and less to political process) than a model of partial benevolence. This would be the case, for example, if 'invisible hand' processes were more effective in markets than in politics: political process might be more demanding of a minimal benevolence than markets are and, indeed, it may be that markets can work tolerably well without any benevolence at all. If this is so, then the choice of the *homo economicus* assumption as the universal model of agent motivation may in itself constitute a source of bias in institutional comparison and more generally in institutional design. Consider, for example, and merely as a matter of conceptual possibility, two kinds of institutional device that might be ruled in if agents are partly benevolent and be ruled out if strict egoism applies:

1. If motivations are heterogeneous, and specifically if some agents are more 'publicly interested' than others, then it may be possible to use 'selection devices' that will determine who the relatively publicly spirited agents are and allocate these agents to those arenas in which their relative 'virtue' is most socially productive. On this view, public-interested motivations may be somewhat like human capital – a resource like physical capital which can be allocated to its highest social

---

[10] Buchanan (1984).

value uses. The way in which various institutions assist in recognising and allocating persons with this kind of motivationally embodied social capital becomes an important feature of those institutions' performance and hence becomes an object of specific attention in normative institutional analysis. Note that any argument for a particular institutional arrangement along such lines would meet the onus of proof that Buchanan lays down in relation to 'motivational symmetry' in political and market processes. But no such argument could ever get off the ground if everyone were assumed at the outset to be a Humean knave.

2. If agents with different motivations are differentially rewarded in the politico-economic system, then it may be that different institutional arrangements will lead to the differential 'production' of different motivations. Adam Smith, for example, believed that the market system had this effect with respect to trustworthiness: on Smith's view, the Dutch were more trustworthy than the English, and the English more trustworthy than the Scots precisely because commercial society was better developed in Holland than in England and in England than in Scotland.

These two suggestions illustrate the possibilities that might arise in a setting in which the *homo economicus* motivational assumption is relaxed in favour of something that is a little less 'dismal' (and a little less extreme) about human nature. We do not suppose that these two examples exhaust the variety of ways in which institutions and motivational assumptions are interconnected. Nor do we take it for granted that the particular lines of reasoning embodied in these examples are unproblematic. After all, they depend on the capacity of agents to discern the motivations of others, in circumstances where there may be incentives for agents to pretend that they are motivated in ways other than they actually are. Our claim at this point is the more modest one that such possibilities are worth considering: they should not be simply ruled out *a priori*.

It is worth emphasising in this connection that there is ample evidence – both in the empirical literature and in the emerging accumulation of experimental results – that there *is* a significant degree of motivational heterogeneity and specifically that some agents are more egoistic than others. Somewhere between one-third and one-half of subjects routinely 'co-operate' in *n*-person prisoner's dilemma situations, for example.[11] The only plausible argument for ignoring this evidence would be that motivational assumptions do not really matter – that somehow the *homo*

---

[11] On the experimental literature, two useful synoptic views are provided by Ledyard (1995) and Sally (1995).

economicus abstraction captures everything that is relevant about motivations for the purpose of institutional analysis. But certainly on the face of it, no defence of the *homo economicus* construction on purely empirical grounds seems available.

Moreover, motivational neutrality across institutional forms does not imply *behavioural* neutrality. Different institutions lead to different consequences by virtue of what might be termed generalised relative price effects – the idea, that is, that different institutions associate different costs and benefits with the actions available to the individuals operating within them. Indeed, tracing out the impacts of such relative price effects lies at the heart of the economic analysis of institutional choice. However, public choice orthodoxy has tended to interpret the scope of those relative price effects rather narrowly. In particular, as one of us has argued at length elsewhere,[12] there are good reasons to suppose that voters will *not* routinely vote for policies that they expect to leave them better off – in precise contrast to consumer choice in the marketplace. In this respect, market and political processes differ. The reason for this particular difference lies in the fact that individual consumers are decisive in the market over the options they consume, whereas individual voters are characteristically non-decisive: voters operate, as it were, behind a 'veil of insignificance'. Voters are thereby led to discount the instrumental aspect of rival policies and attend differentially to the intrinsic benefits and costs attaching to lending support for one candidate rather than another. Ideological loyalties, moral convictions and/or the aesthetic properties of the options seem, on this basis, likely to play a much more extensive role in voting behaviour than they do in market behaviour. Equally, conceiving political action as a kind of scramble for the promotion of individual interests seems likely to present an extremely partial and analytically misleading picture. Because standard means–ends notions of rationality do not apply to the connection between vote cast and political outcome preferred, we ought to expect electoral and market processes to be rather different. Note that this claim makes no assault on individual rationality – with rationality appropriately abstractly understood. But there is an assault on the simple idea that voter behaviour can be rationally explained as an attempt by the individual voter to promote her instrumental interests. What rationality entails in the political arena is more complex – and certainly less familiar – than in the marketplace and any proper rational actor political theory must, in our view, accommodate that fact. In this sense, the arguments elaborated in earlier work[13]

[12] See Brennan and Lomasky (1993).
[13] Specifically, in Brennan and Lomasky (1993).

have coloured our approach to the analysis of democratic 'desires', though what we argue here goes beyond, and moves in rather different directions from, that earlier work.

In summary, in the treatment of the various democratic devices we examine, we bring to bear our distinctive conception of democratic desires. We use our account of political motivations/behaviours to assess the significance of diagnoses of political failure standard in normative public choice theory. In the process we add to that list some diagnoses of our own. And with the diagnoses of the problems of democracy appropriately amended, we proceed to examine the selected devices, noting in particular as we go the possibility of the effects of these devices both as tools of selection and as tools for promoting and rewarding certain motivational dispositions.

There is, finally, a conceptual reason, beyond the descriptive and analytic ones, for choosing a more moralised picture of agent motivation than public choice analysis usually allows. This is that, in accepting the force of the motivational asymmetry challenge, we want to be careful not to arrogate to ourselves as writers – or, for that matter, to our readers – a monopoly on normative concerns. This book, like much else in political theory, (whether of the rational actor type or otherwise) is an exercise in normative analysis: our ultimate concern is to explore how democracy may be made to work better. We address this book to readers who, we believe, will share that kind of normative concern. We believe, therefore, that our general conception of agent motivation had better make allowance for this possibility. It is not entirely clear what a book on the institutions of politics written by total egoists and for an audience of total egoists would look like – but this is not that book. On the other hand, it is not a book for an audience of saints either. What we believe of ourselves and of our readers and of the ordinary agents we write and read about is that they lie in that huge range between moral perfection and unmoderated venality. We have, all of us, a desire to make the world a better place; but this desire is not the only one we have.

A reader's guide

We begin with desires. The six chapters that make up part I of this book are concerned to establish and explore our view of the motivational structure of political agents. Chapter 2 states our theme that the precise formulation of motivations matters, and that the adoption of *homo economicus* motivational assumptions distorts the normative analysis of political institutions. We outline an alternative position that grants morality a foothold in the motivational structure of individuals without in any way suggesting that individuals are essentially moral. Indeed, we see our suggestion as a simple way of capturing some of the tension between moral and other motivations. Chapter 2 also addresses a number of preliminary, but important, issues such as whether the detailed specification of individual motivations will be important in analysing the properties of social institutions, and the relationship between individual motivations and normative theory. Throughout our discussion of democratic desires we will adhere to the principle that the basic motivational structure of individuals should be unified – in the sense that, at any one time, agents should be conceived as having just one set of desires regardless of the range of institutions that they operate within. This fundamental commitment should not, however, be taken either as a commitment to the proposition that agents necessarily *behave* similarly in different institutional settings, or as a commitment to the proposition that desires may not change over time in response to institutional forces.

The idea that moral motivations may be of particular significance in political (as opposed to market) settings is further explored in chapter 3. The argument here also serves to introduce the idea of dispositions. We take dispositions to be an important aspect of the typical agent's motivational landscape – even though it is one that is treated with considerable scepticism by economists. Roughly, a disposition is a type of commitment strategy – an indirect means of achieving overall ends that may not be directly accessible. Dispositions are ultimately based on desires, but are not themselves desires – rather they are structures that partly determine the individual's decision-making process. Chapter 3 presents an extended discussion of dispositions in the context of the case of trust, and argues that dispositions – and moral dispositions in particular – are likely to play a particular role in the analysis of political behaviour.

Moral motivations and dispositions provide the vocabulary of virtue. Chapter 4 attempts to articulate this vocabulary: to both identify an appropriate conception of virtue, and explore the idea of economising on virtue in institutional design. Economising on virtue is carried to its logical extreme in the traditional economic approach where virtue is completely ignored so that institutions must substitute for virtue. A basic theme of chapter 4 is that once virtue is admitted, several senses of economising on virtue must be distinguished – not least because they may have very different institutional characteristics and very different implications.

Chapters 5, 6 and 7 then take the basic motivational apparatus outlined in the three earlier chapters and begin the process of directing this apparatus toward institutional concerns. Chapter 5 provides an analysis of a variety of ways in which institutions may engage with individual motivation – the range of mechanisms by which institutional devices can work. A central point here is that the recognition of motivations of the type identified as specifically 'democratic' desires opens up a range of mechanisms that are suppressed under the narrower interpretation of motivations associated with *homo economicus*. Chapter 6 then provides a more formal discussion of the possible interaction between these institutional mechanisms and dispositions. The model presented in that chapter addresses the question of whether a reliance on private incentive mechanisms – the standard economist's mechanism for 'economising on virtue'- may serve to undermine virtue in society. In crude terms, the question is whether the use of market-like mechanisms may tend to make citizens less concerned with civic virtue. Although the model we present is very simplified, it serves to illustrate the range of considerations on which answers to questions of this sort can depend. As the final element of part I, chapter 7 then offers a discussion of a variety of approaches to the central issues that arise in the design of democratic political institutions. Without a clear diagnosis of the problems of democratic politics it would be difficult to identify with any precision the diseases for which the various institutional devices on offer may be cures. But diagnosis depends on the background assumptions made, and these background assumptions include assumptions about the motivation of individuals. We suggest that the motivational model that we propose provides a distinctive lens through which to view the problems of democratic politics, and one that offers diagnoses rather different from those associated with the more traditional public choice literature.

Democratic devices move to centre stage in the five chapters that make up part II of this book. The structure here is very simple. Each chapter concentrates on a major aspect of what might be termed the archetypal liberal democratic constitution. Chapter 8 takes as its subject the most basic element of democracy – voting – and recasts the discussion of voting in the light of our discussion of democratic desires. The emphasis is on constructing a simple analysis of electoral equilibrium that draws on the idea of expressive behaviour by individuals which is in turn seen as a rational response to the institutional setting. This discussion of voting then feeds into the discussion of political representation in chapter 9, where the distinction, critical to the idea of representation, between voting for policies and voting for candidates is brought to the fore. The starting point here is to question the normative relationship between direct and representative democracy. Standard rational actor analysis typically assumes representative democracy as the prevailing practice, while holding up direct democracy as a relevant normative ideal. Our discussion, based on our model of motivation, not only provides a distinctive argument for the normative superiority of representative democracy but also points to a different idea of representation from the essentially statistical notion that is often taken as relevant. Chapter 10 moves on to consider the institution of political parties that so dominate the landscape in many democratic countries. Just as the standard rational actor analysis often obscures the distinction between policies and candidates, so that analysis also obscures the distinction between candidates and parties. Indeed, we argue that political parties are often mis-analysed both within the rational actor tradition and in other traditions of political analysis. Again, our perspective on motivation provides us with a treatment of parties that, we believe, sits comfortably with practical politics, at least as we perceive it.

Chapters 11 and 12, taken together, turn to the (rather less precisely specified) set of institutional arrangements that correspond to the idea of the 'separation of powers'. In fact we distinguish two broad ideas at work here and label them the separation of powers and the division of power. Roughly, the separation of powers applies to institutional devices that serve to unbundle powers and place each power in the hands of different agents or bodies, while the division of powers relates to institutional devices that attempt to spread a single power across a number of individuals or bodies. The separation of powers between a legislature and an executive may, then, be either a 'separation of powers' or a 'division of power' depending on the details of the institutional arrangements. Bicameralism provides another example of the same ambiguity. In these areas there is so little pre-existing analysis that there is little agreement on what the standard rational actor analysis of politics has to say on the separation and division of powers. These chapters, then, are an attempt to frame relevant questions about the 'arithmetic' of powers and provide some preliminary steps towards a more fully rounded analysis. The relatively preliminary nature of our discussion in these chapters indicates that while they mark the end of this book, they certainly do not constitute the final word.

PART I

Democratic desires

2

On human nature: beyond *homo economicus*

The supposition of universal venality in human nature is little less an error in political reasoning than the supposition of universal rectitude. The institution of delegated power implies that there is a portion of virtue and honor among mankind, which may be a reasonable foundation of confidence. And experience justifies the theory. It has been found to exist in the most corrupt periods of the most corrupt governments.

(*Federalist* papers, 76, Alexander Hamilton)

Motivation in politics

It seems self-evident that any account of the operation of democratic political institutions must depend on assumptions made about human nature – and specifically about human motivation. After all, within the analytic tradition that we will be working in – the rational actor tradition – human behaviour is understood as the outcome of rational choices, and rational choice is understood in terms of agents' beliefs and desires. The rational option, in the standard Humean/Davidsonian account, is just that option that maximises the agent's desire satisfaction, given the agent's beliefs (beliefs, say, about the consequences of alternative actions). Economists may, in most settings, talk about preferences rather than desires, but the Humean story – or something very like it – underlies virtually all modern economics and correspondingly all rational actor political theory.

Not all scholars admire the rational actor approach to politics. Their criticisms are varied and we will not try to address them all in this book. There is, though, one line of criticism of the rational actor approach – at least, of rational actor political theory as actually practised by most of its exponents – that we do wish to engage explicitly: engage and support. This criticism revolves not so much around the assumption of agent rationality as around the assumed nature of desires – not, that is, around the general idea that human action is purposeful but around the more specific idea that the purposes in question are essentially selfish and exhibit a narrowly economistic, venal character.

The truth is that rational actor political theory, at least in its predominant 'public choice' variant, typically distinguishes itself by the assumption that all the players in the political game are of the *homo economicus* type – 'egoistic, rational utility-maximisers', to use Dennis Mueller's terminology. Indeed, Mueller consistently asserts in his various surveys of public choice theory that this assumption is '*the* basic behavioral postulate of public choice'.[1] If so, then what follows in this book is not public choice. Or at least, it is only half public choice. Because while we shall retain the assumption of rationality, we shall jettison the assumption of unmoderated egoism. And we shall also be concerned to show that the rationality assumption, taken seriously, does not translate directly into 'rational action' in any simple 'behavioral' sense. In other words, our assault on the use of *homo economicus* in political analysis operates at two levels. Our attack on egoism is direct and explicit. We think, for reasons that we shall explore in these chapters, that this assumption is not only empirically wrong but conceptually problematic and practically misleading.[2] Our position on rationality is more complex. We are critical of what we take to be an excessively simple-minded view of what rationality implies – a view that is common in rational actor political theory. However, our adherence to the basic idea of rational choice remains firm. We think that the requirements of rationality are less obvious than most public choice theorists admit; but we see this as grounds for revising public choice orthodoxy, rather than as grounds for rethinking the claims of rationality.

Having said this, we should immediately emphasise that we do not intend to replace *homo economicus* in rational actor political theory with *homo heroicus*. To see the choice over motivational assumptions as one between pure egoism and pure benevolence (as public choice theorists often have) is to present an entirely false dichotomy. Between those two extremes, there is a huge expanse of middle ground. And it is that middle

---

[1] Mueller (1989), p. 2, our emphasis.
[2] We emphasise from the outset that the views on motivation in politics and in the analysis of constitutions developed here mark a clear departure from the views presented by one of us in earlier writing – for example Brennan and Buchanan (1980a, 1985).

ground we intend to inhabit. And indeed, we will inhabit that ground at the sceptical end of the range. But in the course of the discussion that follows, it may often seem otherwise because we shall be drawn to emphasise those aspects of our rational actor analysis that distinguish it from its more familiar and more extreme cousin. We will argue that even a modest move in the direction of 'morality' or 'virtue' (we shall be more explicit about our meanings of these words in chapter 4) can make a major difference when it comes to understanding the operation of political institutions and, therefore, when it comes to questions of institutional design. At this point, we simply want to insist that in rejecting the extreme *homo economicus* assumption that characterises orthodox public choice theory, we are not thereby embracing a romantic, idealist view of human nature of the kind that public choice theorists have sought so vigorously to suppress. Helpfully, Alexander Hamilton has expressed exactly the position we want to take – which explains the choice of epigraph for this chapter. We think that Hamilton has put it exactly right. The assumption of universal rectitude is a totally unsatisfactory one in political reasoning. But the assumption of universal venality is scarcely less bad: it *is* less bad, but not by much. The political theorist can do better than either of these suppositions, Hamilton thinks, by recognising the middle ground. We agree.

Specifically, we shall formulate our basic motivational assumptions as follows. We will assume that, among the desires (the motivational triggers) that agents have, the desire to behave morally is one. Importantly, however, the desire to act as morality requires will be only one desire among many. That particular desire must jostle for recognition among desires with a more familiar economistic cast. Moral considerations will weigh in the deliberations of agents but may be outweighed by considerations of a more self-interested kind.[3] But, as with other desires, the desire to act morally will be more likely to be decisive the lower is the opportunity cost in terms of other desire fulfilment forgone. Morality – and more particularly moral action – will be subject to a downward-sloping demand curve. Moreover, as with other desires (or preferences), there is no reason why all agents will exhibit the desire to behave morally

---

[3] Schmidtz (1995) provides a detailed argument to support the view that self-interested and moral considerations can fit together in an account of rational human motivation. See also Smith (1994), Brennan and Hamlin (1995b), Hampton (1997), Slote (1997). We do not wish to be read as taking an extreme stance in the debate between 'internalist' and 'externalist' accounts of the relationship between morality and motivation. We maintain that at least some moral beliefs may act as motivations for action for at least some individuals, but make no more general claim.

to the same extent, or assess its detailed content in exactly the same way. Some people will be more impelled than will others by the desire to act as morality requires; and exactly what action is understood to be required by morality in any particular case may differ to some degree from person to person. In short, we should expect some moral heterogeneity. Moral homogeneity is a very strong assumption, and an implausible one.

It is important to note that we do not intend here either to reduce morality to rationality, or to reduce rationality to morality. Rather, we see rationality and morality as two distinct but equally fundamental aspects of an agent's character – with rationality imposing a structural connection between the individual's desires, beliefs and actions, while morality speaks to the substantive content of the individual's desires and beliefs.[4]

It is also worth noting that the inclusion of a desire to act as morality requires will provide a basis for 'persuasion' (a mechanism for making moral considerations more salient in choice) and for moral reasoning (a mechanism for enquiry about what actions one's moral position would recommend). In this sense, our picture of agent motivation allows room for the broad enterprise in which this book is engaged. We can take it that normatively driven arguments about the operation of alternative institutions – of the kind we shall present in this book – can have purchase, without implicitly denying the model of agent motivation on which the analysis is based.

Do moral motives really matter?

We began this chapter with the suggestion that motivational questions are a natural point of departure for the study of democratic devices. We wrote that it seems self-evident that the workings of these devices will depend on underlying assumptions about human nature, and about desires specifically. But is this claim *really* self-evident? The simple fact that people are influenced to some degree by moral considerations is not sufficient to imply that this fact ought to figure in the analysis of institutional design. In an enterprise as general as rational actor political theory aspires to be, only significant facts should register: one cost of painting on a grand scale is that some details must be lost. We need to make the case for the proposition that moral motivations, and hetero-geneity in moral motivations, matter.

In fact, there are several reasons why morality might *not* matter – we will pick out four. First, there may not be enough common content in the

---

[4] Compare this with the discussion of the 'rational' and the 'reasonable' in Rawls (1993) pp. 48–54.

moral positions actually held by individuals to allow moral motivations to have any systematic effects at the aggregate, 'social' level. The lack of moral consensus would mean that moral motivations would be of little use in ensuring political compliance, or in providing any particular pattern to political action. Why, after all, should I submit to norms or political decisions that I believe to be morally wrong? The fact that some others believe them to be morally right (or good) cannot in itself provide an argument for such compliance. This is, on one interpretation, the view that Arrow takes in framing the requirement of 'universal domain' in his famous 'impossibility theorem'. For Arrow, values, like preferences, can in principle be in conflict over anything at all, so that no pattern of consensual values can be taken as fundamental.[5]

Second, morality might not matter because, although the *desire* to behave morally might be almost universal, and although the *content* of morality might be widely agreed, the desire to act morally is just too weak to have much influence on behaviour in any circumstances of interest. This is essentially the view taken by Stigler, Tullock and probably many other enthusiasts for *homo economicus*.[6] Their point is that it is only where interests and morality pull together that morality is apparently effectual. On this view, moral motivations may exist, but play no real or significant role in the determination of behaviour, so that the simpler model which assumes the complete absence of moral motivations should be preferred.

Third, morality might matter behaviourally – but still not assist in any way in promoting good outcomes. This is one interpretation of Mandeville's position on 'private virtue'. Mandeville's argument is that the prevailing view of what morality requires is both behaviourally effective and quite wrong. From an explanatory point of view then, morality plays a role: but the idea of structuring political institutions to allow those prevailing moral judgements full play is a counsel for disaster. In Mandeville's lexicon, *homo economicus* can be understood as the motivational structure that actually corresponds with the proper application of the correct justificatory norms. However, since agents do not properly understand this – since they often allow their egoistic inclinations to be clouded or corrupted by false views about 'virtue' – the proper role of good institutions is to suppress those false views and encourage rational

---

[5] This being so, it is an interesting question as to what authority his other
     normative requirements can claim – i.e. non-dictatorship or Pareto optimality. A
     moral consensus is presupposed for *those* desiderata. Values, then, cannot be quite
     like preferences after all. For further discussion of the Arrow impossibility
     theorem, see chapter 7 below.
[6] See, for example Stigler (1981), Tullock (1971).

egoism.[7] It is worth emphasising that on the Mandevillean view, morality does indeed matter – both the false morality of private 'virtue' and the true morality promoted under narrow egoism. The former matters behaviourally; and the latter matters normatively – in a nice reversal of common intuition.

Or, fourthly, morality may not matter because desires more generally do not matter – because, despite all appearances to the contrary, the operation of political institutions does not much depend on the nature of agent motivation. This fourth possibility requires some elaboration.

Economists have traditionally resisted any attempt to reduce social explanation (and normative political theory, by implication) to matters of psychology. Indeed, considerable professional ingenuity has been devoted to finessing as much of the psychological detail as possible. The object has been to make the weakest, most abstract, most general assumptions about motivational questions consistent with the rational actor framework itself and the explanatory and normative agenda at stake. Consider, for example, the logic of interaction laid out in the standard 'prisoner's dilemma', or the 'battle of the sexes' or any of the other familiar two-person, non-co-operative, non-zero-sum games. It is not necessary to enquire as to the content or currency of the pay-off functions – whether pay-offs are in cash, or years in prison, or the pleasure of someone's company (all of which feature in the standard descriptions of these games) – in order to identify the *logic* of interaction that actually characterises the games. Interest in the prisoner's dilemma derives not from an interest in the specifics of this or that example, but because the pattern of interaction throws light on a whole range of social situations. Of course, we need to know *something* about agent motivation to establish this pattern (and to recognise those situations to which it might apply). But the 'something' that we need to know is fairly coarse-grained – that agents can rank different outcomes, for example – and does not depend on any fine-grained knowledge of the precise basis of their rankings.

In the same way, propositions about the comparative static effects of changes in relative prices will apply to virtually all goods and activities without requiring a detailed specification of agents' preferences. The properties of the demand curve for a good can be derived from relatively coarse-grained assumptions about the structure of preferences, without

---

[7] Mandeville's distinctively satirical form of argument does not lend itself to clear or simple interpretation, and experts differ on his ultimate meaning. We offer our rendering as a convenient label for a position we believe some economists hold, rather than as a claim about Mandeville's intentions.

the need for detailed, fine-grained information about the content of preferences.

Or again, in the case of the median voter theorem, we do not need to know the precise content of voters' preferences to conclude that one-dimensional, two-party electoral competition will lead the contending parties to locate at the median of the ideal points of voters, if those parties seek to maximise their chance of being elected (and granting other assumptions). Again we need to know only relatively coarse-grained facts concerning the structure of political preferences (and specifically that preferences are 'single-peaked').

The lessons that underlie this catalogue of examples are generally pragmatic: first, that the requirement for specific information about desires, and the kind of psychological detail that one needs, varies from case to case; and second, that much can be achieved without recourse to any fine-grained psychological assumptions. We accept both of these lessons. We see rational actor theory as providing a grammar of argument – an abstract 'logic of choice', to use Buchanan's (1979) terminology – which can do a great deal of explanatory work despite its abstract quality. But we believe that rational actor theory, in at least some cases, has pursued abstraction in this particular direction too far, and has attended less to motivational realism than is sensible. Moreover, in practice, many applications of rational actor theory (particularly in the political context), have proved unnecessarily tendentious: they have attached themselves to particular, and ostensibly implausible, models of agent motivation solely on the methodological grounds that simplicity is to be favoured. If, after all, the particular motivational assumptions do not matter much, it seems to court unnecessary confusion to adopt an extreme form of egoism as the basis for analysis. On the modest grounds (normally so popular with economists) that one should never adopt a strong assumption when a weaker one will serve, the *homo economicus* construction in rational actor political theory ought to be softened in the direction of greater generality and psychological plausi-bility. If the introduction of some more moral element into agent motivations makes no real difference to the analysis, then no harm is done and a line of criticism is deflected. And if it does make a real difference, then *homo economicus* is not as innocent as the abstraction defence alleges, and the move to more plausible motivations is war-ranted on substantive grounds.

In the face of these four reasons why moral considerations might not matter – and other reasons that might be adduced – we want to argue for the contrary view. We deny the claim that there is inadequate consensus in moral beliefs to make moral argument interesting in social

theory.[8] We dispute the charge that moral considerations are too weak
to exercise influence on behaviour in at least some relevant circumstances (see below and chapter 3). We reject the Mandevillean view that
all common morality is mistaken. And we shall argue at some length
(beginning in chapter 4), that abstracting from moral considerations
does considerable violence to the task of political and institutional
analysis: it limits the array of institutional devices to which one might
appeal and it ignores the possibility that some institutional devices may,
through negative feedback effects on motivations, do more harm than
good.

In the remainder of this chapter we want to advance and defend two
independent propositions, both of which support the relevance of moral
motivations to the task of normative political theory. Neither of these
propositions is empirical: both are conceptual. We know well enough
that empirical evidence of the practical importance of moral motivations
is unpersuasive. Any catalogue of instances of apparently morally motivated behaviour can be met by a series of arguments which show, with
some ingenuity, that these pieces of behaviour can be derived from self-
interest. Economists, in particular, are often good at constructing such
arguments. To avoid this sterile debate, we take the more conceptual line.

The two propositions that we want to advance and defend are these:

- that the extreme *homo economicus* formulation of agent motivation
  makes it difficult – arguably impossible – to make sense of genuine
  normative theorising;
- that the internal logic of rational action suggests that moral considerations, once admitted, are likely to play a disproportionately significant
  role in democratic political processes, so that moral motivations that
  may lie dormant in market settings may be strongly relevant in political
  settings.

In chapter 3 we will then take up a very different line of argument
concerning the link between our basic motivational structure and political
action, a line of argument that begins from the observation that the logic
of rational action may actually require departures from egoism in at least
some interesting cases. We will argue that the step from that observation
to the idea of moral dispositions is a relatively short and attractive one.
Chapter 4 will then build on the ideas of morally motivated behaviour
both by discussing the ways in which institutions might economise on
virtue, and by offering some more detailed comments on moral heterogeneity. These three chapters, taken together, are intended to introduce

---

[8] For detailed discussion of the idea of a shared morality and the process by which
we form and reform our value judgements, see Griffin (1996).

our basic motivational apparatus, defend it against some lines of criticism, and spell out its significance for action in the political sphere. We make no claim to offer anything like a full defence of our motivational model – this is not a book devoted to moral psychology. The basic idea of individuals characterised by a desire to act as morality requires, among other desires, remains an assumption of our argument, not a conclusion.

Homo economicus and normative theory

Most economists believe that the normative advice that they offer ought to have some influence. Indeed, it is difficult to see how they could coherently think otherwise. If, after careful study, you come to believe that an option (a particular policy, perhaps) is the best available, it is hard to see how it could be the case that you would not also believe that those in authority should take notice of your advocacy of that option. In fact, many economists seek to justify their professional activities by appeal to the value of their influence. But the models of behaviour from which their policy advice is derived, deny the possibility that normative advice could be influential in this way. Moral considerations play no direct role in the rational deliberations of *homo economicus*. Real economists and the real people to whom their advice is offered may care about the morality of their actions, but this is not a characteristic shared by the agents who populate economic models, who care about nothing but their own interests.

This dichotomy between economists' own behaviour and their assumptions about the behaviour of others has been a point of departure for much public choice scholarship, and a critical part of the informing spirit of the whole research agenda. Public choice theory offers a vigorous critique of the standard approach to economic policy, in the form of an attack on the 'benevolent despot' model of government that is seen to underlie that approach. Implicit in the policy economist's offer of normatively derived policy advice, so the critique goes, are two assumptions: first, that political agents are motivated predominantly (perhaps exclusively) by a desire to promote the public interest (the 'benevolence' assumption); and second, that political agents have the capacity to act benevolently, unencumbered by any political constraints (the 'despot' assumption). Neither assumption, say the public choice critics, is at all plausible. If the first were true, then the economist would be promoting an implausible schizophrenia in agents' motivations – totally selfish in markets, totally benevolent in politics – or claiming an even more implausible moral distinction between agents, with some agents (politicians and the economists themselves) totally selfless while others are totally selfish. The economist would also be logically committed to a normative position in which all democratic and electoral constraints are presumptively *bad*, serving only to place obstacles in the way of benevolent politicians and their advisers. If the second assumption were true, then economists would be obliged to conclude that democratic political institutions were not worth promoting or defending for a different reason – there are surely no persuasive arguments for institutional arrangements that do no work.

A response to the public choice critique of the benevolent despot might be to argue that, while political agents should properly be conceived along the lines of *homo economicus*, well-designed democratic political institutions transform political process into an invisible hand mechanism, so that one can analyse politics *as if* political agents (and their advisers) were benevolent, even though they are not. But this is a substantive claim about democratic political process, to be demonstrated not merely asserted. And demonstrated, moreover, in a manner consistent with other assumptions in economics and, not least, the assumption that all agents are motivated solely by their private interests. The claim would, in other words, have to be demonstrated as a proposition in orthodox public choice theory. In an important sense, this issue – whether or not democratic political process works as an invisible hand mechanism – has been the central preoccupation of normative public choice scholarship. And it has to be said that the results, on the whole, are not encouraging. Of course, some simple models can be found in which democratic politics does operate in the hoped-for manner, but these models are neither general nor robust – for reasons to be explored in more detail below.

However, the issue here is not whether democratic politics operates as an invisible hand, but a more basic concern about economists' normative theorising: one of inconsistency between *homo economicus* as a behavioural model and normative theorising of any recognisable kind.

The point is that in a world of unrelieved egoism, agents cannot even recognise the category of 'the normative'. Even the idea of an 'invisible hand' is based on an essentially moral idea and could not make much sense to *homo economicus*. Moreover, even if agents could recognise moral categories, they could certainly not grant them any reason-giving status. To put the same point in other words, in an egoistic universe agents are committed to a language in which 'good' can only mean 'good for me' or more particularly, 'in my interests' (or, conceivably, in the interests of a small set of identified individuals such as a family). In that world there is simply no meaningful possibility of distinctively moral or justificatory argument. Justification could only be a redundant repetition of motivation – an action can only be justified (to me) if it is in my interests, and its being in my interests is a reason for me to act. Without a distinctive moral sense of justification, there is no work for normative theorising to do.

One possible response to this problem is to accept the logic, but to point to circumstances in which the distinction between justification and motivation might re-emerge, so that the possibility of normative analysis would also be restored. These circumstances involve uncertainty and are taken to the limit in the famous Rawlsian construction of the original position behind a veil of ignorance. But whereas in Rawls the veil of ignorance plays the role of a conceptual tool designed to inform our conception of justice within an explicitly normative framework, here the veil of ignorance is intended to operate as a means of introducing a moral component into an otherwise self-interested story. It does this by setting each individual in the context of choosing the 'rules of the game', without knowing which cards each will be dealt. This interpretation of the veil of ignorance is most familiar from the work of Buchanan. However, the strict normative limitations of this exercise must be recognised. Perhaps, as a matter of fact, the shift in the domain of decision making from actions to rules will induce a rational egoist to choose those rules that promote the interest of the average citizen (or some other idea that might be rendered as the 'public interest'). But this fact in itself cannot provide any *reason* for anyone (that is, any rational egoist) to prefer or promote the constitutional level of decision making over the in-period or 'action' level. Nor can it provide the social analyst with any reason to claim that the rules that would be chosen behind the veil of ignorance are in any way morally justified. Such reasons can only be derived from some explicitly normative base. Nor can the facts about choice of rules at the constitutional level provide the in-period individual with any reason to accept, internalise or comply with those rules.

The economist might react to this by claiming that the idea that 'good' can only be rendered as 'good for me' is the ground on which the normative criterion known as the Pareto criterion flourishes. The Pareto criterion ranks social state *A* above *B* if and only if everyone is at least as well off (in their own estimation) in *A* as they are in *B*. No aggregative idea of the public interest is implied here. But even the Pareto criterion is a substantively moral idea and, as such, we would argue that it can have no meaning or role in a world populated entirely by *homo economicus*. Simply put, the point is that no rational and purely egoistic agent could recognise the idea that the Pareto criterion provides a justification for any particular policy or action, and nor could such an agent be motivated to achieve a Pareto improvement that offered her no personal benefit. The

Pareto criterion can be *defined* in a world of rational egoists, but it could play no justificatory or motivational role. And the same is true for any normative criterion.

In fact, the motivational base required for real normative analysis may be quite minimal. It may involve little more than a modest commitment to some definition of the 'public interest' as one thing that one ought to promote – for itself and not by reason of any indirect promotion of self-interest. That commitment would provide one with reason both to promote the constitutional level of decision making above the in-period level, and to pay some attention to the rules chosen at that level in considering alternative in-period actions. But without some such normative commitment, no such reasons seem to be available.

Moreover, granting this moral element to motivation liberates us from any anxiety about whether the veil of ignorance is complete or only partial. Because agents can be presumed to have a reason for promoting the public interest, all we need to note is that the shift to a more abstract level of constitutional decision making amplifies the possibility of public interest considerations being effective. The constitutional move itself has an 'invisible hand' character, and the normative commitment to the 'public interest' allows us to both recognise and value that fact.

Note, too, that the reference to the 'public interest' here involves no informational demands that are not already present in any argument about constitutional choice. Questions concerning the limits of knowledge about the interests of others have historically played an important role in economists' arguments about alternative normative frameworks. We do not wish to engage such questions here. We simply note that the constitutional move only makes sense if some things about the interests of others are knowable – either by virtue of abstract institutional analysis or by introspection or by some other means. If we cannot know anything about how different citizens will fare under different institutional regimes, we cannot hope to provide an account of constitutional choice. Whatever that set of knowable things is, we see no reason why it cannot also provide an adequate basis for an understanding of the 'public interest' that operates at both the constitutional and in-period levels. Extreme solipsism is just as devastating for constitutional contractarians as it is for any simple utilitarianism.

To summarise the argument so far, we believe that any normative analysis must be committed to two propositions: first to the idea that normative analysis has an audience in the sense that agents can comprehend the logic of justification; and second to the idea that that audience not only comprehends but is also inclined to respond appropriately to the force of normative reasoning. We think that the original public choice critique of economic policy analysis was correct, but that it resolved the conflict between the nature and content of the economists' arguments in the wrong way, by seeking to extend *homo economicus* assumptions universally. That particular move, in the limit, rules out normative analysis. The benevolent despot must go, but he cannot be adequately replaced by *homo economicus*. For consistency, we need a behavioural model in which moral motivations play some role.

In any event, our own ambitions in this book are essentially normative. We want, simply put, to investigate whether particular, familiar pieces of political and institutional fabric help democracy to 'work better'. And by this we do not mean 'better for Brennan and Hamlin', but 'better' in the more natural, normative sense that informs most political analysis. Since we start from such a normative stance, simple requirements of coherence and generality require us, we believe, to extend such a normative stance to the agents we model.

It would, of course, be logically possible to extend normative motivations to only a restricted subset of persons – some elite of philosopher kings (and their economic advisers). It would be foolish to deny that such a strategy has had an active life in political thought. Plato's guardians, Macchiavelli's Prince, even perhaps Adam Smith's 'wise sovereign', exemplify. In this tradition, the issue in relation to the great bulk of humanity is how to manipulate them for their own good – to indulge in a variant of what has come to be known as 'government house utilitarianism'. We reject this possibility. We see no plausible reason for believing that either moral sensibility or moral conduct should be seen *ex ante* as the monopoly of any one group, class or caste – and certainly not the monopoly of the governing class. That possibility seems both empirically implausible and politically distasteful.

On the other hand, we do want to concede something to the spirit of this view, at least on the question of motivational heterogeneity. There is a temptation to respond to the proposition that only the rulers are concerned about or can discern the public interest with the no less extreme hypothesis that everyone is concerned with the public interest to exactly the same extent. This alternative is neither logically required, nor is itself particularly plausible. Some actors will be more responsive to moral issues than others. Furthermore, one might hope that political institutions might tend to allocate the relatively moral to those areas where their morality can do the most good, so that *ex post* there might be some correlation between social roles and the motivations of the role-holders. Indeed, we will spend considerable time and effort in discussing precisely these possibilities – beginning in chapter 3. What we want to rule out is any unargued presumption of moral governance – any kind of

anti-Actonian claim that power sanctifies, and absolute power sanctifies
absolutely. Governors are not moral *because* they are governors; but it is
at least possible, if institutions are designed appropriately and work well,
that persons are selected as governors because they are relatively moral.

Now, it is one thing to argue, as we have in this section, that the
possibility of justificatory argument demands some moral element in
agent motivations. It is quite another to resolve the question of the
precise link between justification and motivation once these two are
separated. One thing, at least should be clear; the link between justification and motivation must be partial and indirect. If justification and
motivation are too tightly bound together, we are either returned to the
world of *homo economicus* or we enter the world of a compliance theory
of politics, in which moral justification is taken to imply the presence of
the relevant motivation, a solution that we take to be logically neat but
practically uninteresting.

We have already suggested how the link between justification and
motivation might work. The desire to act morally might be construed as
one desire, among others, which each agent possesses. The fact that the
agent possesses this desire at all explains why she is capable of moral
action and is potentially responsive to normative argument. The fact that
this desire is only one among many explains why the agent does not
always behave morally and so distances the account here from any simple
compliance theory of politics. A model of motivation of this general type
seems to be required if we are to *allow* moral action without making it
universal, and in particular if we are to study the relationship between
motivation and action in the context of alternative political institutions.

Ethics and democratic politics

Once moral considerations are admitted as potentially relevant, are they
likely to play a disproportionately significant role in democratic political
processes, so that moral motivations that may lie dormant in market
settings may be strongly relevant in political settings? We believe that the
answer to this question is yes; and we offer two very different lines of
argument in support of this answer. The first line of argument hinges on
the nature of the democratic electoral process and the rational response
to that process by citizen voters. It is an argument from expressive voting.
Because this line has been extensively argued elsewhere by one of us in a
different collaboration[9] we will not develop it at length here. However, it
is important to sketch the argument briefly, because it provides the

---

[9] Brennan and Lomasky (1993).

starting point for some of the discussion of democratic institutions in subsequent chapters.

In the economic theory of politics it has been standard to extrapolate directly from market behaviour to political behaviour. This extrapolation has never been seen to require much in the way of explicit argument. The simple observation that the agents who buy and sell in the marketplace are the same agents who also vote in the polling booth has typically been seen as sufficient to rule out any systematic motivational difference. As public choice scholars are prone to remark, the onus of proof would seem to lie with those who argue for motivational non-neutrality. And, with motivations interpreted suitably abstractly, this is surely correct. But neutrality with respect to the basic motivational structure of agents does not imply neutrality with respect to *behaviour* – or indeed to the particular desires that will be engaged in different institutional settings. It may be that systematically different desires are engaged in market and political contexts in a manner totally consistent with agent rationality. This, in fact, is what we believe.

This picture of differential engagement of desires as between the market and the polity is, as we see it, a key aspect of democratic, and specifically electoral, politics. The essential observation is that no individual voter can reasonably expect to affect the outcome of any practical electoral competition, whereas each individual in the market directly determines her own consumption bundle. Except in the extremely unlikely event of an exact tie among other voters, your vote will not determine the electoral outcome. If you made a mistake in the polling booth and voted for the 'wrong' candidate, that mistake would almost certainly not alter the electoral outcome – though, presumably, it would remain a mistake from your point of view.

There are, let us suppose, two types of reasons for voting: because you want to express your support for one or other candidate; and because the victory of a particular candidate serves your interests. These may seem like the same reason. But that cannot be right. If the two reasons collapse to one, you will rarely have any reason to vote at all because your influence on the victory of a particular candidate is asymptotically negligible. Call the first reason for voting, expressive, and the second reason instrumental. Public choice scholarship has focused almost entirely on instrumental voting. On the instrumental view, voting behaviour depends on the expected effects that different policy options will have on your income, or your consumption of public goods, or your interests more generally. But these instrumental costs and benefits, we argue, are more or less irrelevant, on the argument that they do not depend on your voting behaviour. What *are* relevant are the expressive considerations. Of course, these expressive considerations may be correlated with the instrumental in at least some cases, but the categories are conceptually distinct, and are likely to differ in practice in many significant cases.

To give an example. Suppose that you believe that a certain policy is a good policy, morally speaking. Let us further suppose that by 'a morally good policy', you mean one that promotes the 'public interest'. You think that this is a policy that you *ought* to support – a policy that the government *ought* to follow. But suppose also that this policy is one that will imply net costs for you – extra taxes or whatever. If you are to make a truly rational calculation in deciding whether to vote for or against this policy, what should you do? On the benefit side of the ledger you will include the benefit from expressing your moral convictions, weighted in some way by the strength of your desire to behave morally. But what on the cost side of the ledger? Certainly *not* the net costs to you of the policy going ahead, because the policy going ahead is not the matter under decision. The matter under decision is just how you will vote. The relevant ledger entry is rather the net costs of the policy weighted by the probability that your vote will be decisive in bringing the policy about. This probability is so small as to be negligible in almost all cases. On this calculus, it is rational to vote to express your moral approval of the policy, despite its instrumental costs.

Now, one might respond that if the instrumental cost is negligibly small, so is the moral benefit. How can one take any moral satisfaction from voting for a policy if doing so does not actually bring the morally desired policy about? How can one feel any moral satisfaction from such a cheap gesture? But that question suggests its own answer – gestures are more common when they are cheap. Actions do indeed speak louder than words. That is, a systematic account of what people say would be rather different from a systematic account of what they do. Action typically carries responsibility for consequences – words are often inconsequential. And that is precisely the point. Electoral process is much more like the world of speech-acts than it is like an idealised market in which each actor bears the full consequences of her action. The fact that voting is almost certainly an inconsequential action encourages the expressive use of the vote.

A 'veil of insignificance' (the phrase is originally Harmut Kliemt's) surrounds the act of voting. It is not the same as the 'veil of ignorance' familiar from the work of Rawls and other contractarian writers, but the two 'veils' share one feature – namely, both serve to suppress the role of particularised self-interest. It would, however, be quite wrong to suppose that the veil of insignificance promotes only moral considerations in electoral choice. In fact, it will promote any consideration that is expressive in nature. Such considerations might include: the candidate's appearance or personality; the voter's identification with, or loyalty to, a particular party or ideology; and indeed any other affective consideration. The important point is that the voter's instrumental interests will play only a minor or indirect role. Moral considerations will be only one variety of expressive consideration, but even so we have reason to suppose that moral considerations will be more engaged in voting than in market trading where the weight of private interests is likely to be predominant.

We will say no more about this line of reasoning here,[10] but there is a simple lesson to be drawn from this 'expressive' argument: motivational considerations that are relatively insignificant in the market context – or in any context of directly instrumental choice – may become extremely important in the context of democratic politics. Accordingly, a model of motivation that is perfectly satisfactory in market and other similar contexts may go badly awry in the political setting. More particularly, moral considerations, including specifically questions of the 'public interest', seem likely to play a disproportionately significant role in electoral politics, even where private interests play the predominant role in market settings.

---

[10] We develop some implications of the expressive line of argument further below – particularly in chapters 7, 8 and 9. Readers interested in the *a priori* argument for expressive voting are referred to Brennan and Lomasky (1993).

3

Moral dispositions

It may be a reflection on human nature, that such devices should be necessary to control the abuses of government. But what is government itself, but the greatest of all reflections on human nature? If men were angels, no government would be necessary. If angels were to govern men, neither external nor internal controls on government would be necessary.

(*Federalist* papers, 51, James Madison)

Rationality and trust

We have, in the foregoing chapter, suggested one reason why moral motivations might play a disproportionately significant role in democratic politics: the mechanics of democratic elections may engage expressive rather than instrumental concerns, and the expressive calculus is more likely to promote moral action. In short, the veil of insignificance reduces the price of moral action in the political arena relative to the market arena, so that we would expect more moral action in politics. We now want to turn to a different line of argument, which has the same general ambition – namely to suggest that moral motivations may be especially relevant in the setting of democratic politics. This line of argument stems from the idea that rationality might require departures from egoism: that *homo economicus* is self-defeating in a range of circumstances of relevance – and self-defeating in a way that is hospitable to certain accounts of morality. We will present our argument in three steps. First we will argue that the project of making one's life go as well as possible, in the terms that *homo economicus* admits, may require a non-egoist dimension of agent motivation: that it may be rational to adopt an alternative disposition as the proximate determinant of behaviour.[1] With this argument established, we will then take the second step to introduce distinctively *moral* dispositions, based on our assumed desire to act as morality requires. The third and final step will then be to argue that moral dispositions can be expected to be especially relevant in the political arena.

The argument at stake in this chapter connects with the rapidly growing literature on 'trust';[2] and our own presentation will be formulated in these terms. Although familiar in some areas of debate, much of the reasoning to be presented here does not seem to have connected much with rational actor political theory. Our aim here is to make this connection.

It is useful to begin with a clarification of what can count as an 'action' in rational actor political theory. There is a potential ambiguity here that should be resolved. In the process, it will be helpful to introduce some terminology to distinguish importantly different cases. Simply put, we wish to extend the conventional domain or scope of rationality axioms. Accordingly, we shall use the term *option* to define the domain of choice: rationality addresses the choice between options. Ordinary choices – which bundle of goods to consume, which candidate to vote for, etc. – we shall designate as choices between actions where actions are to be thought of as a subset of options. (We shall also include in the set of actions the category of speech-acts, so that the choice of what to say or write or what view to express is the choice of an action in our sense.) However, we also wish to identify as a possible option a disposition which is not an action in our sense. A disposition picks out a particular mode of decision making which may then be applied to the choice among possible actions; a disposition involves a procedure or mechanism that allows a set of decisions on *actions* to be bundled together and made according to a particular rule. Thus a disposition identifies both a class of choice situations and a choice rule, and involves the application of the specified rule in the specified situations.

Seen in this way, self-interested calculation over actions (together with some specification of the class of actions to which it should apply) is itself a *disposition*: the disposition of rational egoism. This disposition tells you to take that *action* which, of those actions that are available to you, makes your life go best for you (i.e. maximises your expected lifetime pay-off).

---

[1] This step of the argument is clearly related to arguments put by Parfit (1984) and Gauthier (1986) among others.
[2] See, for example, Baier (1986), Gambetta (1988), Jones (1996), Hardin (1996) Becker (1996). Hollis (1998) in particular presents an account of trust that involves relaxing the strict idea of rationality associated with *homo economicus*.

But the disposition of rational egoism is not necessarily the disposition that will make your life go best for you. Your expected lifetime pay-off may be larger if you were to have a different disposition. If this is true, the disposition of rational egoism (the *homo economicus* disposition) is self-defeating in Parfit's sense; and it would be in your own interest to choose a different disposition if only that were possible.

An ambiguity in the denomination of 'rational actions' then arises from the contrast between an action that has been chosen under the disposition of rational egoism, and an action that has been chosen under some other disposition that was itself rationally chosen. This ambiguity can be the source of much confusion. Accordingly we will reserve the term 'rational action' for actions that are directly chosen under the disposition of rational egoism, and use alternative terminology to indicate actions taken under alternative (rationally chosen) dispositions.

This ambiguity in the meaning of rational action also serves to highlight the distinction between the position typically adopted in rational actor political theory and our own position. We do not understand rational actor political theory to be limited to the study of rational action. In our account, it is the actor who is rational, not each and every action. We will take seriously the possibility that rational actors may, in at least some circumstances, adopt dispositions other than rational egoism. Furthermore we will argue the case for distinctively moral dispositions based on the acceptance of moral argument as an influence on the rational choice of dispositions.

All of this may be clarified by an extended example of the kind of predicament in which dispositional choice might be effective. The following subsections provide a discussion of such an example – the case of trust. We will first lay out the nature of the predicament, and then canvass three complementary approaches to that predicament, including one that draws on the idea of dispositions. We will then examine the plausibility of the moral disposition approach, and indicate why we believe that moral dispositions are particularly relevant to the design of political institutions. Our discussion in many of these sections will be brief. Our aim is not to provide a complete analysis of these topics, but rather to establish the broad lines of such an analysis and thereby to provide further support for our modification of the *homo economicus* assumption, and further understanding of its implications.

The reliance predicament

Consider the predicament set out in extensive game form in figure 3.1. There are two players: *A*, who moves first, has a choice as to whether to

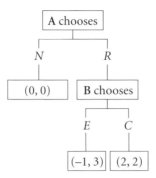

Figure 3.1 The reliance predicament

rely (*R*) on the second player (*B*), or not to rely (*N*). If *A* chooses *N*, the interaction ends and each player receives a pay-off of zero. If *A* chooses *R*, however, player *B* is brought into play and faces a choice between exploiting (*E*), in which case *A* receives a pay-off of -1 and *B* receives a pay-off of 3; and co-operating (*C*), in which case each player receives a pay-off of 2.

This reliance game is similar in some respects to the prisoner's dilemma, although it differs most obviously in the fact that the players move in sequence, so that there is no question of symmetry between the players. One clear similarity is that the unique equilibrium under rational action is suboptimal. That is, if both *A* and *B* are rational in the *homo economicus* sense, and this fact is common knowledge, then *A* will argue that if she chooses *R*, *B* will certainly choose *E* giving *A* the pay-off of −1. With this in mind, *A* will certainly choose *N*. *A* will not 'rely' on *B*, since it is 'rational' for *B* to exploit reliance. Yet both *A* and *B* would be better off if they chose *R* and *C* respectively. This Pareto improvement is simply inaccessible to rational *homo economicus* players. In particular, *B* cannot credibly commit to choosing *C*, since *A* knows that such a promise will carry no weight in *B*'s decision making – it is simply 'cheap talk'. We should perhaps emphasise that the 'problem' here is *not* that *A* is exploited. Indeed, no exploitation occurs in equilibrium. The problem is rather a lack of reliance or trust. *B* is not trusted because she is not trustworthy, and this fact restricts the pay-offs to both players.

Within the grammar of argument that rational actor analysis admits, any resolution of the reliance predicament must be based on some change to the nature of the game being analysed. The logic of the analysis of choice within the original game – defined by the nature of the players, their information, the strategies available to them and the pay-off structure – is not in doubt. We distinguish between three types of change

to the underlying game, which correspond to three distinct approaches to
the reliance predicament.[3]

Approaches to the reliance predicament – repetition

One standard move in the analysis of games such as the reliance
predicament is the move from the one-shot game to an indefinitely
repeated game. If the interaction between *A* and *B* is to be repeated, and
this fact is common knowledge, *B* may have an incentive to build a
reputation for choosing *C*, and this possibility will be known to *A*. And if
the repetition is indefinite, *B*'s incentive will not unravel under backwards
induction. Under certain circumstances, this can lead *A* to choose *R* and
B to choose *C*, so that the Pareto-optimal outcome is realised.[4]

All of this is both true and important in many cases, but it does not
represent a response to what we see as the basic difficulty. The fundamental logic of the reliance predicament is untouched by this type of
argument. Even in the presence of reputational considerations, there can
still arise cases in which the rationality of *homo economicus* will be a
barrier to trust, and a sufficient barrier to prevent the realisation of
mutual benefits. What is at stake is the ability of agents to keep promises,
and it is the opportunistic, forward-looking expediency of rational *homo
economicus* that makes him untrustworthy. Arguments such as the
argument from the indefinite repetition of the game will certainly reduce
the number of cases to which the predicament applies. It is an empirical
question as to whether the cases that remain are sufficiently numerous, or
sufficiently important, to merit concern. We believe that numerous
important cases remain, and that they are particularly likely to arise in the
political arena. We shall return to this point below.

Approaches to the reliance predicament – enforcement

A second possible resolution of the reliance predicament involves varying
the objective pay-offs associated with the different strategy choices. This
possibility is uninteresting in itself, since it is obvious that by arbitrarily
changing the pay-off structure we can transform the reliance predicament
into a wide variety of different games. But there is a more specific and
interesting interpretation. In the face of a social predicament, we might

---

[3] These three approaches are not mutually exclusive, so that emphasising any one of
them does not involve arguing against the other two.
[4] This result can be extended in a number of ways, for example to certain cases in
which the players at each point in time are drawn from a given population: see
Kandori (1992), Ellison (1994).

seek to employ social institutions to provide solutions that are not accessible to individually rational action. In particular, institutions might be put in place that impose penalties on players taking certain actions, or provide rewards to other actions. Fines can be imposed, subsidies paid and so on. However, although such social institutions are conceivable, they must pass at least two tests of feasibility. First they should be institutions that work within resource limits. If an institution is to offer additional rewards to certain actions, the resources required to finance those rewards must come from somewhere, and from somewhere within the model. And second, they should be institutions that could be designed and operated by people of the type that populate our model – in this case by *homo economicus*.

The most obvious type of institution that might resolve a reliance predicament is an institution that penalises player B if she takes action E. If this penalty is large enough (in our example, if it is greater than 1), B's rational response to A choosing R will be to choose C. Knowing this, it will be rational for A to choose R and the Pareto-optimal outcome will be realised. Such an institution does not require major resources since it offers no rewards (indeed, in equilibrium penalties are never paid either), but the credible threat of penalties is sufficient to change behaviour. And if the institution is somewhat costly to maintain, it is likely that these costs could be financed out of the real gains enjoyed by the players. Furthermore, this type of institution would also seem to be capable of being designed by *homo economicus*: since the institution offers a Pareto improvement, it would be approved by all potential players of the game *ex ante* – even if they did not know which of the two roles they would be playing.

But can such an institution be operated by *homo economicus*? As public choice critics have rightly insisted, to simply assume that there exist public institutions that are themselves reliable (i.e. run by benevolent dictators) is to assume the real problem away. The difficulty here is that we are introducing a third 'player' into the game – the enforcer – without explicitly modelling her choices. If the enforcer is herself a rational egoist, the simple fact that the act of enforcement benefits the two original players does not provide her with a reason to act in that way. If the enforcer is granted powers sufficient to ensure compliance by B, she must be assumed to use those powers to maximise her own pay-off, regardless of the impacts on A and B. There is nothing to show that the enforcer's pay-offs are connected to A's and B's in the relevant way; and postulating a further tier of enforcement simply extends the problem.

We shall discuss the problem of enforcement in a rather more general context in chapter 5 below. We do not believe, as some public choice scholars seem to, that this problem is necessarily insoluble, but we do believe that it imposes a strict limitation on the range of institutions that can be sustained in a world of rational egoists. In short, all institutions must ultimately be self-enforcing. That is, while some enforcement may be possible *within* an institution, the institution as a whole must be self-enforcing in the sense that it operates only by channelling the self-interest of the individuals who act within it. Invisible hands are the only kinds of hands that are allowable in this world of unrelieved egoism. While we would certainly not wish to deny the importance of invisible hand mechanisms, they clearly have their limits. And to insist that only invisible hand mechanisms are available is itself, as we shall argue, extremely restrictive. We will return to this question in chapter 4 below. At this point we simply note the problem.

Approaches to the reliance predicament – dispositions

We come now to the third and, for our purposes, most significant way in which we might modify the reliance game in order to resolve the underlying predicament – that is, by modifying the assumed nature of the players to allow them access to dispositions other than rational egoism. There are two issues involved here. The first relates to our distinction between choice of actions and choice of dispositions. The second relates to the distinction between moral and non-moral motivations of the choosing agent. We wish to involve both issues, but we will begin with an extreme case in which only the first is relevant, so that all agents are conceived as rational egoists in the sense that all their basic desires are essentially self-interested.

Suppose that anyone can have a surgical operation performed on the brain which will ensure that any promises made are faithfully kept. Suppose further that this possibility is common knowledge. Suppose also that the operation is irreversible and leaves the person with a distinctive scar on the forehead – a scar that is impossible to fake. The operation has no other effects or risks and is costless to perform. It seems clear that it would be rational for egoists to undergo such an operation to the extent that they expect to be involved in the reliance game in the player B role.[5] Player A will have rational grounds to trust a scarred player B, and so the Pareto-optimal outcome will be realised, leaving B in particular better off. Furthermore, if there is any element of choice in the formation of

---

[5] Of course, an irreversible commitment to promise keeping may be costly in situations other than the reliance predicament, and the rational egoist contemplating the operation would balance expected costs and expected benefits.

partnerships, potential A's will seek out scarred players as partners, so that profitable interactions will be more plentiful for the scarred than the unscarred. The scarred will then do better than the unscarred in terms of lifetime pay-offs.

Note that, just as the common knowledge of rationality is important in the standard game-theoretic analysis, so the common knowledge of the operation and the observable signal of the scar are important here. A's have good reason to trust scarred players on rational grounds – that is, they trust them because they are identified as trustworthy. Common knowledge of the possibility of the operation plus the scar together constitute a perfect signal: the operation makes trustworthiness both credible and transparent. If we change the details of the story, we will get different results. If there is common knowledge of the possibility of the operation but no scar, and everyone knows only that a proportion (p) of individuals have undergone surgery, without knowing who the trustworthy types are, all A's will face a gamble. With probability p strategy R will carry a pay-off of 2, and with probability $(1-p)$ strategy R will carry a pay-off -1. If A is risk neutral and must choose a pure strategy (i.e. she cannot randomise between N and R) she will choose R if and only if p is greater than 0.33. But notice that in this case, individuals will have no reason for undergoing the operation. Whether you will be trusted is completely unrelated to whether you have had the operation. You will do best where p is relatively high, so that A's will be more likely to 'trust' their partners, but where you yourself have not had the operation so that you are free to exploit these trusting A's. This is a classic free rider problem: everyone would like p to be high (i.e. they want others to have the operation), but will not have the operation themselves.

While the case of brain surgery illustrates the possibility of purely egoistic commitment, it lacks any element that bears on morality. It might be that an egoistic commitment gives rise to behaviour that is apparently moral, as with promise keeping in the brain surgery example, but it would be just as plausible to construct an example in which there are good egoistic reasons to adopt a commitment that generated behaviour that was apparently immoral. There can be no general presumption that commitments adopted on egoistic grounds lead to morally appropriate behaviour.

The brain surgery example uses the device of surgery as a means of commitment and represents the limiting case of a disposition where the commitment is hard-wired, transparent and irreversible. Despite these limitations, the surgery example does point to the necessary requirements for any disposition to work. A disposition must be credible, translucent and long-lived. Brain surgery was assumed to carry all of these properties to the limit, but a workable disposition does not need limiting values. Nevertheless, there is an obvious question as to whether such workable dispositions are possible: that is, do techniques exist to support commitment that are accessible to rational individuals? We shall take up this question below. But first we must take the second step in our discussion of the dispositional approach to the reliance predicament and introduce the idea of a moral disposition.

Consider the possibility that there are at least some agents in the community who perceive the keeping of promises to be a morally charged matter. They feel, we might suppose, moral guilt and shame if they fail to keep their promises.[6] Whatever the details, promise keeping is an issue that triggers their desire to act as morality requires – independently of the impact of promise keeping on their other interests. Such agents may wish to adopt a disposition to be trustworthy by reference to this moral desire. We term such a disposition a moral disposition. The disposition is moral in the simple sense that it is morally grounded: it involves an essential appeal to moral categories relating to the goodness or badness of acts. Two obvious questions arise in connection with such moral dispositions: how do moral dispositions operate in relation to interests, and how can they be acquired?

To begin, let us simply suppose that a moral disposition to keep promises exists. If so, then it operates just like any other disposition. All dispositions operate to reconfigure decision making over actions. A moral disposition differs from an egoistic disposition in its grounding, not in its mode of operation. But we would point to one particular aspect of the relationship between moral dispositions and interests. In the case of the reliance predicament, a moral commitment to promise keeping has an important, though contingent, property: namely that life may go better in terms of her own interests for an agent with such a moral disposition than it would in the absence of such a disposition. In this case, then, a moral disposition carries no cost in terms of the sacrifice of interests. Indeed, on the contrary, the moral disposition actually promotes the agent's interests in a manner that is inaccessible to a disposition of narrow self-interest. To put the point in other words, the moral disposition is behaviourally equivalent to the disposition that would be chosen by the rational egoist if only there existed a credible and translucent means of commitment (as in the case of brain surgery). We

---

[6] We do not mean here to commit to a moral psychology in which it is an anxiety about bad feelings consequent on a bad action that induces the agent to act morally. It may just be that the agent feels that exploiting reliance is wrong: that view would in itself count against acting in that way. Guilt and shame are simply convenient heuristics to employ in depicting the agent's rationality.

do not claim that all moral dispositions have this property. Clearly, in other contexts, moral considerations might pick out dispositions that would carry costs in terms of the sacrifice of interests, and differ from the disposition that would be chosen by the rational egoist. The point is simply that there can be no general presumption that moral dispositions are always costly in terms of interests.

We now turn to the question of the acquisition of moral dispositions. Again our general point here is that the acquisition of a moral disposition is broadly comparable to the acquisition of any other disposition: a disposition is rationally acquired in the light of the agent's full range of underlying desires and beliefs. The key difference is simply that a moral disposition depends crucially on the desire to act as morality requires, and on beliefs about the specific content of morality. An agent will have a reason to acquire a moral disposition to the extent that she believes that morality requires action of the particular type picked out by that disposition, and to the extent that the strength of her desire to act as morality requires is sufficient to overcome other pressures. This last point links to the discussion of the relationship between moral dispositions and interests. Where moral dispositions actually promote interests, we might expect such dispositions to be relatively widely chosen, since they require little moral strength – the simple belief that morality requires actions of the relevant type will be almost sufficient. In cases where moral dispositions carry costs in terms of interests, we might expect such dispositions to be less widespread, since they require greater moral strength: that is, a stronger desire to act as morality requires. In this way we might expect to observe heterogeneity in the dispositional make up of the population, with some agents being 'more moral' than others.

Moral and non-moral dispositions raise similar issues. Essentially these relate to the feasibility of rationally acquired dispositions. In particular, two questions seem to arise: can dispositions be sufficiently translucent. And can dispositions be rationally accessible? We will consider each in turn, focusing on moral dispositions in each case.

Translucency

The issue of translucency revolves around the question of the extent to which knowledge of an agent's disposition is accessible to others. We reckon that a sufficient degree of translucency is at least plausible – and offer two arguments in this connection, one negative and one positive. First, we would suggest that the proposition that individuals are entirely opaque – that individuals cannot know anything about other individuals except their actual behaviour – is deeply unconvincing. This proposition is sometimes endorsed by economists – often inappropriately, since much of economics requires that universal rationality is itself common knowledge (i.e. totally transparent). But the point is not just that standard economics requires a considerable degree of motivational translucency. The point is rather that radical solipsism is an extreme assumption that claims too much. If we can have no non-behavioural knowledge of each other, it seems difficult even to make sense of the idea of trust (as distinguished from a purely statistical expectation of behaviour) or of many other ideas that are common to our understanding of human interaction. The idea of trust seems to be connected essentially with some degree of understanding of the motivations of others.[7] And the same point would carry over to all ideas that derive from trust or are parasitic on it. For example, the idea of a confidence trick, or of fraud, are both parasitic on the idea of trust in that they describe cases in which trust is abused. Neither idea could make sense to a radical solipsist. Equally, debates on the likely correlates and causes of trust can make no sense. Questions such as whether trust is more common in 'dense relationships' which involve more face to face interactions over a wide range of issues, or in more specialised 'linear relationships', in one society or another, or at one time or another would be simply meaningless. Complete opacity does not seem to us to be at all plausible as an option. The real question is not so much opacity versus transparency, but the *degree* of translucency.

Second, and more positively, it will clearly be in the interests both of those adopting dispositions, and of those who will interact with them, that such dispositions be (at least) reasonably translucent. Without sufficient translucency, the dispositions will not be signalled and both parties may suffer. To the extent that translucency can be supported or enhanced by technology or social behaviour, there will be an incentive on both sides to support translucency. It might be thought that there will be some who would face the opposite incentive – those who hope to free ride by pretending to be trustworthy, for example. But this is a mistake. Even would be confidence tricksters will have reason to support translucency (but not, in their case, total transparency) since it is only if trustworthiness is established that there will be trusting behaviour for the trickster to exploit. In short, everyone has a rational incentive to promote translucency. Of course, the trustworthy have a further incentive to distinguish themselves from the expedient egoists, but this simply adds to the pressure for translucency. That such private incentives exist is not sufficient to show that means for making motives translucent can be

[7] See, particularly, Becker (1996).

found; demand does not necessarily create its own supply. But the absence of demand would surely be a problem.

Given that translucency of some degree seems essential to our understanding of social life, and that most, if not all, agents will have an incentive to ensure translucency to a sufficient degree, it seems reasonable to allow that the appropriate degree of translucency is at least plausible.[8]

Rational access

But how, exactly, are dispositions brought into existence? We hope that we have established that, if the degree of translucency is sufficient, an individual will have a rational reason to adopt a disposition to behave in a trustworthy fashion. But how does this reason become effective? Unless an external technology (such as the brain surgery of our earlier example) exists that serves the relevant purpose, what resources does the individual have to commit to a disposition?

Note that there is a particular problem facing the egoistic agent who seeks to develop a disposition – namely that the very reason that impels him to acquire the disposition is the same reason that gives him grounds to break with that disposition in the arena of action. I 'choose' to adopt a disposition to be trustworthy because I will be better off if people trust me: but if they should trust me I will be better off still by exploiting their trust. Perhaps an individual can habituate herself to the action of always keeping promises, exploiting the force of habit and putting out of her mind the reasons why this was a good habit to have. But there does appear to be at stake here an element of self-deception; the advantages of being trustworthy emerge as one of Jon Elster's category of 'necessarily incidental consequences of an action undertaken for other reasons'. Having the disposition to be trustworthy can be 'psychologically rein-forced' by the benefits it brings, but there are problems if those benefits are the reason why the disposition was chosen.

Now, compare the task of supporting a moral disposition with that of supporting an egoistically acquired disposition. These two tasks seem to parallel each other in most respects: whatever resources are available to the non-moral exercise are available to the moral exercise. But there is one key distinction between the two projects, one resource that is available to the moral exercise that is not available to the non-moral – namely moral argument. Whatever the strength of the agent's moral

---

[8] Detailed discussion of the mechanisms by which character and emotion may be rendered translucent in a broadly economistic framework is provided by Frank (1988).

beliefs, they give her an additional source of support for a moral disposition. Lacking any fundamental normative support, non-moral dispositions will be susceptible to unravelling in a way that does not threaten genuinely moral dispositions. Whatever the prospects for establishing dispositions, we would suggest that they are more promising for moral dispositions than they are for their more egoistically grounded cousins.

Consider, for example, the calculus of a parent, engaged in the exercise of influencing a young child's dispositional make up. Suppose that parent desires that the child's life go as well for the child as is possible, understood in purely egoist pay-off terms. Given the requisite degree of translucency, the parent will then inculcate in the child the disposition to keep promises, and in searching for reasons to ground this disposition in the child will look for reasons other than egoist ones. Assuming that the child has some nascent moral sense – some access to categories of 'good' (that which you should do) and 'bad' (that which you should not) – it will be to that sense that the parent is likely to look. The parent will want the child to act in a trustworthy way for its own sake, and will want to use the entire repertoire of accessible reasons to bolster that disposition – aesthetic, moral, identity-related and so on. So the child will, to the extent that it can be 'programmed' in this way, come to believe that being trustworthy is a morally good thing. And now, the next generation of parents will have two reasons, not just one, for inculcating in their own children a disposition of trustworthiness – first, because that will make their children's life go better in egoist terms; and second, because they believe that being trustworthy is morally right.

A moral disposition has its origins, at least in the account we have given, in a belief – the belief that a particular type of action (keeping promises, for example) is morally required. Of course, that belief is not sufficient in itself to induce a moral disposition, but it is necessary. Without the belief, the disposition cannot be moral in the appropriate sense and the disposition cannot be robust to temptation to the same extent as a truly moral disposition is. But then will it not be rational for an egoist individual simply to adopt the belief that promise keeping is morally required and, by this means, gain the extra resources that may help her to adopt a 'moral' disposition of trustworthiness? And if this is so, how can a moral disposition be distinguished from an egoistic disposition?

Our response here is, in part, to rely on the Humean account of rationality. Beliefs are not the objects of unconstrained rational choice but are the background against which rational choices are made. Coming to a belief is route-specific: it depends on one's coming to see something as true, and 'true' here means something much more than simply 'convenient to treat as if it were true'. A simple desire to believe a proposition (whether moral or otherwise) cannot work as evidence for the truth of that proposition. Of course, rational egoists may wish they had access to moral dispositions (in those cases where moral dispositions also generate private returns) and may do what they can to come to hold such a disposition. But the belief must be genuine if the disposition is to be robust. Any attempt at deception (including self-deception) will be vulnerable to reflection that recognises that the very reason for the attempt to generate the disposition is also a reason for departure from the disposition once others have come to trust you. In short, the egoist attempting to impersonate someone acting under a moral disposition of trustworthiness will always face the temptation to exploit trust, because the argument for impersonation and the argument for exploitation appeal to the same currency, self-interest. Only when the belief that trustworthiness is morally required is genuine will the disposition be reinforced by a moral argument that acts to buttress the agent against the temptation to exploit. In that case, the disposition will not be vulnerable to reflection on its underlying motivation. Though it will, of course, be vulnerable to the clamour of other desires, including most notably purely egoistic desires.

This may make it seem that the choice of dispositions – and particularly moral dispositions – is entirely beyond influence; that dispositions are in some sense 'natural' – determined by native beliefs and desires that are themselves entirely beyond explanation. This is not so. While beliefs cannot be willed, dispositional choice can be influenced by, for example, the structure of social institutions. Changes in the structure of social institutions can affect agents' beliefs about what actions morality requires by the simple means of varying the relationship between actions and their consequences. If social institutions are designed in such a way that actions of a particular type – say the keeping of promises – are particularly productive of morally desirable consequences, then individuals may come to believe this (since it is true); and this belief may, in turn, influence the determination of dispositions.

The foregoing discussion should serve to indicate our view that there is an irreducible moral element in rationally supportable moral dispositions. Such dispositions require a 'moral' element in two senses – first, that they depend on a genuine belief that particular actions are morally required, and second, that they require in the agent a desire to act as morality requires. We recognise that acquiring such a moral disposition as a matter of expressly rational choice is problematic, and that moral dispositions, once acquired, are unlikely to be perfect. But neither of these facts supports the extreme claim that moral dispositions cannot arise – and in cases where the possessors of such moral dispositions flourish *vis-à-vis* their rational egoist cousins, the moral disposition seems likely to flourish correspondingly.

Are moral dispositions important?

The model of the reliance predicament set out above represents a class of two-person interactions that is often used to depict in a simple form the idea of interpersonal exchange for mutual advantage that is the basic building block of economic analysis. To be sure, not all market transactions will have a profitable exploitation option for player *B*. But many market transactions are of this general type – especially where payment and delivery of goods are separated in time or space, or where one party has information about the exchange that is not available to the other.

Whatever the situation in the market context, the reliance predicament is certainly important in the setting of democratic politics. In the design of political institutions that is of central concern in this book, one of the key issues is the extent of citizen reliance on political agents. The essential character of any democratic social order involves 'each' citizen ceding power to 'all' – with the 'all' normally operating through the medium of some agent or agents.[9] But how much power should be ceded? And how much discretion should political agents be allowed? These fundamental constitutional questions clearly engage questions of 'trust' – the trustworthiness of political agents and the trust of citizens.

If this is so, and versions of the reliance predicament are a recurring theme in the structure of democratic politics, it is no less true that these political instantiations of the predicament tend to be less amenable to the strategies of repetition and enforcement than are the predicaments encountered in the economic sphere. While repetition, for example, clearly has a role to play in understanding some political institutions – most obviously the discipline imposed by periodic re-election – there are many political settings which lie outside the scope of repetition. Indeed, some institutions seem to pull explicitly in the opposite direction – most obviously the limitations on repeated candidature that are imposed in many constitutions. Similarly, the idea of external enforcement mechanisms seems to have little relevance to the design of political institutions

---

[9] The idea that the relationship between the polity and their representatives – between principal and agent – identifies the key problem of democratic politics is discussed in chapter 7 below. The topic of representative versus direct democracy is treated at length in chapter 9.

which form the basic structure of political society. Enforcement mechanisms may operate well to solve particular issues *within* a political framework, but it is difficult to see how they can support that framework itself.

Now, if trust were a purely political phenomenon, arising in no other aspect of life, it might seem unlikely that the capacities to commit to a moral disposition of trustworthiness, and to discern trustworthiness in others, would be particularly well developed. But the fact that trustworthiness is also privately profitable to ordinary agents in a variety of everyday market transactions lends plausibility to the claim that trustworthiness will emerge as a significant factor in social interactions generally. To this extent, we believe that the complementarity between the three approaches to the resolution of the reliance predicament is important. Patterns of trust may develop in some settings as a result of the repeated nature of the relevant game, or as a result of enforcement within a self-enforcing institutional structure, or as a result of the adoption of appropriate dispositions. Whatever their explanation, these patterns will make the idea of trust salient and will also tend to develop the ability to signal trustworthiness in a reasonably reliable and translucent manner. And this background provides a good setting for the adoption of the moral disposition of trustworthiness since it provides direct evidence of the moral value of trust. The view that it is morally wrong to betray trust, in environments where others have come to rely on you and will be harmed by your betrayal, will be widely held. And, on the general account offered here, the fact that one believes an act to be morally wrong gives one a direct reason for avoiding that act. Further, in arenas (such as politics) where one is especially vulnerable to exploitation by others, one will have special reason to look out for trustworthy persons to occupy the relevant positions.

We take our discussion of trust to suggest support for three broad conclusions. First, that trustworthiness as a disposition may be privately profitable to those who possess it and are identifiable as such. In itself this provides the basis for the prediction that trustworthiness is likely to emerge, although its scope may be limited and its foundations relatively fragile. Second, that trustworthiness is best understood as a moral disposition that gains further support from broadly egoistic considerations. And third, that the moral dimension of trustworthiness will have genuine behavioural consequences.

We would also suggest that everything that we have said about the example of trust, will apply with only detailed modification in other relevant examples. Trustworthiness is by no means the only moral disposition that is relevant to politics. We suggest that all such dispositions may be rationally accessible to agents with a basic desire to act morally. However, the extent to which such dispositions are realised in practice will depend not only on the strength of the underlying moral commitments, but also on other factors such as the presence of relevant institutional support.

We hope that we have done enough to render plausible three claims: a fundamental desire to act morally can be parlayed into a disposition that is an effective determinant of action in particular settings; that such moral dispositions can, in certain circumstances, be complementary with private interest; and that these possibilities are especially relevant in the political context. If these claims are accepted, then a political analysis that leaves morality entirely out of account seems somewhat implausible – and seems especially so for anyone who is disposed to think that at some basic level, self-interest plays a significant role in motivating behaviour.

4

Economising on virtue

The aim of every political constitution is, or ought to be, first to obtain for rulers men who possess most wisdom to discern, and most virtue to pursue, the common good of the society; and in the next place, to take the most effectual precautions for keeping them virtuous whilst they continue to hold their public trust.

(*Federalist* papers, 57, James Madison)

Motivation and morality

In the two preceding chapters we have advanced a general model of human motivation that incorporates a desire to act morally alongside other desires, where that desire may operate either as a direct determinant of action or as a ground for the adoption of a moral disposition. We wish, in this chapter, to push the argument forward on three distinct fronts.

Our first concern will be with the idea of economising on virtue – the idea that institutions should be designed in such a way that they do not rely on the virtue of the individuals who act under them, so that the emergence of satisfactory results arises not only through the virtue of individuals but also is supported by the force of other motives, including self-interest specifically. This idea is an old one, dating at least from St Augustine's discussion of private property as a *remedium peccatorum* (guard against sin) – though, as is well-known, it receives its most extensive development and application in the work of Adam Smith, David Hume, Montesquieu and the American authors of the *Federalist* papers.

On the face of it, the idea of mobilising an entire range of diverse motives to support the good working of the social order seems self-evidently a good thing. Why depend solely on citizen virtue, when arrangements can be set in place that will secure the desired results from agents whose 'virtue' is weak? In fact, however, the idea of economising on virtue is, at least in some versions and some contexts, highly controversial. For example, the idea is often used to justify reliance on markets to allocate resources in areas where markets are widely regarded as somewhat dubious. A particular case of some salience involves the market in blood which became a minor *cause celebre* with the publication of Richard Titmuss's *The Gift Relation* in 1970. Analogous issues are at stake in markets for transplantable organs and potentially adoptive children, and are engaged in less striking terms in many current debates on privatisation in areas where privatisation is an issue. Many scholars who might be expected to be generally sympathetic to the idea of economising on virtue seem anxious that it may be carried too far. Part of the reason for this anxiety may well be terminological: the very phrase may well invite the suspicion that various institutions economise on virtue in the same way that a liar economises on the truth. And perhaps the phrase 'economising on virtue' is misleading. We use it here only because it has a certain currency in institutional analysis circles – deriving in part from the rhetorical force of Dennis Robertson's famous essay.[1] In any event, as we shall argue, there is much more at stake in anxieties about economising on virtue than mere terminology.

Our discussion of the idea of economising on virtue will be presented in two steps. In the next section we will introduce the idea of virtue and link it to our discussion of the rational choice of moral dispositions. We will then provide an analysis of the idea of economising on virtue – identifying a number of senses of the phrase, analysing their interrelationships and picking out the broad structure of the idea that will inform our subsequent discussion.

Our second general concern in this chapter will be the heterogeneity of motivation across individuals. We have already alluded to this idea on several occasions, but we need to say more about the role and importance of the assumption of heterogeneity in our analysis of political devices. Our third concern will be to discuss more fully the substantive content of morality that might underlie our model of virtue. We do not intend to argue for one particular moral theory over all others – rather we seek for a formulation of agents' moral desires that is consistent with a wide

---

[1] Robertson (1956), particularly pp. 148–54.

variety of substantive moralities, and one that is particularly suited to the analysis of democratic political institutions.

The nature of virtue

Despite the recent resurgence in virtue ethics, there seems to be no generally accepted approach to the definition of virtue or virtues.[2] We do not intend to address this issue in any foundational way. We take virtue to be dispositional in the sense that we have outlined in chapter 3. The virtuous agent is one who has chosen the disposition to act as morality requires *because* that is the act that morality requires, in at least some relevant contexts. The agent is, in short, motivated directly by moral considerations when facing the choice among actions in relevant settings. Note that, for the moment, this idea of virtue is independent of any particular substantive moral theory in that it merely requires the agent to be appropriately motivated relative to the relevant substantive concept of the good (or the right). This simple account of the virtuous agent is intended to stand in sharp contrast to the interested agent, who acts under the disposition of rational egoism. Of course, many other dispositions are possible, and even with respect to these two dispositions we should think of a continuum of possibilities between these two extremes; but the stark contrast between the virtuous agent and the interested agent will allow the argument to be sketched in simple terms.

Similarly, we do not intend to deny that there are, in fact, many particular virtues in addition to the single overarching virtue stipulated here – or that the multiplicity of virtues and the dispositions that go with them are likely to be important in any detailed account of democratic political institutions. Our intention here is just to retain the simplest possible structure that we believe capable of capturing the basic idea of a virtuous disposition. We can then investigate the sort of work that this idea can do in the context of the design of democratic political institutions.

If virtue is the disposition to act as morality requires in at least certain circumstances, we should also be clear on the question of the value of virtue. There are two parts to this question – one concerning the value to the individual, and one concerning the more general social value.[3] At the level of the individual, the virtuous disposition is valuable to the extent

---

[2] See, for example, Anscombe (1958), Geach (1977), Foot (1978) and MacIntyre (1981).

[3] We do not intend this phrase to imply any particular commitment to any theory of social value – see below.

that it serves the basic desires of the relevant individual – including, but not limited to, the desire to act as morality requires. The virtuous disposition would be rationally chosen only if the expected value of having that disposition exceeded the expected value of having other feasible dispositions.

At the level of society we take the value of virtue to be the increase in the value of social outcomes brought about by virtuous dispositions. Virtue, on this account, is not its own reward, but is socially valued only as a means of serving substantive ends. This view is adopted in part to focus on the possible trade off between alternative institutional means of serving normatively derived ends – some of which may rely upon virtuous dispositions while others operate by economising on virtue in one of the senses to be identified below.

Although we do not see ourselves as staking out a particularly restrictive view of the nature of virtue, there is one, reasonably common, conception of virtue that we want to question. This particular conception identifies virtue as a sort of 'moral muscle'.[4] Virtue, on this view, is like muscular strength or certain skills: it develops with use and withers from disuse. And this view might gain some support from that tradition that links the acquisition of virtue to the development of 'good' habits where constant use prevents the force of habituation from eroding. There are perhaps Aristotelian and Humboltian echoes here: *omne ageus agenda perficitur*. However, the moral muscle conception of virtue invites certain misconceptions and carries certain implications that we think are highly questionable.

A strict interpretation of the muscular analogy carries with it, for example, not only the importance of muscle-building by exercise but also the possibility of muscles becoming tired with extensive use, and requiring periods of rest. On this view, in the longer run, virtue may depend positively on the extent of virtuous action in previous periods, but virtue will be fixed and exhaustible in the short run. This conception likens virtue to a stock in the short run and, as we indicate below, this is not a conception we find plausible.

Moreover, to the extent that habituation plays a role in determining or supporting virtue, one needs to take care in specifying precisely to what it is that the agent becomes habituated. If, for example, agents become habituated to the performance of particular actions, then any institution that encourages these actions will be desirable, regardless of the details of the institution or the motivations that induce the actions, in so far as the conditions that render those actions desirable remain in place. For

---

[4] Hirschman (1985) provides a discussion.

example, Adam Smith's famous butcher and baker who find themselves in a market institution which ensures that public and private interests pick out identical actions may become habituated to those actions. The baker may, that is, become habituated to providing high-quality bread under the discipline of a competitive market, and may continue to maintain that high quality even when the discipline is relaxed and opportunities to use cheaper materials without reducing price present themselves. Equally, an institutional arrangement that develops muscular strength by building exercise into activities pursued for other reasons need be no less effective at promoting muscular strength than arrangements that provide access to gymnasia: there need be no systematic advantage to arrangements that operate only through an agent's desire to get fit for its own sake. In this way we would suggest that if habituation operates at the level of actions, there can be no presumption that particular motivations matter, or matter much. If virtue is as virtue does, institutions that induce and habituate the actions associated with virtue seem to be perfectly acceptable substitutes for virtue itself.

If this conclusion is to be avoided, the moral muscle argument seems to require that individuals become habituated not to actions but to modes of deliberation or calculation – at the level of dispositions, in our terms. On this version of the argument, motivations are indeed central and the moral or virtuous disposition is threatened by lack of exercise. The anxiety is that individuals who routinely adopt self-interested modes of deliberation in a wide variety of settings will lose the ability for moral deliberation where it is required. We take this anxiety seriously, but the argument itself is by no means self-evident. The force of the anxiety lies in the presumed causal connection between institutional settings and the disposition that is operative under them – so that market settings, for example, induce self-interested calculation. No grounds are offered for believing that such a causal connection exists. We will offer a more detailed analysis of this possibility in chapter 6. As we shall show there, the anxiety itself can be grounded, and investigated, without muscular analogies and within a dispositional conception of virtue.

The idea(s) of economising on virtue

There seem to us to be two basic questions at stake in viewing the relationship between virtue and institutional design. We may think of them as the static and dynamic questions, or as the direct and indirect questions. The static, direct question is how best to design institutions given a particular distribution of dispositions (virtuous and interested) in the population. That is, holding virtue constant, how best can we structure our institutions? The dynamic, indirect question then concerns the possibility of feedback effects from institutional design to dispositional choice. Do certain types of institution promote the choice of virtuous dispositions, while others undermine virtue? If such feedback effects arise, and are predictable, they too should be included in the overall analysis and evaluation of institutions.

There is no easy conclusion that the answers to these two questions will pick out the same institutional arrangements as desirable, or that one of these questions always dominates the other. It might be the case that the answer to the static question pulls in favour of one type of institution while the answer to the dynamic question pulls in favour of another type, and if this were the case, the further question of balancing these two effects would arise. Our aim is to provide a simple framework for such balanced analysis: one that allows both the static and dynamic aspects to be studied, and for various strategies in the design of institutions to be assessed. Economising on virtue identifies one family of strategies available to the institutional designer.

One thing should be clear from the outset. To justify institutions that economise on virtue in no way requires that everyone be wholly egoistic. Indeed, if all agents were wholly egoistic, there would be no virtue to economise on; or, to put the same point in other words, economising on virtue would be inevitable. Equally, if virtue were universal, there would be no need to economise on it. The strategy of economising on virtue is only relevant in a world in which virtue exists but is scarce. To be sure, if most individuals are overwhelmingly self-interested then institutions that make only modest demands on agents' virtue will be more crucial to a well-ordered society than if most people are virtuous most of the time. In other words, economising on virtue is likely to be a more relevant consideration where individuals are more self-interested, but economising on virtue must be an option of interest in any world in which virtue is scarce.

But what exactly does it mean for an institutional arrangement to economise on virtue? There are at least four different aspects to the idea of economising that we wish to isolate. We will discuss each in turn. The first of these we will dispose of quite briefly. Our main attention will be focused on the three remaining aspects, because these are the aspects that we see as bearing on the key issues of institutional design.

Economising on a stock

Consider some fixed stock of some good that can be used up or stored, like a quantity of a non-renewable resource such as coal or oil.

Economising on the stock of coal means saving coal up now so that more will be available in the future. The application of this idea in the case of virtue might be that each person has a certain stock of 'virtue', and that when that virtue is used up, she has to act egoistically or maliciously thereafter. The straightforward argument for arrangements that economise on virtue would then be that such arrangements free one up to be more virtuous in other arenas.

It should be clear that this notion of economising, in treating virtue like a stock of coal, sits rather oddly with our formulation of virtue as a disposition. We do not normally think of a disposition being consumed by use, and we are not inclined to see this concept of economising on virtue as a useful way to make sense of the metaphor. We mention it here only to dismiss it.

Economising in use

Consider some 'virtuous act'. By definition here a virtuous act is one that not only has the appropriately 'moral' content, but is also chosen under a virtuous disposition. Now, as we have already noted, it is a matter of basic economic logic that this act will be undertaken more extensively (or will be more likely to be undertaken) if it is less costly to the actor in terms of other desired things forgone. That is, the demand curve for the virtuous act is downward sloping.

For example, a voter is more likely to go to the polls if the journey is pleasant than if the journey is unpleasant. A judge is more likely to find fairly in a case in which he has no financial interest. A public official is more likely to allocate a contract to the best tender if she does not own shares in any of the tendering companies. A jury member is more likely to assess a case on its merits if the accused is unknown to her. And so on.

When economists talk of economising on virtue, it is usually this case of economising in use that they have in mind. This fact may not be entirely obvious, however, because economists routinely discuss such issues in extreme settings where virtue is assumed to be irrelevant to individual behaviour. In particular, in the context of pure invisible hand mechanisms, agents can be expected to perform the act required by public interest out of considerations of pure private interest – or not at all. To return to the case of Adam Smith's butcher and baker, the simple point is that the competitive market requires no virtue on the part of the baker to produce the wherewithal for the dinners of others. But the baker may still be virtuous. Smith does not rule out the possibility that the baker may delight in serving the dining needs of her community, and cannot do so on *a priori* grounds, because it is not possible to tell from the baker's actions what motivation is in place.

Of course, should the invisible hand process be imperfect at the margin, behavioural differences will emerge. The virtuous baker will refrain from profitable but anti-social strategies, the interested baker will not. Virtue may make a difference. But there are two points to be emphasised: first, the standard point that the good working of the market does not depend on virtue to any great extent – even opportunities for price fixing and fraud may be limited by the freedom of entry and the discipline of continuous trading; but second, and more importantly in the present context, one cannot induce from the fact that the competitive market does not require virtue that virtue will be driven out. Virtuous persons will flourish alongside their more interested cousins because they each do what the competitive market rewards: that is part of what it means to say that institution of the competitive market economises on virtue.

In more general cases where invisible hand mechanisms are absent or only partially successful, virtuous action will be more costly to the actor who pursues it: to behave virtuously will be to act morally in cases where things will go less well for you if you do. However, this cost will be lower where the institutional structure succeeds in economising on virtue. Economising on the use of virtue in this sense seems straightforwardly to reduce the price of virtuous action and so encourage such action. This aspect of economising on virtue is extensively studied. It remains fundamental.

Economising in allocation

A critical element in any first-year course in economic principles is the theory of comparative advantage – the idea, that is, that trade permits agents to specialise in things they are (relatively) good at. Indeed, this allocational issue is, on some views, the central consideration in any economising ambition. Thus, for example, the idea that the market mechanism encourages the division and specialisation of labour, with each worker employing his skills and abilities in their most highly valued use, is fundamental to the claims of the efficiency of the market mechanism.

There is a direct application of this allocational aspect in the context of economising on virtue. Efficiency will require that virtuous individuals be allocated to roles that are particularly reliant on virtue – that individuals should be selected, at least in part, by reference to their motivational dispositions; and further, that institutions should be designed and assessed with this aspect in mind. Interestingly, however, this aspect of economising is almost entirely absent from the economist's theory of institutional design. There are at least two possible reasons for this. One is that the focus on Smithian invisible hands has directed attention to incentive mechanisms almost exclusively. The second is that economists have been very reluctant to depart from the *homo economicus* assumption and the attendant implication of motivational homogeneity. Only if there is some virtue in the population and only if that virtue is unevenly distributed across persons can there be any possibility of selecting the more virtuous agents for particular roles.

Economising on virtue in this allocational sense might be thought of as an alternative to economising in use – both attempt to extract the greatest value from a given level of virtuous motivation. But the ideas in play are very different, and can be variously related. In some cases, the incentive aspects of an institutional device (focusing on 'economising in use' in our sense) and the selection aspect (economising in allocation) might operate in complementary fashion, while in other cases, the two aspects might operate against each other. It is an important element of the task of the analysis of institutional devices to view the nature of this interaction in specific cases, and where possible to choose institutional arrangements that minimise any conflict.

Economising in production

If some technology were found for producing more steel from a given amount of iron ore at no extra cost (or at an additional cost that did not outweigh the value of the extra steel) we might refer to that technology as economising on iron ore. That is the spirit of economising on virtue in use, discussed above: virtue is conceived as an input into producing outcomes, and reliance on that input should be reduced where this is both feasible and cost-effective. But, to return to the steel analogy, iron ore also needs to be extracted, and a technology that generates more ore for less effort and energy is no less an economising technology for steel production – but at one remove.

Economising on virtue in production, as we term it here, is taken to refer to the generation of virtue itself. Any social process that inhibits the generation of virtue, other things equal, will not economise on virtue in production. It is at this level that the dynamic or indirect question identified above arises: do some institutional arrangements reduce or erode virtue in production? Are there institutional arrangements that encourage the supply of virtue? And how do these institutional arrangements relate to those institutions that economise on virtue in use or in allocation?

Our interest here is less in explaining why dispositions are as they are, and more in showing how we might expect dispositions to respond to changing institutional arrangements. In particular, we are interested in cases where institutions that attempt to economise on virtue in use (or in allocation) will *undermine* the production of virtue, conceived as a chosen behavioural disposition. This case is one in which virtue would be 'crowded out', to use Bruno Frey's terminology.[5] Here, we point, again, to the simplest relative price propositions of standard economics. Specifically, we take it that persons are less likely to adopt virtuous dispositions – for themselves or for their children – the less well their lives will go as a result, and obversely. That is, if adopting the disposition to be virtuous becomes more costly, virtue will be eroded.

The implication is that a shift to institutions that economise on virtue in use will tend to erode virtue only if being virtuous is made more costly thereby. But, on the face of it, precisely the opposite seems to be the case. Institutions that economise on virtue in use serve to arrange matters so that interests and virtue indicate the same actions. But in such circumstances, the virtuous disposition becomes *less* rather than more costly – more, rather than less, likely to be chosen. Why, then, might one be concerned that virtue would be eroded? If honesty is the best policy, people will choose the disposition to be honest more often – and purely expedient egoists will also be led to be honest. Honest action is consistent *both* with direct calculative egoism and with dispositional honesty. At the very least, there does not seem to be any more reason to think that honest people will become increasingly expedient than that expedient persons will adopt the disposition to be honest. Of course the matter deserves more explicit consideration, and we will provide this in chapter 6, where we also consider institutions that economise on virtue in allocation. But there seems to be no general presumption that economising on virtue in use will necessarily erode virtue in production. In this sense, the widespread anxiety about reliance on market-like arrangements on the grounds that they tend to 'crowd out' virtue seems out of place. More needs to be said about the possibility of conflict between alternative aspects of virtue-economising, but there is nothing to indicate that such conflicts will arise as a matter of course.

To summarise, we have identified four possible senses in which we might speak of economising on virtue. The first of these – the simple notion of

5 Frey (1997a, 1997b).

economising on a stock – we have dismissed from further consideration: but the remaining three are all of continuing relevance. Economising on virtue in use requires us to make the best use of whatever virtue exists by means of designing institutions that operate as invisible hands, or otherwise by reducing the effective cost of virtuous behaviour. Economising on virtue in allocation requires us to make the best use of whatever virtue exists by channelling or selecting virtuous individuals into those social roles that are particularly demanding of virtue. Economising on virtue in either of these senses may be in conflict with the economising on virtue in production. That is, institutions that economise on virtue in use or in allocation may erode the base of virtuous dispositions and so turn out to offer a 'false economy'. But nothing we have said so far suggests that such conflicts are any more likely than are complementarities. Creating economic incentives to act in the way virtue requires, and/or selecting relatively virtuous agents for roles where much virtue is required, seems at least as likely to encourage people to adopt virtuous dispositions as to discourage them from doing so.

Dispositional heterogeneity

It should be clear enough from our discussion of the idea of economising on virtue in allocation that heterogeneity of motivational dispositions will play an important part in our account of democratic institutions. We believe that recognition of a range of dispositions – even the two basic dispositions of our simple model – is both warranted and necessary if the rational actor approach to political institutions is to be rich enough to account for the variety of institutional devices that we encounter in the political sphere. But we should be clear about exactly what is being assumed. It is at the level of dispositions that we incorporate heterogeneity, with some individuals adopting the disposition of rational egoism while others adopt virtuous dispositions. But these dispositions are themselves endogenous on our account; they are rationally chosen in the context of particular institutional settings. At the most basic level of individual desires, we adhere to the idea of structural homogeneity of desires. That is, we conceive of all individuals in terms of a set of desires including the desire to act as morality requires. Within this homogeneous structure, however, we allow interpersonal variations in the relative strengths of the basic desires, and we assume that this variation is sufficient, in most institutional settings, to ensure some variety in the dispositions that are rationally chosen.

There is no formal difference here from the standard economic approach to consumer behaviour in which all consumers are endowed with the same structure of preferences and desires – a common form of utility function, as it might be – but allowed detailed interpersonal variations in the parameters of their utility functions so that each may choose a different bundle of consumption goods.

At the deepest level, then, we do not depart from the standard assumption of motivational homogeneity. We depart from standard practice only by introducing a desire to act morally as one desire among many, and by emphasising the intermediate level of the choice of dispositions which stand between the basic motivational desires that characterise individuals, and the choice of particular actions in particular institutional contexts.

There is a well-known quotation from Hume that is often invoked in connection with the appropriate motivational assumption to adopt when considering institutional design:

> in contriving any system of government, and fixing the several checks and controls of the constitution, every man ought to be supposed a knave, and to have no other end, in all his actions, than private interest. (Hume, 1985, pp. 42–3)

Setting aside the question of whether this quotation accurately reflects Hume's views on the matter, and focusing simply on the analytic method implied, there are three independent claims made here: first, that everyone ought to be assumed to be identically motivated; second, that the identical motivation ought to be that of pure private interest; and third, that private interest motivations are equivalent to knavishness (i.e. egoism is the root of all evil). All three claims ought to be contested. Certainly, we would contest them and we believe that plenty of relevant supporting argument could be found in Hume himself. But here we want simply to emphasise how restrictive these claims are. In particular, they serve to rule out entirely any consideration of the allocative dimension of economising on virtue.[6]

We do accept what we take to be one important aspect of the Hume quotation – namely, that one ought to reject any simple compliance theory of political motivation. We should, in other words, avoid solving the compliance problem by assuming non-compliance away. As we have noted, within any pure self-interest model the possibility of economising on virtue in allocation is entirely closed off from analysis. At the other extreme, under any compliance theory of motivation, the possibility of

---

[6] It should again be stressed that this marks a sharp departure from earlier writing on the topic for one of us – compare for example Brennan and Buchanan (1980a, 1985) where the assumption of self-interested motivation is defended in the constitutional context.

economising on virtue (in any of its senses) is simply irrelevant. We seek a path between these two extremes. Once a desire to act as morality requires enters into the basic motivational structure attributed to individuals, and the possibility of the choice of dispositions is recognised, the way is open to analyse the resulting heterogeneity of dispositions, and in particular how that heterogeneity both influences and depends upon the design of institutional devices.

Substantive morality

We come, at last, to the question of the nature of the morality that informs our agent's basic desires. We have deliberately left this topic until last because we believe that almost all of our discussion of the rational choice of moral dispositions, of virtue, and of the strategies of economising on virtue, is independent of any particular specification of the underlying substantive morality. Our discussion, as we have said before, is more concerned with the structure of rational and moral choice than with its detailed content. We have also said that we do make certain structural requirements on morality: most obviously that it should be broadly agreed in the sense that the content of morality is reasonably common across individuals – common enough for there to be a shared moral code covering at least the major aspects of moral behaviour. In this section we want to be a little more specific about both the structure and the content of morality that we have in mind. We will begin by underlining two further structural points.

The first point concerns the distinction between morality and self-interest.[7] For many writers this distinction is fundamental, with morality being characterised as a concern for others.[8] Of course, this characterisation does not amount to a substantive theory of morality, since it leaves open the important questions of the form of the concern and the identity of the relevant others; but the contrast between self and other – between self-interest and altruism – seems to many to be the key step towards defining morality. This view is in sharp contrast with an alternative conception of morality that attempts to soften this contrast and to view morality and self-interest as mutually dependent. This alternative conception is most obviously present in the Aristotelian tradition in which the virtues are seen as indispensable and constitutive parts of the good life for

[7] Throughout, we use self-interest in the narrow sense of the individual's self-regarding interests. Of course, if the individual has, as we assume, a desire to be moral, then one could speak of morality being in the individual's self-interest in the broader sense that it is an interest that the 'self' has.
[8] This might be termed the Humean view – as expressed by Williams (1973).

any individual, but also in some parts of modern contractarian thought where morality is brought within the scope of interests.[9]

We do not need to take sides in this debate, but we would point to the implausibility of either extreme position. At one extreme, self-interest and morality are seen as identical (or one is seen as reducible to the other); at the other extreme, morality requires an absolute selflessness and there is no place for the personal in the moral. The more interesting possibilities lie in the middle ground, where self-interest and morality may overlap to some extent without the distinction being altogether lost. We believe that our formulation is consistent with a wide variety of positions in this middle ground.

A second structural point relates to the authority of morality. On some accounts morality is taken as authoritative in the sense that moral arguments and moral reasons always outweigh or trump their non-moral counterparts. If morality requires you to undertake action *A*, then action *A* is what you *should* do all things considered. But this can be true without morality actually motivating you to *do A*. Our framework does not assume that agents do what they believe they should do, either at the deep level of the choice of dispositions or at the level of the choice of action. In each case, the demands of morality are just one type of demand, which must be balanced by the agent against other demands. And different agents will weigh moral considerations differently. Some will be 'more moral' in the sense that they grant moral considerations greater weight in their rational deliberations, and these agents are both more likely to select virtuous dispositions, and more likely to act morally than their 'less moral' counterparts. The weight placed on moral considerations by agents is part of the fine-grained detail of agent motivation, and is not stipulated by anything that we have said.

So all that is required for our purposes is that there is a roughly shared moral code which permits fine-grained differences in both the precise interpretation of what morality requires, and in the weight with which moral considerations enter into rational deliberation. This shared moral code does not reduce morality to individual interests but we would expect that it would include a concern for the 'public interest' defined in terms of the private interests of all individuals. Incorporating this idea of the public interest need not commit us to any simple utilitarianism – we have no need to insist that the public interest is defined as a simple sum of individual utilities, still less do we need to insist that the idea of the public interest constitutes the whole of morality. Rather we incorporate the specific idea of the public interest as a common element in moral

[9] Most obviously, Gauthier (1986).

motivation so as to provide a minimal substantive content to our moral structure in a manner that seems most appropriate to the study of democratic political institutions. Democracy has many dimensions, but two that seem to be fundamental are that it involves both government *for* the people, and government *by* the people. A shared morality that is at least sensitive to benefits and costs that arise *for* the people seems to be a sensible prerequisite for any account of the ways in which specific institutional devices operationalise the idea of government *by* the people. To put this point in other words: we see ourselves as engaged in the task of analysing and evaluating democratic politics from the inside, that is, from within an essentially democratic framework. Such a framework requires a normative structure that supports the basic idea of democracy. A shared morality of the type we have described – one that includes, but is not limited to, a concern for the public interest – seems like a minimal specification of such a structure.

Recalling our own motivation for the inclusion of a moral element in agents' motivational structure, one thing at least should be clear – that the content of the moral dispositions at the level of the individual agents should be connected to the content of the normative scheme of evaluation that is to be applied to social states or the processes that produce those social states in assessing alternative institutional arrangements. To take a simple example, if outcomes in possible prisoner's dilemma situations are to be evaluated by reference to the Pareto-dominated pay-off structure that the interaction generates, then that same concern with *total* pay-offs should constitute the content of agents' conceptions of virtue. A 'virtuous' agent in a prisoner's dilemma setting will be one who is disposed to act to produce the Pareto-efficient outcome. Just what action this will require is itself a complex matter; the virtuous agent need not be required to sacrifice herself to the self-interest of her playing partner by co-operating uncontingently. More generally, how the desire to act as the normative evaluative system requires translates into a recipe for particular actions will involve estimates of how others will act and how one's own action maps into relevant outcomes. The disposition to act virtuously will include a capacity to make those calculations, or at least, to act as those calculations would suggest. But at some level, coherence between the content of 'virtue' and the ultimately justifying scheme of evaluation of political institutions is obligatory.

Overview

Homo economicus is a powerful construct. But we believe that it is not the appropriate construct on which to build normative political analysis. In the limit (as we argued in chapter 2), a strong commitment to *homo economicus* leaves normative theory empty and pointless. But if *homo economicus* is not the appropriate model of individual motivation, nor is the entirely moral construction of compliance theory. A fully compliant motivational psychology implies a political life that is unrecognisable.

In these three chapters we have outlined what we believe to be both a plausible and an interesting middle way. In summary, our preferred motivational model is one in which individuals count the desire to be moral as one of their desires, and are rational in the sense that they choose among the options available to them by reference to their desires and beliefs. Among the options available to these individuals are dispositions which serve to partially commit future decision making. These dispositions may be chosen on moral grounds, and such rationally chosen moral or virtuous dispositions will be behaviourally effective within limits. Morally motivated action may arise either through the operation of a virtuous disposition, or under the disposition of rational egoism where the opportunity cost of moral action is sufficiently low. Furthermore, although dispositions are relatively fixed, they remain sensitive to choice in the long run, and the extent to which virtuous dispositions are maintained may depend on the institutional environment.

We think that this formulation of individual motivation is plausible partly because it allows us to make sense of a wide variety of claims and arguments that seem to fit badly in either the *homo economicus* or the compliance theory model. This formulation also seems to accord with some of the most common intuitions about what it means to be both rational and moral without attempting to reduce either to the other. We think that this formulation is interesting since it provides a basis for the analysis of a range of significant questions that are not accessible to rational actor political theorists in the *homo economicus* tradition – and these questions are significant because we think the moral aspect of motivation is likely to be particularly relevant in political settings. But the proof of the pudding is in the eating. The majority of the remainder of this book is concerned with using our model of motivation alongside the more familiar apparatus of rational actor political theory to address questions of the design of political institutions. It is in that context, as much as by *a priori* argument, that the model should be judged.

5

Political mechanisms

This position will not be disputed so long as it is admitted that the desire of reward is one of the strongest incentives of human conduct; or that the best security for the fidelity of mankind is to make their interests coincide with their duty.

(*Federalist* papers, 72, Alexander Hamilton)

Introduction

Our major reason for departing from economic orthodoxy in the matter of the motivational structure of individuals derives from a concern to extend the scope of rational actor analysis to include a range of ideas which are relatively familiar in the literature on constitutional politics and which seem to us to be central to any rounded constitutional analysis. Chief among these ideas is the concern to view constitutions in terms of the design of institutions which strike a balance between three considerations: the limitation of government powers; the expression of political opinion through processes of deliberation and representation that refine private opinions and select the most virtuous for office; and the maintenance of an environment which encourages individuals to participate in politics in an appropriate spirit.[1] While an entirely orthodox economic analysis of constitutional design can easily recognise the first of these three elements, and can provide valuable insights into means by which power may be constrained, it seems destined to fail to provide an

---

[1] This concern is distinctly Madisonian; see the discussion by Elkin (1996) and in Elkin and Soltan (1993), for example, as well as the *Federalist* papers.

account of the second and third elements, since it cannot recognise the relevant categories. As a result, economists tend to provide an unbalanced analysis of the role of constitutions, while non-economists tend to dismiss economists' efforts as missing the point.

The remaining chapters in this first part of our book are intended to make the transition from our account of personal motivation to the more detailed discussion of the institutional devices associated with representative democracy. In this chapter we aim to provide an account of the mechanisms by which democratic devices might exercise influence on social outcomes. These various mechanisms are the primary attributes of any particular device and differ in the ways in which they engage with individual motivations to generate social outcomes. In the case of any of the particular devices to be discussed below, these mechanisms form a checklist against which the operation of the device may be assessed. We will draw attention to five possible mechanisms: sanctioning, screening, virtue producing, virtue enhancing, and aggregating. Although any specific institutional device may operate via a combination of these mechanisms, we think it important to identify the mechanisms separately in the first instance, so as to establish the vocabulary of our discussion. The final section in this chapter considers the possible interactions between these mechanisms.

In chapter 6 we set out a simple model intended to illustrate the interactions between institutional mechanisms and dispositional choice that may arise in particular institutional settings. This model draws the discussion of political mechanisms together with the analysis of the strategy of economising on virtue discussed in chapter 4. Chapter 7 then provides a discussion of alternative conceptions of democratic politics and the key problems faced by democratic institutions.

Sanctioning

Sanctioning is perhaps the most obvious of the mechanisms to be considered and is probably *the* mechanism that most people have in mind when they think of the rational actor approach to institutional or constitutional design. The sanctioning aspect of institutional operation is certainly the aspect stressed in the orthodox economic analysis of constitutions. Essentially, the sanctioning argument emphasises the role of positive and negative private incentives in the decision calculus of individual agents, and so stresses institutional devices which offer or reinforce such incentive structures. Examples of the analysis of institutional devices that appeal primarily to the sanctioning or incentives argument include the standard economic analysis of competitive democratic elections, and the range of models which stress the principal–agent structure of many political and social institutions.[2]

All sanctioning devices seek to structure the interaction between individuals in such a way that, for each individual who is party to the interaction, there is a positive correlation between the perceived private benefits accruing to the actor and the wider normatively approved or 'moral' benefits. Securing this correlation is no simple matter, not least because both the private and the moral benefits associated with a particular action by a specific individual will often depend on the actions taken by others. Nevertheless, the broad strategy is clear enough. Within this broad strategy, two forms of incentive devices are of particular relevance in a principal–agent setting, one based on *ex ante* competition and the other on *ex post* monitoring. Although these two will often work together, they work in rather different ways and in rather different circumstances.

The *ex ante* competition form of an incentive mechanism is most easily illustrated with a simple example. Suppose that a society must appoint someone to operate a fresh water spring which forms the only source of water to the community. Wary of the obvious threat of monopoly power and high water prices, the society allocates the right to operate the spring by a competitive auction, with candidates asked to bid for the right in terms of the price that they will charge for the water. The force of competition in this *ex ante* auction is to provide each bidder with a private incentive to reduce the price in an attempt to increase the probability of winning the operating licence. Under ideal circumstances, this type of *ex ante* competition will yield an outcome identical to the outcome that would be realised in a fully competitive market for water. Even when circumstances are not ideal, competition among bidders will tend to result in a lower price than would have prevailed without competitive tendering.

There are clear links from this simple story to the standard economic analysis of competitive elections, in which rival candidates offer to the electorate specific policy platforms in an attempt to maximise their probability of victory. Such a contest will, in ideal conditions, operate in much the same manner as a competitive market, with each candidate facing a private incentive to offer a platform that is collectively beneficial. But what are the 'ideal conditions' that are required for *ex ante* competi-

---

[2] For a survey of economical models of the election process see Coughlin (1990). For an example of the analysis of a political institution in a principal–agent framework see Weingast (1984). These ideas will be discussed in more detail below.

tion of this type to operate well? Most importantly for our present discussion, these conditions include the requirements that all relevant parties are reasonably well informed and that candidates are able to make credible commitments concerning their future actions.

The significance of the requirement for relatively full information can be illustrated by reference to our simple spring water example. If there is uncertainty about the true costs of operating the spring, but all potential bidders have the same information and are risk averse, we would not expect bidders to be willing to offer prices as low as those that would emerge from a competitive market, since this would involve the risk of a loss. In these circumstances, prices (and profits) will be higher under *ex ante* competition than under market competition. However, if potential bidders have different expectations about the costs of the enterprise we might expect the bidder with the most optimistic view of potential profits to win the auction and to do so at a price that may be *below* the competitive price and which involves losses to the firm. This is the idea behind the well-known 'winner's curse'. Furthermore, if there is uncertainty about the quality of the water to be supplied, and quality is costly to the operator, candidates in the *ex ante* auction may face an incentive to bid prices and quality down below the socially efficient levels. Of course, these difficulties with *ex ante* competition can be overcome in principle. Candidates might be offered some form of insurance against unforeseen cost variations; or candidates may be asked to commit to quality levels as well as prices. But complicating the structure in these ways is likely to introduce further problems – and not least additional information costs.

Another important feature in establishing the effectiveness of *ex ante* competitive mechanisms involves the ability to commit to specified future action. If candidates cannot effectively commit themselves to future pricing policies, their promises will be incredible; there will be no real constraint on the successful candidate's post-auction behaviour. It may be possible to generate the effect of *ex ante* competition through repetition of the interaction or the discipline of continuous trading. That is, even if in a single auction of the type discussed the candidates will have no reason to honour their promised pricing policy, such a reason can be provided by repeating the auction at intervals. In this repeated version of the story, the winning candidate will have a reason to honour price pledges to the extent that any attempt to deviate from this strategy is expected to imply losing the licence at the next auction. Again this argument has a clear link to the analysis of elections, where the repeated nature of electoral competition is thought to reinforce the incentive to deliver policies that are promised. We should also note that the commitment problem may be two-sided. In our example, it is not only the bidders that need to commit to pricing policies: the government also needs to commit to its side of the bargain, by allowing the winning firm to operate that pricing policy without further intervention. Having auctioned off an unencumbered monopoly right to the highest bidder, there will always be gains to voter-consumers by subsequent regulation to reduce price and /or to increase quality.

An alternative to *ex ante* competition is *ex post* monitoring. Imagine a government agency (a civil service department, perhaps) populated by individuals presumed to be privately motivated. The task is then to design an institutional structure which will ensure that the agency acts in the public interest, somehow defined. One obvious possibility is to construct a system of personal advancement and promotion within the agency which rewards activity of the relevant type. If individual activity can be monitored and rewarded in this way, it is clear that this institutional structure will act as an incentive device, with private and moral benefits showing the required positive correlation. We require no public-interest or moral motivation on the part of the civil servants: indeed, the more privately ambitious they are, the better the public performance of the agency. But we do require that monitoring is possible, and this in turn requires that we can distinguish 'good' actions from 'bad' actions; that we can associate actions with individuals; and that those that reward/punish are themselves appropriately monitored and rewarded. If any of these conditions breaks down, the capacity to design and operate a satisfactory monitoring and incentive system will be reduced and, in the limit, destroyed.[3]

Sanctioning devices – whether based on *ex ante* competition, *ex post* monitoring, or some combination of the two – can be relatively subtle in their operation, and, indeed, devices introduced for independent reasons will often have sanctioning/incentive effects. Such devices do not depend on the crude manipulation of personal rewards and punishments. Any shift in institutional structure may induce changes in the incentives facing agents operating within that structure.

Although monitoring systems and competitive systems will operate well under rather different circumstances, there are clearly some circumstances under which neither can be expected to work well. Situations in which team work is important so that it is difficult to provide appropriate incentives at the individual level, or where the actions of individuals are

---

[3] There is a clear link between sanctioning devices and two of the strategies discussed in the context of the reliance predicament in chapter 3 above. Essentially the approaches based on the repetition of the game, and on enforcement would underpin the design of sanctioning devices to resolve the reliance predicament.

not easily observed or easily identified as 'good' or bad' (as in the case of unobserved quality) provide examples of situations in which incentive-based systems are unlikely to perform well. In these cases, and others like them, other devices must be found to promote the right action. Direct moral argument – 'preaching', as public choice has tended to describe it – might be one such mechanism. Although preaching can be supported by institutions, it is not itself an institutional device. Nevertheless, institutions can serve to mobilise moral motivations, in a variety of ways. This is the possibility to which we now turn, with the intention of indicating some of the relevant variety.

Screening

We do not always think of an election as an indirect means of choosing preferred policies or as a means of disciplining or monitoring politicians, and it does not always seem appropriate to reduce the discretionary power of a politician or official. The idea of representation, as opposed to delegation, captures the thought that an elected or appointed person is entrusted with discretionary power and allowed to display qualities of leadership and vision.[4] The traditional rational actor approach to politics can make little sense of this view of politics, but the modifications in the background motivational assumptions discussed above provide the basis for a rational actor analysis of this aspect of politics.

One argument, which we term the screening argument, revolves around the idea of sorting agents into social and political roles by reference, *inter alia*, to an underlying criterion that picks out relatively virtuous dispositions. Screening devices of this type have not to date been much discussed in the economic literature on constitutional design, but it seems clear that this idea of screening is central to many of our social institutions, including the procedures used to select individuals in particular areas such as the judiciary or civil service, where direct private incentive mechanisms seem either inappropriate or ineffective for one reason or another.

The basic idea is simple enough. In a standard economic example, such as the labour market, individuals might be assumed to vary in their abilities and talents (even though in these standard models they will be assumed to share a standard, self-interested motivation). The principle of comparative advantage will then imply that each individual should specialise in that job in which her particular talents are best rewarded. A

---

[4] The idea of representation is analysed in more detail in chapter 9 below.

competitive labour market will provide a mechanism which effects such an allocation – sorting individuals into relevant occupational groups.

Once we drop the assumption of homogeneity of individual motivation, we open up another dimension in which screening may operate – that of agent motivations and dispositions. A motivational screening device would serve to allocate individuals to social roles in which their dispositions, as well as their talents, grant them a comparative advantage. To oversimplify, we would seek to allocate discretionary power to those who are relatively trustworthy and virtuous.

Of course, it may be *desirable* to allocate individuals in one way or another across social roles; but we still need a mechanism which can achieve such an allocation (at least with some degree of accuracy greater than the random). One obvious problem here concerns the observability of dispositions. We argued in chapter 3 that dispositions must be reasonably transparent if they are to work at all, but the form of transparency discussed there was transparency to other individuals in face to face settings. It might be the case that dispositions are relatively transparent in such settings but still relatively opaque in more impersonal, institutionalised settings. This is not, however, the end of the story: some devices may be able to screen effectively even in circumstances where dispositional character is relatively opaque. In the economic case of the labour market, one such screening device builds directly on a straightforward sanctioning device. The income that an individual can earn in the job that matches her comparative advantage will be greater than the income on offer from alternative employment, so that the individual will have a private incentive to take up her most socially productive role. Consider an employer who offers piece rates for the production of widgets. Even if the capacity to produce widgets is unknown to the employer *ex ante*, that employer can be reasonably confident that the piece-rate salary structure will ensure that those who are most productive in widget manufacture will be those who will seek employment with the firm.

However, such a simple incentive-based structure is unlikely to be useful in the constitutional context since the roles which require trust and offer discretion are, by their very nature, likely to attract both the trustworthy and the untrustworthy; the one attracted by the moral benefits associated with the role and the other attracted by the prospect of private benefits. Agents who lack the disposition to be trustworthy will rationally pretend to be trustworthy in order to be assigned the discretionary power – which they can subsequently exploit. But this very observation points to one possible solution to the difficulty – a solution that depends on what we label a 'currency effect'. Imagine a situation in which there are two types of person, distinguished by their true motivational dispositions which are, however, externally unobservable *ex ante*. We wish to recruit persons into a role in which one dispositional type is more socially productive than the other. How can we ensure that the relevant type is recruited disproportionately into the role when we cannot observe the characteristic that distinguishes the types? If it is possible to distinguish the types once they take up the role, it might be appropriate to recruit at random and then dismiss the inappropriate type once they have revealed themselves. Indeed, such a practice might deter inappropriate-type individuals from applying in the first instance, so that *ex post* dismissals might actually be rare. But in important cases, it may be costly to use the *ex post* identity test: the damage done in the process of identification may be exactly the damage one seeks to avoid. If the test of a defective pacemaker is the death of the patient, the test is no solution to the information problem. In other cases, it may be costly or even impossible to distinguish types even *ex post* (notice the connection here with the idea of *ex post* monitoring in the context of sanctioning devices), and in these cases it will be necessary to attempt to screen *ex ante*. Moreover, the *ex post* argument presupposes that those doing the dismissing will themselves be appropriately motivated. A 'currency effect' is an attempt to operate a differential incentive mechanism which rewards the appropriate type of individual to a greater extent than the inappropriate type. This is possible in the case in hand, only because the two types have different *dispositions* and so may value a given offer differentially. If one type values rewards paid in one 'currency' rather than another, then offering rewards in the favoured currency would have the effect of making it more likely that appropriate individuals would be recruited. Effectively the choice of currency would provide an incentive for the appropriate types to reveal themselves in a way that was reliable (that is, would not be subject to inappropriate individuals masquerading as appropriate in order to gain access to the role); the appropriate type would self-select because the reward package would be worth more to the appropriate type than to the inappropriate.

Currency effects of this type might be in play when civil servants are offered job security or social prestige and honours, rather than high monetary reward, or when academics are offered increased research support rather than increased salary. Notice that the argument for possible currency effects runs counter to the standard economic argument for payment in cash rather than in kind, effectively by claiming that non-cash payments can be used to distinguish between types of individuals. Clearly, for a currency effect to work, it must be costly for the agent being rewarded to transform payments made in one currency into the other currency. For example, when the academic researcher seeks to sell off academic support in exchange for cash, she must receive less in cash than the academic support actually cost. Complete fungibility undermines the currency effect.

Currency effects are not, of course, the only means of institutionalising screening. Screening may be based on direct observation and identification of the relevant characteristics, so that mechanisms of investigation, scrutiny, information seeking and processing will also be significant. And these mechanisms will play both a direct role in selecting candidates for particular positions and an indirect role in creating incentives for aspirants to acquire the relevant characteristics, including dispositions.[5]

Now, in the examples we have given, it may seem that since both sides in the potential exchange stand to gain from the acquisition of information about types, if the type is good, then we can rely on private action to reveal whatever information is available. But this is not necessarily the case. The difficulty is that the technology for distinguishing types may have the character of a public good. Any particular pair of agents may face an incentive to free ride on the information providing activities of others, and so less information will be acquired than would be efficient. In this way, a case for some kinds of public institutional intervention to assist the provision of information to agents may be warranted.

Within the political setting, the case for such institutional intervention seems particularly strong. It is in the nature of representative democracy that individuals will face inadequate private incentives to acquire relevant political information: some ordinary citizens may be well informed about some aspects of political affairs, but many will be rationally ill-informed. In the face of this failure of private incentives, the argument for institutional arrangements that promote the provision and dissemination of political information seems likely to be persuasive. We do not intend in this book to focus on such informational devices – but we emphasise that our failure to discuss them in no way indicates a belief that they are unimportant. Public support for such institutions as independent academic and journalistic commentary, freedom of information, a free press, and so on, may be significant in ensuring the better operation of political processes. But such institutions are auxiliary to the political process itself, and it is on the institutions that constitute the political process that we focus our attention.

Screening effects can be negative as well as positive, and the recognition that institutional devices may carry screening implications may be as important in identifying institutional failure as it is in constructing

---

[5] This indirect effect is an example of a virtue producing mechanism; see section 5.4 below, and the model presented in chapter 6.

institutional success. The possibility of 'adverse selection' is widely recognised in a range of economic models – the basic idea is that under a particular institutional structure there may be a tendency for individuals of different types to act differently, and in ways which adversely affect the overall operation of the institution. A classic example is provided by insurance markets in which individuals have private information concerning their own risks. If an insurance company cannot distinguish between individuals with different risk characteristics, it can only charge everyone the same premium. But at this common price, only relatively high-risk individuals will find the insurance attractive, and so the market will adversely select these high-risk individuals. Such a market may not be sustainable, and so a potentially important market may fail to exist. Notice again that the key point in this simple story is the existence of private information – or, to put the same point another way, the unobservable nature of some important individual characteristic.

Screening devices may complement sanctioning mechanisms in several ways. We have already suggested that, in the case of currency effects, the introduction of screening extends the range of incentives in play. But more importantly, screening devices are capable of offering constitutional options in those circumstances where incentive-based sanctioning mechanisms may be weakest. If, for example, there is no basis for credible commitment, or no possibility for the discipline of continuous trading, or no opportunity for *ex post* monitoring of individuals, then it may be more appropriate to think in terms of the empowerment of appropriately selected representatives. At least, this will be so if there are available screening procedures that reasonably command some measure of confidence.

Virtue producing

It is customary in economics to distinguish between two ways in which an agent's behaviour might be altered: by changing external circumstances such as the relative prices or other incentives facing that agent; and by changing the agent's preferences. Economists are clear that the focus of their attention is on the former. Similarly, public choice theorists seek to investigate and design political institutions taking people 'as they are': anything else is inclined to be described as 'preaching' and is seen as not the economist's business.

As our discussion of dispositions in chapter 3 shows, however, the preference/incentive divide is itself problematic in a variety of circumstances. One does not have to see 'preaching' as the model for all induced changes in behaviour that operate via changes in agent motivation. One can offer an entirely conventional, even incentive-based, account of how the motivations relevant to the arena of action may be influenced by the design of external institutions: the issue is simply one of recognising incentive effects at the level of the choice of dispositions, as well as at the level of the choice of actions. For example, a device acting as a screening mechanism may also act as an incentive mechanism at the level of dispositional choice. If, for example, judges are selected on the basis of probity as well as legal expertise, then it will pay aspiring judges to acquire the disposition of probity along with their legal training. A law school that has a reputation for producing upright lawyers as well as clever and knowledgeable ones will tend to attract more and better students and prosper thereby. And so on. It is worth emphasising in this connection that the screening mechanism operates in a manner rather different from that of a dispositional incentive mechanism. Screening or selection mechanisms require motivational heterogeneity – whatever the source of that heterogeneity and whatever the process that leads individuals to have this or that motivational structure. Dispositional incentives operate in ways that depend entirely on the way in which dispositions are arrived at, and may work even where there is motivational homogeneity.

A virtue producing mechanism is simply an incentive mechanism operating at the dispositional level to encourage the adoption of virtuous dispositions. The obvious general point is that an institution will act as a virtue producing mechanism to the extent that it raises the attractiveness of virtuous dispositions relative to other dispositions, or reduces the corresponding cost. There may be a wide range of social institutions which operate as virtue producing mechanisms: religious organisations, the educational system and families are all obvious examples. But again, we will not focus attention on this broad class of institutions. Our aim is not to examine all those institutions which play a role in virtue production. Our principal aim is the analysis of distinctively *political* institutions. Nevertheless, virtue production is relevant because the institutions that define the political process may encourage or discourage the production of virtue in the sense indicated, and we are keen to recognise such effects.

Virtue enhancing

So far, we have identified two types of mechanism relating to virtue: screening, which attempts to sort the virtuous from the non-virtuous; and virtue producing, which attempts to increase the stock of virtuous individuals. A third type of mechanism may be identified which attempts to enhance or amplify the social effect of whatever stock of virtue there may be in society. The mere existence of virtuous individuals – at least beyond some critical number – may be enough to allow such mechanisms to operate. In this section we wish to identify and discuss two rather different versions of such virtue enhancing mechanisms.

Quis custodiet ipsos custodes?

The ancient challenge 'who shall guard the guardians?' has often been taken, in public choice circles and elsewhere, to demonstrate that appeal to external enforcement procedures as a way of resolving social dilemmas is question begging – relying on enforcers seems no solution to the problem of the general unreliability of agents. We touched on this point in chapter 3. But the question begging nature of external enforcement depends on the background assumptions concerning motivation. The presence of just *some* virtuous individuals in society may change our view of enforcement – not only because of the prospect of screening more virtuous individuals into the role of enforcer, but simply as a result of the possibility that any enforcer selected at random will be virtuous.

To be more specific, we will reconsider the reliance predicament introduced in chapter 3 and reproduced as figure 5.1. Begin with the standard case in which everyone is a rational egoist. As we said in chapter 3, to be effective, enforcement must punish player *B* if she takes action *E*. If the punishment is large enough (greater than 1 in our example) it will be rational for *B* to choose *C*, and so it will be rational for *A* to choose *R*. If sufficient punishment can be relied upon, the threat of punishment will substitute for trust so that agents will act as if they are trustworthy and thereby induce trusting behaviour. Of course, if all act in this way under the threat of punishment, the punishment will never be invoked in equilibrium.

How might such an effective punishment regime be designed? The problem is the classical one of how to limit the powers of the enforcer. The obvious way to provide the enforcer with an incentive to punish would seem to be to allow the enforcer to retain (a share of) the 'fine' imposed. But the enforcer then has an incentive to 'fine' agents regardless of their actions. One step seems obvious: the enforcer should only be brought into play when requested by the injured party – enforcement should be 'reactive' rather than 'proactive' in this sense. Let us assume that this idea can be institutionalised. Figure 5.2 illustrates the modified version of the game. *A* now has an additional choice. If *A* chooses *R* and *B* chooses *E*, *A* must now choose whether or not to call in the enforcer. She will do so only if enforcement is beneficial to her (that is, if $x < 0$). If

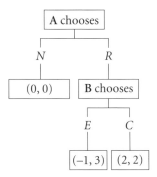

Figure 5.1 The reliance predicament again

enforcement is at all costly to *A*, it would be irrational for her to call in the enforcer even though this would punish *B* sufficiently to ensure that *B* would not choose *E* (i.e. $y > 1$). In short, the threat of calling in the enforcer is not credible unless $x < 0$ and, if the threat is not credible, the potential for enforcement will not affect the way the game is played, so that it will still be rational for *A* to choose *N*. We conclude that while purely egoistic enforcement can help to realise the Pareto-efficient outcome, it will only do so in very specific and somewhat limited conditions.[6]

How is this discussion of enforcement altered if we admit the existence of some virtuous individuals? Assume that a non-zero proportion *p* of the population are virtuous, but that dispositions are totally opaque so that we cannot select for virtue. In the role of *B*, a virtuous individual always chooses *C*. In the role of enforcer, a virtuous individual will act to compensate *A* in the event that *B* chooses *E*, and fine *B* to finance this compensation and, perhaps, to cover costs (*z*).

If no institution of enforcement is available, the presence of virtuous individuals may allow the Pareto-efficient outcome to be attained. As we noted in chapter 3, the basic example of figure 5.1 is such that a risk neutral *A* will choose *R* if $p > 0.33$, and the Pareto-efficient outcome will then be achieved if *B* is virtuous. Thus, provided that $p > 0.33$, the Pareto-efficient outcome will be reached in a proportion *p* of cases. If $p < 0.33$ the Pareto-efficient outcome will not be reached.

Now, if reactive enforcement is available, there is a probability *p* that

---

[6] In the setting of a repeated game an enforcer has an incentive to build a reputation for 'fair' enforcement and so may credibly deliver a zero (or even negative) x. But this type of resolution of the dilemma by recourse to repetition is also available to the players directly, so that, again, the impact of the self-interested enforcer may be small.

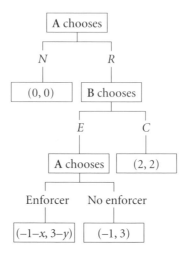

Figure 5.2 The reliance predicament with purely egoistic enforcement

the enforcer, if called into play, will turn out to be virtuous. This case is illustrated in figure 5.3. The expected benefit to A from calling in the enforcer if B proves unreliable is now $(2p+(1-p)(-1-x))$, and this will be greater than the -1 pay-off to not calling in the enforcer if $x < 3p/(1-p)$. This, then, is the condition for the threat of enforcement to be credible. Assuming, as before, that $y > 1$, an egoistic B will choose C if the threat of enforcement is credible. Thus, whenever the threat of enforcement is credible, the Pareto-efficient outcome will be realised.

So, in the case of partially virtuous enforcement, the Pareto-efficient outcome can be achieved in all cases provided that $x < 3p/(1-p)$. This condition ties together critical values of the damage that can be done to the innocent party by a self-interested enforcer (x) and the probability that an individual chosen at random will be virtuous (p). Recall that in the purely egoistic case, enforcement improved the outcome of the predicament only if $x < 0$. In the case of partial virtue but no enforcement, Pareto efficiency could only be reached with probability p, when $p>0.33$. But with partial virtue and 'reactive' enforcement, the Pareto-efficient outcome can be reached in every case even if $x > 0$, or $p < 0.33$, provided that $x < 3p/(1-p)$. For example, even if $x = 1$, the requirement is only that $p > 0.25$, so that any proportion of virtuous individuals above one-quarter would be sufficient to realise the Pareto-efficient outcome universally.

The point that we wish to emphasise is that the recognition of the *existence* of virtue can help to cut through the problem of 'guarding the

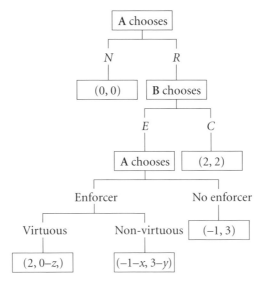

Figure 5.3 The reliance predicament with possibly virtuous enforcement

guardians'. Of course, there are still issues to resolve in the design of enforcement mechanisms. There is a need to limit the harm that egoistic enforcers can inflict on 'innocent' parties (x), and the need to ensure that enforcement is reactive. But the mere existence of some virtuous individuals renders the institution of enforcement much more viable – even when there is no possibility of selecting for virtue and no attempt to increase the stock of virtue. Enforcement can be a virtue enhancing mechanism: that is, hierarchical institutions of enforcement can serve to magnify the impact of the limited virtue that is around and make everyone act as if they were virtuous.

Condorcet jury theorems

A second class of mechanism that acts to enhance virtue is illustrated by the 'jury theorems' originally developed by Condorcet.[7] The context in which these theorems were developed involved determining the truth or falsehood of a proposition – whether or not the defendant committed the crime, for example – in circumstances where each individual's judgement is imperfect but more likely to be right than wrong. The theorems

[7] For discussion of Condorcet's original formulation, see Baker (1976) and McLean and Hewitt (1994). For recent related work see Feddersen and Pesendorfer (1998) and references therein.

represent a version of the central limit theorem or 'law of large numbers'. Specifically, if the probability of a randomly selected individual's judgement on the matter at hand being correct is greater than 0.5, then the probability that the majority of a jury of, say, n persons will be correct may be made arbitrarily close to 1 by increasing the size of the jury, n. Similarly, if the probability of, say, a politician being virtuous is greater than 0.5 then the probability that a majority decision within a house of, say, 100 such politicians will reflect such virtue will be large, and may be made arbitrarily close to 1 by increasing the size of the house. This direct translation of the jury theorem to the political setting simply replaces the accuracy of a judgement of fact, with the normative desirability of a judgement of policy.

In this simple application of the logic of the jury theorem, majority voting acts as a virtue enhancing mechanism provided that there is a sufficient stock of virtuous individuals (more than 50 per cent). But the relevance of the jury theorem idea is not restricted to this case. Most obviously, the same logic would operate in the case of qualified majority voting with appropriate stocks of virtue – two-thirds majority voting in a large house will deliver virtuous policy if the stock of virtuous individuals is at least one-third, and so on.

The point we wish to stress is just that the statistical theorem underlying the Condorcet analysis bears no less on issues of motivation than on issues of judgements of fact. In this sense, we may be able to institutionalise a reliance on virtue even when we believe virtue to be relatively scarce and difficult to detect. The law of large numbers ensures that we do not need everyone to be virtuous all of the time to develop arrangements that will produce desirable social outcomes almost all of the time. But equally, we do need there to be *some* minimal level of virtue (which may vary from case to case) for such institutional mechanisms to get off the ground at all.

Aggregating

The final mechanism of institutional influence to be discussed here focuses on the way in which different social institutions aggregate the individual pieces of which the 'social' is composed. A simple example illustrates. One obvious difference between markets and democratic politics lies in the different weighting schemes that each institutional framework utilises in aggregating from the individual to the social. In the market, each agent's preferences carry a weight determined by that agent's expenditure: each pound or dollar of demand counts for the same, so that individuals will count for different amounts. By contrast, in the voting booth, each enfranchised agent's vote carries the same weight. Accordingly, if we were seeking to explain the impact of transferring decision-making on some issue from the market to politics, or *vice versa*, the differences in the aggregating properties of the two systems offer one clear line of argument. Even if there is no change in relative prices or other incentives, no screening effect, no virtue production or enhancement, the simple shift in the mechanics of aggregation may be expected to have an impact on the social outcome.

Differential aggregation mechanisms may also be in play in the more fine-grained comparison of alternative political institutions. Proportional representation voting systems will systematically produce representative assemblies with a very different composition from those produced under single-member constituency elections with a simple plurality voting rule. Voting outcomes within a legislative assembly seem likely to depend systematically on whether individual members are free to vote as they choose or are subject to party discipline; or on whether the assembly is divided into two houses. In these and other examples, we do not deny that there may be influences other than aggregation at work. The change from one system to another may involve a shift in incentives, virtue enhancement, or whatever. We simply point to the pure aggregation effect as one relevant aspect of institutional performance.

Aggregation is a staple of the standard economics and public choice literatures. The choice between aggregation rules involving more inclusive and less inclusive decision criteria was a central theme of Buchanan and Tullock (1962), and an enormous literature is devoted to the comparison of alternative voting rules.[8] As is well known from the work of Arrow, Sen and others, attempts to aggregate individual preferences, opinions or values into a single 'social' preference, opinion or value are deeply problematic.[9] However, these social-choice theoretic problems are not our major concern here. We simply wish to locate such problems in our overall map of the analytic terrain. If we think of the key problem of democratic politics as a kind of principal–agent problem – a problem of attempting to control and constrain political agents[10] – we had better recognise that the 'principal' in the political relationship is essentially multiple, with different principals having different interests, opinions and values. So conceived, aggregation issues arise most clearly at the level of the relationships among the principals, or alternatively at the level of the

---

[8] See, for example, Dummett (1997), Levin and Nalebuff (1995), Myerson and Weber (1993), Myerson (1995), Tideman (1995), Young (1995).

[9] Arrow (1963), Sen (1970). For a selection of important papers see Rowley (1993).

[10] This and other conceptions of democratic politics will be discussed more fully in chapter 7.

relationships among the agents, rather than the relationships between the set of principals and the set of agents.

The issues at stake in aggregative mechanisms are, therefore, quite different from those we have emphasised in connection with sanctioning or screening mechanisms. While sanctions and screens might be seen as the opposite sides of a coin – the one concerned with restricting discretionary power in the hands of agents and the other concerned with allocating appropriate individuals into positions of discretionary power – aggregative mechanisms attempt to pre-empt questions of discretionary power by making decisions directly and so making delegates and representatives unnecessary. Alternatively, we might think of aggregative mechanisms as operating at a stage after all questions of delegation and representation are institutionalised – when the topic is the final decision-making among the set of delegates/representatives.

However, the distinction between aggregation mechanisms and sanctioning or screening mechanisms is not always clear cut. Consider the classic problem of the prisoner's dilemma. The problem lies with the lack of correlation between the perceived private benefits of the alternative actions open to each individual and the associated spillover benefits to other players. In this sense, the prisoner's dilemma is an example of a perverse sanctioning mechanism. But we might also think of the prisoner's dilemma as an example of a perverse aggregative mechanism. Under this description, the rules of the interaction can be seen simply as rules by which we aggregate individual preferences into a social outcome.

It is also clear that we can imagine institutional solutions to any particular example of a prisoner's dilemma which may rely on sanctions or on screens or on aggregative mechanisms. A simple sanctioning device would be to institute punishments for defection (or rewards for co-operation) which change the private pay-offs in such a way as to establish the desired correlation between private and spillover benefits. A screening device might attempt to ensure that only individuals of a genuinely co-operative disposition encounter each other in the setting that would otherwise be a prisoner's dilemma. Finally, an aggregative device would attempt to change the aggregation rule so that, for example, the individuals could express their preferences over outcomes rather than their preferences over actions, and these outcome preferences could be the basis of the determination of the final outcome. Our comments here are intended only to reinforce the idea that in isolating the three identified institutional mechanisms, we are identifying three distinct ways of viewing any particular social interaction – alternative perspectives rather than distinct pictures.

Indirect and interaction effects

In drawing to a close this discussion of the political mechanisms that may be recognised and analysed within our rational actor approach to constitutions, we would re-emphasise two points – one concerned with the potential indirect effects associated with these constitutional mechanisms, the other concerned with interaction effects.

In outlining our characterisation of individual motivation, we have been keen to rule out the possibility that individuals' characters depend directly on the particular institutional role in which they find themselves – governors are not moral simply because they are governors. However, in ruling out any such *a priori* institutional effect on dispositional character, we are equally keen to leave open the possibility of an indirect or feedback effect from institutional environment to dispositional character. Indeed, we see it as one of the key advantages of the approach we advocate that it can recognise and offer an account of such feedback effects.

To reiterate, what we have in mind is the possibility that a particular constitutional framework may induce or support the choice of particular dispositional characters over time. Such feedback effects may, of course, be either positive or negative. Some institutional frameworks may induce the dispositions which support that institutional framework, while other institutional frameworks may undermine the dispositions on which they depend. In this way, some constitutions may be more stable than others. This understanding of the motivational stability of a constitutional order relates directly to the Madisonian idea of the maintenance of an environment which encourages individuals to participate in social and political life in an appropriate spirit.

The fact that mechanisms of the types identified here can work together harmoniously might be taken to suggest that they always work well together. That is, that mechanisms of all types can be mixed and matched in any combination to produce an effective set of institutional devices – a constitution. This is not our view. Any serious attempt at constitutional design must take care to account for potentially perverse interaction effects between institutions and the mechanisms they employ. A simple example will serve to illustrate. Imagine the role of a senior civil servant. We might seek to structure that role by use of sanctions or by means of screening. Each approach is likely to yield imperfect results. In the case of sanctioning mechanisms, it is unlikely that the actions of the incumbent can be monitored and evaluated sufficiently accurately to effect a fully efficient *ex post* incentive system, while it is equally unlikely that *ex ante* competition for the post can exert sufficient control.

Similarly, it is unlikely that any practicable screening device could ensure that the incumbent was always disposed to act as morality required. Nevertheless, it may be a mistake to believe that one can improve the constitutional position by invoking both types of mechanism in tandem, since, in this case, they operate on opposed principles. If the screening device is employed, it will work only to the extent that the incumbent is indeed trusted with the discretionary power associated with the role. Minimising this discretionary power by the use of sanctioning mechanisms will effectively reduce the power of the screening device to produce socially desirable outcomes. In short, the screening mechanism relies on the incumbent being given space in which to exercise discretion, while sanctioning mechanisms operate by restricting such space. Of course, it is still possible that a balance of screening and sanctioning institutions will be optimal, but it is also possible (and perhaps more intuitive) that it is optimal to rely on just one type of device – even if it is imperfect in operation – and discard the other. The rational actor approach to constitutional design is not predisposed to either solution.

Real social and political institutions do not normally conform to the ideal types of sanctioning institutions, screening institutions, virtue producing and enhancing institutions and aggregative institutions. Rather, any particular institution is made up of a blend of these various mechanisms. Any social interaction can, therefore, be analysed in terms of its sanctioning, screening, virtue producing and enhancing and aggregative properties and the interactions between these properties. Our approach to constitutional design provides a framework within which all these aspects of social and political interactions can be recognised and analysed in a consistent manner and incorporated into an institutional recommendation that offers the best resolution of all the relevant effects. This framework includes, but is not exhausted by, the analysis of incentive effects of the kind that in most other formulations of the rational actor approach are an exclusive concern.

6

Mechanisms and dispositional choice

Ambition, avarice, personal animosity, party opposition, and many other motives not more laudable than these, are apt to operate as well upon those who support as those who oppose the right side of a question.

(*Federalist* papers, 1, Alexander Hamilton)

A simple model

In this chapter we take up the question – first broached in chapter 4 – of the relationship between the operation of institutions that seek to economise on virtue in use or in allocation, and the dispositional choices of individuals. The basic question is whether – or in what circumstances – institutions that economise on virtue in either of these senses may undermine or erode the virtue that they economise on. We will begin by sketching what we consider to be the simplest possible version of a model that is capable of capturing the feedback effect from institutions to dispositions; that is, a model that incorporates both dispositional choice and a structure of political institutions that operate as both sanctioning and screening mechanisms. In this context we will investigate the question of the conditions under which such an institutional structure has virtue producing properties, and the conditions under which the institutional structure may act to destroy virtue. Some of the limitations of this simple model will be addressed in the following section, where we will also outline some generalisations.

The basic model is organised around the choice between dispositions in the face of an imperfect screening device and an imperfect sanctioning device. The screening mechanism economises on virtue in the allocative sense (introduced in chapter 4), but operates imperfectly in the sense that it cannot identify dispositions perfectly. The sanctioning mechanism economises on virtue in use, but operates imperfectly in the sense that some areas of social life lie beyond its reach.

For simplicity, individuals may take on just one of two possible dispositions – they may be virtuous (disposition V) or egoistic (disposition E). An individual's disposition, once entered into, is assumed to be fixed for life. Society is made up of a number of generations of individuals – each with a disposition selected at the beginning of his/her life. For the moment we will consider a steady state population of size N, with one person joining (and leaving) the population each period (so that each person lives for N periods): we will relax this restriction later.

There will be two sectors of employment (or spheres of activity) labelled M and P (they might be thought of, loosely, as the market and politics respectively). The M sector is characterised by a perfect sanctioning device, so that this sector operates on the basis of an invisible hand mechanism. It might be that there is perfectly effective monitoring in this sector so that there is no problem in ensuring that employees discharge their functions appropriately. By contrast the P sector lacks effective monitoring, and all other invisible hand mechanisms, so that employees in P have some residual discretion – it is in this area that the sanctioning device is significantly imperfect. Assume that there are N jobs available in total so that there is full employment, and that a proportion p of those jobs are in sector P. Individuals with disposition V employed in sector P use their discretionary power to promote the public interest, while individuals with disposition E employed in sector P use their discretionary power to promote their own interests. The two types of individual act identically in sector M employment, despite their different dispositions, by reason of the perfect sanctioning device.

We assume that there is no way – either *ex ante* or *ex post* – to distinguish V-types and E-types at the individual level but that, nevertheless, there is an imperfect screening device which operates at the point at which individuals are allocated between sectors. This screening device results in an increased representation of V-types in sector P. Think of the labour market as operating as follows. Each period all individuals are allocated between the two sectors. Since there is no benefit to be derived from considering the past history of any individual, all individuals enter the labour market in each period on equal terms. From the point of view of any individual (whether V- or E-type), if allocation between sectors were entirely random the probability of entering sector P in any given period would simply be p. The imperfect screening device then operates by ensuring that the probability of entering sector P for a V-type is

$(p + \varepsilon_V)$, while the relevant probability for an E-type is $(p - \varepsilon_E)$, where ε_V and $\varepsilon_E > 0$. Loosely, in line with the idea that the two sectors pick out the market and the political process, we might think of the screening device as a form of election that operates in such a way as to ensure that those elected to the political sector are more virtuous than a purely random sample of the population.[1]

We model individual choice in terms of 'motivation functions' (analogous to the utility functions of standard economic analysis) which reflect the disposition of the individual. Hence:

$$M_i = f(y_i, Z) \text{ if } i \text{ is type } V,$$
$$M_i = f(y_i) \quad \text{ if } i \text{ is type } E,$$

where y_i is the money income of individual i, and Z reflects the public interest motivation of the virtuous. Let y^m and y^P represent the per period money payment in sectors M and P respectively, and z be the additional per period reward to virtuous workers employed in sector P (measured in a money metric). Furthermore, assume that the motivation function is simply additive for the virtuous in sector P so that:

$$M_i = (y^P + z) \text{ for all } i \text{ who are type } V \text{ in sector } P.$$

Type E individuals selected for sector P enjoy discretion which they use to pursue their own interests. Let b be a money metric measure of the per period value of the discretionary rent enjoyed as a result of employment in P by an E-type, so that:

$$M_i = (y^P + b) \text{ for all } i \text{ who are type } E \text{ in sector } P.$$

For the moment we shall ignore any costs associated with dispositional choice. We may also abstract from issues of discounting on the assumption that all individuals share the same discount rate. The expected per period benefit from a virtuous disposition is then given by:

$$\text{EXP}(V) = (p + \varepsilon_V)(y^P + z) + (1 - (p + \varepsilon_V))y^m,$$

while the expected benefit from an egoistic disposition is given by:

$$\text{EXP}(E) = (p - \varepsilon_E)(y^P + b) + (1 - (p - \varepsilon_E))y^m.$$

Equating these expected values yields:

$$(y^P - y^m) = \frac{[b(p - \varepsilon_E) - z(p + \varepsilon_V)]}{(\varepsilon_V + \varepsilon_E)}.$$

---

[1] This idea of voting as a screening mechanism is developed in detail in chapter 9.

We may interpret this equation as an equilibrium condition in the sense that it identifies the wage differential between sectors at which individuals would be indifferent between virtuous and egoistic dispositions.

The first point to make in this context is that if there were no effective screening device, so that $\varepsilon_V = \varepsilon_E = 0$, the optimal strategy for the individual at the level of dispositional choice depends solely on the relative sizes of b and z – the cash equivalent benefits from egoistic and virtuous dispositions in the P sector. If $b > z$, all would wish to be egoists while if $b < z$ all would wish to be virtuous – virtue will truly be its own reward. If we restrict attention to the case in which $b > z$, so that egoism is not directly self-defeating, the introduction of the screening mechanism supports the possibility of virtue in the sense that, for at least some configurations of wage rates in the two sectors, it will be optimal for those entering the population to choose a virtuous disposition. This simple proposition identifies one way in which economising on virtue in allocation may encourage the production of virtue.

If both $b > z$ and ε_V and ε_E are both sufficiently small, then:

$$b(p - \varepsilon_E) > z(p + \varepsilon_V),$$

so that the equilibrium wage premium in sector P will be positive. However, as the screening device becomes more efficient, in the sense that ε_V and ε_E become larger, this equilibrium wage premium will shrink and eventually become negative. To see the significance of this, imagine a situation in which the wage rates in both sectors are fixed and consider the impact of varying the efficiency of the screening device. In this situation, the more powerful is the screening mechanism, the more likely are individuals entering society to choose the virtuous disposition. In this way, not only does the existence of a screening device which economises on virtue in allocation make virtue more likely, but the more powerful is the screening device the more virtue is encouraged.

One point is worthy of further emphasis in this connection. An obvious implication of the foregoing argument is that increasing the monetary rewards in sector P will tend to encourage virtue. This may initially seem rather surprising, since it might be thought that the egoists will be attracted to a high wage sector. But this is to confuse two effects. Once dispositions are fixed, increasing the wage in sector P will make that sector more attractive to both E-types and V-types, so that the wage increase by itself would not influence the allocation of types between sectors. But the screening device makes it more likely that V-types will be chosen and, taking this effect back to the level at which dispositions are chosen, it is this increased probability of entering sector P conditional on being a V-type that provides the increased incentive to select the virtuous disposition. In this way, the screening device operating at one level generates an incentive mechanism operating at a higher level. Just as the choice of dispositions can be conceived as a higher order choice, so a screening device of the type discussed here can be conceived as a higher order incentive. So, although our focus of attention is on screening devices as such, the process by which these screening devices interact with virtue production is via a form of incentive effect. If there were no such feedback effect, it is difficult to see how there could be any implication from the operation of the screening device to the choice of dispositions. Once the possibility of such a feedback effect is admitted, the real question boils down to whether this feedback effect is positive or negative.

Even in our very simple model, the answer to this question is somewhat complicated. As we have already noted, in the absence of the screening device (and assuming $b > z$) all who could choose would choose to be egoists. So in a global sense, the feedback effect is positive – the introduction of the screening device acts to introduce at least the possibility of virtue. Furthermore, for any given configuration of wages, the more effective the screening mechanism, the greater the incentive to adopt the virtuous disposition. However, it may still be the case that relative wages are such that the feedback effect is ineffective, so that even with the screening device in place, all new entrants choose the egoistic disposition. Indeed, we may characterise a number of aspects of this simple model in terms of the relative wage rates in the two sectors. On the assumptions that $b > z$ and ε_V, ε_E are small (in the above sense), there are four cases of interest:

1. If $y^P < (y^m - b)$. In this case no one would be willing to work in the P sector, and all disposition choosers will opt for egoism. However, this is not a feasible equilibrium since y^P could be expected to rise to attract at least some workers to sector P.

2. If $(y^m - b) < y^P < (y^m - z)$. In this case, only existing E-types will wish to enter sector P, and all disposition choosers will opt for egoism. So, whatever the initial distribution of E-types and V-types, society will be characterised by a P sector dominated by E-types and a long run decline in V-types. In this case the conjecture that economising on virtue undermines virtue might seem to be doubly borne out in practice since the operation of an institution designed to economise on virtue in allocation would not improve the operation of sector P in the short run, and would result in virtue being driven out in the long run.

3. If $(y^m - z) < y^P < y^*$ (where y^* is the equilibrium sector P wage derived above). In this case both E-types and V-types will seek employment in sector P, but all disposition choosers will opt for egoism. So the

screening device will overrepresent V-types in sector P, but there will be a long-run decline in the number of V-types. Here the screening device is a partial success in that it does improve the behaviour of sector P in the short run, but nevertheless, virtue is driven out in the long run. We suspect that it is a situation of this kind that critics of 'economising on virtue' have in mind.

4. If $y^* < y^P$. In this case both E-types and V-types will seek employment in sector P, and disposition choosers will opt for virtue. So there will be a long-run growth in the proportion of V-types, who will also be heavily represented in the P sector even in the short run. Here the undermining conjecture is entirely overturned: the feedback from economising on virtue in allocation to the production of virtue is entirely positive.

Despite the simplicity of this model, we would suggest that it captures several effects of interest. Most obviously there is the property that the static question of the overrepresentation of V-types in the P sector must be separated from the dynamic question of the evolution of the proportions of E- and V-types. But it is also clear that the answer to both of these questions (i.e. of the efficient allocation of types, and of the supply of types) depends not only on the institutional arrangements that are designed to economise on virtue – or the power of these institutions – but also on the particular wage rates that evolve in the economy. As we have already suggested, for any given and fixed values of the wage rates, screening will tend to encourage (or at least not discourage) virtue, and the more so the more powerful is the screening. But this effect may not be sufficient to ensure that virtue is not eroded – that will depend upon the forces determining wage rates.

Extending the model

While we would argue that this simple model has considerable merit, it is clear that it is also severely limited. In this section, we intend to address some of these limitations and suggest responses.

One relatively minor point may be disposed of fairly quickly. The model as sketched includes no cost at the point of dispositional choice, so that the choice between disposition V and disposition E is made purely by reference to the expected benefits. However, the introduction of such a cost makes little substantial difference to the model. If the net cost associated with choosing to be virtuous is C, the equilibrium equation becomes:

$$(y^P - y^m) = \frac{[b(p - \varepsilon_E) - z(p + \varepsilon_V) + C]}{(\varepsilon_V + \varepsilon_E)}$$

and the arguments developed above go through in only slightly modified form. Since they play no significant role, such costs will be ignored in what follows.

A more important limitation concerns the very particular structure of population and labour market dynamics. If it were the case that the structure of dispositional choice rested crucially on our extreme assumptions concerning the entry of just one person per generation into the population, or a labour market which reallocated the whole population between sectors each period, we could not claim any real significance for our results. But we do not believe this to be the case. Consider the following generalisation. Let the steady-state population be N as before, but now let D persons exit the population each period – with the D individuals selected at random. As before, entrants (D of them, now) make dispositional choices which are then fixed for life. In the labour market, assume that sector M jobs may be held for life, but that workers in that sector can quit at any time (since all workers perform identically in sector M there is no reason for employer-initiated separations). By contrast, jobs in sector P are held on one period contracts – with incumbents having neither an advantage nor a disadvantage in the competition for jobs in the next period. Assume, for the moment, that $(y^m - z) < y^P$, so that all citizens will apply for sector P employment. Then the screening device operates to allocate the jobs available in sector P in such a way that the probabilities of success for V- types and E-types are exactly as before.

In these circumstances, an individual entering the population will have an expected life span of $N/D = n$. If the virtuous disposition is chosen, the new entrant would expect to spend $(p + \varepsilon_V)n$ periods in sector P, and the remainder in sector M. If the egoistic disposition is chosen, the new entrant would expect to spend $(p - \varepsilon_E)n$ periods in sector P, and the remainder in sector M.

If we again abstract from questions of discounting, our two equations describing the expected benefits associated with the alternative dispositions now become:

$$EXP(V) = (p + \varepsilon_V)n(y^P + z) + (1 - (p + \varepsilon_V))ny^m,$$
$$EXP(E) = (p - \varepsilon_E)n(y^P + b) + (1 - (p - \varepsilon_E))ny^m,$$

and it is clear that these imply exactly the same equilibrium condition as before. Hence, this apparent generalisation of the model has no formal impact at all. We take this to suggest that the broad structure of the model is at least somewhat robust to different specifications of population and labour market dynamics.

A further criticism of the simple model is that there is no real account of the social value of virtue. So far we have been chiefly concerned to model the private dispositional choice, and the impact of the screening institution on that choice. If, however, we are to view virtue as instrumental in achieving desirable outcomes, we will need to say something about the connection between the dispositions chosen and the social outcomes that emerge, because only then can we address the question of the desirability of encouraging virtue. As we have seen, it will always be possible to encourage virtue in our model by raising the wage in sector P. But this may be thought of as imposing a cost on society, because wage increases must be funded out of increased taxation or by otherwise increasing the cost of sector P outputs. This cost will be worth bearing only if the benefits are sufficiently great.

We might make a start in considering this issue by supposing that the social benefit of virtue depends on the proportion of V-types in sector P in the manner depicted in figure 6.1. At low levels of virtue, the marginal value of an additional virtuous member might be small, but when a critical mass of V-types is present this marginal value increases, only to fall again as the sector becomes dominated by V-types.

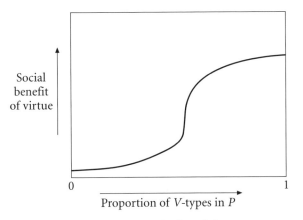

Figure 6.1 The social value of virtue

Imagine an initial situation in which the number of V-types is low – so that there are few benefits to society. There are two extreme strategies to be considered. On the one hand, we might attempt to encourage virtue by raising the wage in sector P so that $y^* < y^P$. While this will lead to a long-run social benefit, in that sector P will perform better, there will be short-run costs in terms of the increased wage bill. The alternative strategy would be to accept egoism, recognising that this will drive virtue out in the longer run, and effectively tax E-types in sector P by reducing wages to the point where $(y^m - b) = y^P$, so that the E-types are indifferent between the two sectors.

Further, less extreme, strategies may also be relevant. For example, if the costs of investing in a virtue producing strategy are too high, it might still be desirable to use the screening device to overrepresent V-types in sector P while accepting that virtue will be driven out in the long run. In this case we might wish to set the sector P wage so that $y^P = y^m - z$.

Clearly the choice between these strategies will be contingent on a wide variety of empirical matters – the various critical wage rates, the discount rate (since the time profile of costs and benefits differs as between the alternatives), the details of the population dynamics and so on – but the general point is clear enough. Even where virtue is socially desirable and where a mechanism exists for the production of virtue, it will not necessarily be the case that virtue should be produced. This conclusion follows directly from the assumption that virtue is valued instrumentally – as an input to the production of social value – rather than intrinsically.

Of course, this story might also be told in reverse. If the initial circumstances were that V-types were predominant, so that once again the marginal social value of virtue was low, there would be an argument for cutting the wage in sector P so as to lower the cost of the sector even though this might reduce virtue in the longer run.

These two ideas might be put together to yield a story of public-private cycles not dissimilar to that offered in Hirschman (1982). Times of public virtue might endogenously lead to reforms (wage cuts in the P sector, in our simplified model) which themselves undermine public virtue; this effect may then be reversed when the level of public virtue reaches some lower threshold at which compensating reforms are introduced (increasing relative wages in sector P). In this way, the society might cycle around some socially optimal level of public virtue for lack of any instrument by which that optimum can be attained and maintained.

A further aspect of our simple model worth reconsidering concerns the question of the determination of wage rates. As we have stressed, it is the interaction between the screening device and the wage setting mechanism that determines whether virtue will, in fact, be produced or undermined. In the last few paragraphs (and elsewhere), we have written as if y^P were a choice variable; but we might wish to endogenise the wage rates to examine the circumstances under which the emergent wage outcomes satisfied the various conditions outlined above. We might make a start on this task by explicitly recognising the demand- and supply-side forces acting on the sector P labour market.

We have assumed in our model that the demand for employment in sector P is fixed as a proportion (p) of the population, so that attention falls primarily upon the supply side of the labour market. We begin by restating the assumption that the screening device is relatively weak, in the sense that ε_V, ε_E are small. The two types of individual will offer themselves for sector P employment so long as y^p exceeds some type-specific critical value, with E-types coming forward at lower wage offer than V-types (provided that $b > z$). The situation is depicted in figure 6.2. There are two cases to consider. If, at a moment in time, the stock of E-types is greater than pN, so that there are at least as many egoists as there are P-sector jobs, then we are in the situation depicted in panel (a) of figure 6.2, and the simple market mechanism would set $y^P = (y^m - b)$. This puts us in the situation of the second of the four cases discussed above – only E-types would offer themselves to the P sector, and all disposition choosers would opt for egoism, so that virtue will be driven out in the long run.

If, by contrast, the number of egoists is small relative to pN, panel (b) of figure 6.2 is more relevant and the simple market mechanism would set $y^P = (y^m - z)$. This would put us in the situation of the third of the four cases discussed above – all will offer themselves to the P sector and the screening mechanism will overrepresent the V-types. Nevertheless, disposition choosers will still opt for egoism so that virtue will still be driven out in the long run.

The basic point is that the simple market wage setting mechanism will always set the P sector wage below the wage in sector M while a necessary condition for a weak screening mechanism to act as a virtue producing mechanism is that the sector P wage is greater than the sector M wage. The combination of a simple market mechanism for P-sector wage setting and a relatively weak screening device will result in the long-run decline of virtue, despite the fact that the basic screening institution is generally supportive of virtue in the ways we have outlined.

Given that a simple market wage setting mechanism will always set the P sector wage below the M sector wage, the only prospect for virtue production is if the screening device is strongly effective in the sense that ε_V, ε_E are large. In that case, disposition choosers may opt for virtue even when the P sector wage is lower than the M sector wage.

Clearly, other specifications of the wage setting process will give different results, but it seems to us likely that any purely market-based method of wage determination which does not account for the social value of virtue is likely to generate wages that undermine virtue unless the ability to screen for virtue is already strongly established. This possibility provides a basis for the conjecture that economising on virtue in use or in allocation may tend to undermine virtue in production in so far as the

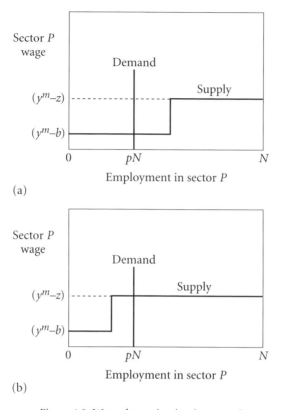

Figure 6.2 Wage determination in sector P

interaction between two institutions – the market mechanism for wage determination and the weak screening device for allocation between sectors, each of which might be said individually to economise on virtue – undermines virtue in production. But our model also points to the contingent nature of this conclusion. There is no necessity for institutions that economise on virtue in use or in allocation to undermine virtue in production; and, if those particular institutions are well designed, they can positively encourage virtue in production.

7

Problems of democratic politics

In framing a government which is to be administered by men over men,
the great difficulty lies in this: you must first enable the government to
control the governed; and in the next place oblige it to control itself.

(*Federalist* papers, 51, James Madison)

The rational actor perspective

In chapter 5 we offered a checklist of mechanisms by which institutional
devices might bear on social outcomes. The discussion there was abstract
in the sense that we were concerned to map out possibilities rather than
analyse particular institutions or their role in particular settings. The next
step in moving the discussion to the more specific analysis of 'democratic
devices' – the institutions of democratic politics – is the diagnosis of the
essential political problems that these institutions are intended to overcome.

Within the public choice and rational actor political theory traditions,
such diagnosis has been a central preoccupation. There are several
reasons for this. One is the economist's general predilection against
promoting 'cures' before the 'disease' is properly understood. As public
choice scholars have insisted in the context of arguments for state
intervention in the face of market failure, the simple recognition that
something is wrong does not provide a licence to intervene in any old
way. After all, scarcity abounds. And this means that the world will
almost always fall short of any abstract ideal. Even in the best *feasible*
state, things will be imperfect. One must accept, from the outset, that real
choices will be choices among imperfect alternatives. To fail to see this is

to fail to distinguish a genuine 'disease', for which some treatment is at least possible, from a 'condition', which one must simply endure.

Democratic politics itself often works to obscure this distinction between diseases and conditions. Politicians are not often elected by counselling endurance. But the failure is not limited to practical politicians. Political idealism – that is, idealism about the capacities of politics – is also alive and kicking in political theory. Indeed, as we have noted before, most traditional political theory is little more than the direct application of moral reasoning to substantive policy questions, as if the mere discovery and pronouncement of what is morally required will be sufficient to induce the relevant behaviour.

In this chapter we want to catalogue what the various strands of rational actor political theory have identified as the essential problems of democratic politics. However, we do not mean to identify or characterise political issues – the substantive topics which politics addresses – but rather the internal or structural problems of politics. Thus, we are not here concerned with debating the appropriate scope for political decision making, or whether political issues can be categorised into those that present co-ordination problems or prisoner's dilemmas. We believe that the discussion of the appropriate assignment of roles to different institutional devices – politics, the market, and so on – can only be approached once we have some clear understanding of the relative operating characteristics of these various institutional arrangements. On this basis, the next step in our approach requires identifying the intrinsic problems of democratic political arrangements, and the contribution that various particular institutional devices might make to resolving them.

The catalogue of problems thus presented provides the diagnoses of the democratic diseases for which particular institutions might offer cures. This catalogue – of the work that we can look to institutions to do – constitutes a sort of intellectual lens through which democratic devices can be studied and appraised. We identify, and will discuss, five distinct problems, all deriving from rational actor analysis of democratic political process. These are: the principal–agent problem; the aggregation problem; the majoritarian cycling problem; the expressive voting problem; and the rent–seeking problem. The discussion will pick up a variety of themes that we have touched on in earlier chapters.

The principal–agent problem

In the economics literature, the principal–agent problem is normally taken to refer to a class of models in which a principal hires an agent to utilise the skills or other abilities in which the agent holds a comparative advantage, but where there is also asymmetric information as between the principal and the agent. The informational advantage enjoyed by the agent allows the agent scope to pursue her own interests at the expense of those of the principal, at least to some extent. The cure for this type of problem is then conceived in terms of the design of a contract between the principal and the agent that will induce the agent to act more closely in the principal's interests or, to put the same point another way, to reveal the private information. However, such cures are rarely perfect, and the agent normally receives an 'informational rent' even under the best feasible contract. The details of such models, and the types of contract that turn out to be useful, hinge on the precise specification of both the informational asymmetry and the task to be undertaken by the agent.

In the general political/constitutional setting, the precise specification of the informational asymmetry may not be obvious, and the nature of the contract between principal and agent may be somewhat unusual in economic terms; nevertheless, the spirit of the principal–agent problem is clearly germane. If government is to be judged, at least in part, against the criterion provided by the interests of the governed – so that democracy, whatever else exactly, should be government *for* the people – and if direct decision making *by* the people is rejected – so that representatives are to act as political agents;[1] then the question of what institutional 'contract' between the people and the politicians is most likely to serve the people's interests must arise as a central concern.

This question is relevant even if most politicians are benevolent most of the time. It is a matter of institutional insurance. To return to our earlier example, when Adam Smith remarks that we do not rely on the benevolence of the butcher, brewer or baker to provide our dinner, it should be clear that Smith is not intent on painting these tradesmen as particularly venal. Smith is claiming that the market provides us with an assurance of appropriate behaviour from these tradesmen even if they turn out not to be benevolent; the market offers insurance against venality. Similarly, when Hamilton (in the passage quoted at the head of chapter 5) notes that institutional and political matters could be arranged differently if all men (and, no doubt, women) were angels, the contrast is not with a society in which all men (and women) are devils, but rather a society made up of both angels and devils and others between these extremes, in which a chief aim of political institutions must be to insure against devilish behaviour. Hamilton's task is the design of institutions

---

[1] We take up the question of representative versus direct democracy in more detail in chapter 9 below.

that best secure 'the fidelity of mankind'; and one explicit element in his approach is that authority should be constrained by means of making the interests of political agents coincident with duty to the greatest possible extent.[2]

This view begins from the recognition of the fact of political power. Representative democracy, for authors in this tradition, necessarily involves the exercise of discretionary power over matters that profoundly affect the governed. The possibility that such discretion will be exercised in the agents' interests at the citizen's expense is a sufficiently serious threat that even the most sanguine institution designer must attend to it.

To take a narrower economic analogy, government is often defined in terms of its monopoly of (legitimate) coercive power. The economist would expect government to exploit this monopoly power in a similar manner to a monopolist in a more standard market setting, *ceteris paribus*. To be sure, the monopolist is not all powerful; in the standard market setting, for example, the monopolist is still constrained by the demand curve for the product. And over some range, consumers' interests and monopolists' interests may be coincident, as they are in the market case over the range of outputs up to the profit maximising output. But still, the monopoly equilibrium involves consumers paying more than they would under competitive conditions, and aggregate welfare is reduced. In the same way, a monopoly government may well have some natural coincidence of interests with its citizenry, over some range – but there will still remain a conflict of interests at the margin, and unrealised gains that might be realised under alternative institutional arrangements.[3]

Accordingly, when public choice scholars have sought to apply economic analogies to the study of politics, one primary object has been to locate institutional arrangements that will bend government-agents' interests to the service of citizen-principals. It is hardly surprising, therefore, that public choice theorists have focused so much attention on electoral competition, for it is one central piece of democratic fabric (possibly the only one) that has an obvious prospect of doing the relevant work. In the simplest case of the median voter model of competition between two candidates within a single political dimension, the fact that electoral competition constrains the two rival candidates to locate at the

---

[2] Hume and J. S. Mill offer further examples of this general line of argument.

[3] It is worth making this point explicitly because some authors – most notably McGuire and Olson (1996) have noted the (partial) coincidence of interests and dubbed it a political 'invisible hand' – mistakenly in our view. This thesis seems better thought of as an elaboration of Hobbes's claim that monopoly government or Leviathan is predictably better than anarchy.

median of citizen-ideal points is often held to be a central and remarkable feature of democratic electoral competition. In that model, governors become mere ciphers for median-voter interests. Within the terms of that model, it would seem appropriate to suggest that political agents are led 'as if by an invisible hand' to promote the interests of the citizenry at large.

For reasons that we will explore below, the simple median voter model of electoral competition may be a rather fragile basis on which to construct a genuine, robust analysis of democratic institutions,[4] but there are certainly some grounds for democratic enthusiasm arising from that model. To be sure, the median voter outcome may not be precisely that which would best serve the aggregate interests of the citizens: the mean of ideal points or some other point might on *a priori* grounds be superior. But this kind of concern would be decidedly second order: within an acceptably small range, the principal–agent problem would be solved.

One point is worth further emphasis. Many critics of public choice orthodoxy are critical because they see public choice as inadequately respectful of democracy. Mark Kelman, for example, refers to public choice theory as 'democracy bashing',[5] and while others may lack Kelman's rhetorical extravagance, they clearly share his general judgement. This judgement, however, seems to us to be mistaken. The basic logic of the principal–agent conception of politics is that, in the absence of institutional safeguards such as electoral competition, citizens must expect to be exploited by government. Public choice theory is not in any way hospitable to despotism, and it is *precisely* because of its analysis of the threat of despotism that it supports institutions that render democracy more effective. To be sure, public choice theory also tends to support the idea of limited government, where the relevant limits may take a variety of forms – substantive restrictions on the domain of political activity, or on the capacity of governments to use debt financing, or procedural restrictions on the internal structure of government decision making. But again, these limitations are derived from an analysis of the best available means to ensure that government serves the interest of the citizens, and in the context of a structure of electoral competition. Those who consider the public choice approach to be anti-democratic in spirit are, we believe, simply mistaken. Both in terms of its central normative structure – the idea that government must be judged by the extent to which it serves the interests of the citizenry – and in terms of its central concern for the process of popular elections, orthodox public choice theory has been unambiguously *pro*-democratic in its orientation. Within

---

[4] Though some, like Wittman (1995), have tried.   [5] Kelman (1987)

public choice theory, the central themes have been to identify how democratic institutions help to improve the performance of government, and to identify those further institutional and constitutional devices that can be expected to help in the work of serving the citizens' interests. To be sure, the support for democratic *process* is contingent – derived from analysis that suggests that such process serves the interests of citizens. But this is simply to say that, within public choice theory, the primary democratic sentiment is that government should be *for* the people; whether specifically democratic institutions are superior to others in achieving this end is and has to be a matter to be derived from relevant analysis. For some democraphiles, this posture towards democratic institutions may seem too provisional, too contingent. But, if this is so, these democratic enthusiasts must offer some reason for supporting democratic institutions even in cases where such institutions are demonstrably inferior to some other political structure in terms of serving the interests of citizens. We do not believe that any such non-contingent defence of democratic process – which would have to elevate the political process to the status of an end in itself – is likely to be convincing.

Having said all this, it is worth noting that public choice scholars do sometimes go awry in the pursuit of their own logic. Public choice is sometimes characterised as an analysis of 'political failure' to set alongside the 'market failure' analysis provided by conventional welfare economics; and, under this characterisation, public choice scholars sometimes make the same mistake that the founders of public choice diagnosed in conventional welfare economics – what we might term the fallacy of the unexamined alternative. Conventional welfare economists, after detailed analysis of a specific market failure, were often tempted to simply assume that 'government' could act to improve the position via the adoption of the optimal policy, without any examination of the process of 'government'. Public choice theorists, after detailed analysis of a specific political failure, seem similarly tempted to assume that some other institutional structure – perhaps the courts – would do better, without any worked-out theory of behaviour in the relevant institutional setting. There is, for example, some enthusiasm in public choice circles (and elsewhere) for the 'depoliticisation' of monetary policy, by assigning powers over the instruments of monetary policy to an 'independent' central bank or some similar authority. Our point is that this enthusiasm is often based on surprisingly little analysis of the expected behaviour of the relevant 'independent' body, or the incentives and constraints that would face it. Of course, we do not want to suggest on some *a priori* grounds that the enthusiasm is misplaced. It may be that a structure can be designed that does endow the independent bank with the appropriate behavioural properties – either via incentive structures or, in our broader motivational landscape, via selection procedures, or otherwise. Our point is rather that to *assume* that the central bank, the courts or any other institutional arrangement will prove superior to political processes on no sounder basis than the observation that political processes are imperfect is to avoid the basic question – in just the same way that assuming a benevolent dictator will solve problems of market failure avoids the basic question. In each case the basic question must be seen as the choice between *feasible* institutional alternatives, with feasibility here understood to carry with it the presumption of some imperfection.

Aggregation and social preference

A characteristic feature of the principal–agent problem in its particular political manifestation is the presence of many principals – principals whose interests diverge from one another.[6] Recognition of this simple fact raises a question as to whether, or to what extent, the standard principal–agent conception of the central problem of politics is coherent. After all, a key idea in the principal–agent conception involves attempting to ensure that the agent act in the interests of the principal(s): that idea is potentially undermined if there is no such thing as the principals' interests. And does not Arrow's theorem show that, in general, there is no 'public interest' or 'social preference ordering' that can be derived from the private interests or orderings of the individual citizens – or at least, no such ordering that does not have some objectionable properties? And even if the Arrow problem can be avoided, does not the issue of how to constitute the idea of the 'public interest' out of the multiple, conflicting individual citizens' interests identify a more fundamental and ineluctably political problem confronting any analysis of political institutions?

It is no deprecation of the Arrovian analysis to doubt that it has the power to undermine other conceptions of normative political analysis.[7] Even allowing that no full social preference ordering may be available, we can often still give meaning to the idea of the public interest and can reasonably hope to identify institutional reforms that might be expected

[6] Of course, some economic principal–agent models also have many principals – the shareholders of a firm, for example. However, it is often possible to finesse the question of divergent interests, or otherwise restrict the variety of interests, in these settings. The political case represents the extreme in which the variety of interests seems essential.

[7] Nor do we mean to imply that Arrow, or others associated with the development of social choice theory, claim that the aggregation problem undermines other conceptions of politics.

to serve the public interest better than specific alternatives. The Arrow theorem points to a problem in the ascription of detailed statements of the public interest, and to the associated problems in aggregating either interests or votes; but it does not pre-empt questions of institutional design. Rather, it sharpens them and provides them with a distinctive orientation.

More specifically, there are two considerations – two distinct lines of argument – that bear on the relevance of the Arrow theorem and the priority of the aggregative view of politics. One line of argument focuses on the formulation of the conditions underlying the Arrow theorem, while the other focuses on their content. Both lines of argument merit brief elaboration.[8]

On formulation, the key point is that in structuring the impossibility theorem, the underlying conditions of universal domain, independence, Pareto efficiency and non-dictatorship are specified as requirements that are either met or violated. The theorem then proves that the four conditions cannot all be met simultaneously. But once the impossibility is established, this formulation tells us nothing about the choice between feasible alternatives. A more standard approach in normative economics would be to specify the normative criteria in the form of a continuous metric across the relevant characteristics. So, for example, rather than construing dictatorship as a dichotomous variable that either does or does not apply to a particular system, we might construe dictatorship as, say, the degree of dictatorial power. The object of institutional choice would then be to minimise this degree of dictatorial power, *ceteris paribus*, over the relevant feasible set of institutional options.

This idea of treating norms continuously seems to us to follow as a natural concomitant of the idea of taking feasibility seriously.[9] In most relevant settings, ideal outcomes or solutions will be unattainable – even if we agree on the definition of the abstract ideal. But this 'infeasibility' result should be considered to be the starting point for normative analysis, not its conclusion. In the case of the Arrow theorem, the 'ideal' is rendered unattainable as a matter of logic rather than as a matter of resource constraints,[10] but the essential point remains. The impossibility

---

[8] We make no attempt to review, summarise or debate the vast social choice literature relating to the Arrow theorem. Key references include Arrow (1963), Sen (1970) and the papers included in Rowley (1993). See also Hausman and McPherson (1996).

[9] For further discussion of the idea of taking feasibility seriously see Brennan (1993), Hamlin and Pettit (1989).

[10] The Arrow conditions are often described as necessary but insufficient for an appropriate social preference ordering, so that the point is still stronger. Of

of the ideal simply points to the need for a metric against which feasible but imperfect alternatives can be judged. And this metric itself will typically be imperfect in the sense that it may not offer a complete or absolutely accurate basis for judgement. The fact that we do not have a precise, fine-grained account of the public interest and its relationship to the interests of individuals should not be taken to mean that we have no account of the public interest, or that the coarse-grained and imprecise account that we have cannot be used to ground a normative analysis in which the notion of the public interest plays a primary role. Research aimed at improving our understanding of the public interest is clearly important, but it is research in ethical theory rather than in normative political analysis. In our view, the Arrow theorem is best seen as a contribution to economics and ethics that identifies an ethical, rather than a political problem.

Our remarks so far have been directed at the structure of the Arrow conditions rather than their content. But their content, too, is obviously relevant. If the theorem is to be granted significant normative force, the normative authority of the conditions must be interrogated. For our purposes, the four conditions may be divided into two pairs: on the one hand universal domain and independence, which seem at first glance to be essentially technical conditions; and, on the other hand, Pareto efficiency and non-dictatorship, which seem more obviously normative. We will comment briefly on each pair.

Universal domain and independence

The universal domain condition effectively requires that any acceptable aggregation procedure must work whatever the individual orderings. Loosely put, there is no individual ordering over any conceivable social alternatives that does not have to be afforded respect and included in the aggregation process. The primary intent behind this condition is clearly methodological – to work in the most general setting with whatever individual orderings might happen to exist and without prior views on the admissibility of particular individual orderings. But whatever the intent, the condition is itself normative. The requirement that all individual orderings are admissible *is* a prior view on the admissibility of particular individual orderings. And there is nothing to suggest that this

course, if the Arrow conditions had turned out to identify a set of admissible social preference orderings, there would also have been a need to define a metric (or introduce further conditions) in order to select from that set. Only if the conditions identify a unique social preference ranking corresponding to any set of individual orderings does the need for a further metric disappear.

requirement itself derives from individual preferences: even if all relevant individuals agree that certain rankings should be inadmissible, the universal domain requirement forces their admission. This requirement is simply imposed. The idea that *all* individual preferences – including those that might be thought malevolent, interfering or just plain evil – must be counted in reaching an appropriate sense of the social ordering or of the public interest, is not one that accords with standard ethical intuitions.[11] Which is simply to say that the universal domain requirement, whatever its methodological attractions, is not normatively compelling. Equally, it might just be the case that in any practical society individual preferences display certain patterns, and that given these patterns of individual references (and the other Arrow conditions) social orderings are possible, so that the force of the Arrow theorem would not be felt in those real societies.

So the universal domain condition is neither normatively nor descriptively compelling. In forcing social orderings to respect arbitrary individual orderings, it imposes a substantive and questionable ethical view on members of the society, while at the same time failing to reflect the patterns of common interest that might be expected to arise within genuine societies.

There is a similar normative arbitrariness surrounding the independence condition. This condition requires that the social ordering of any pair of alternatives depends only on the individual orderings of that pair. Independence has two aspects – one related to ordinality and the other to the relevance of further 'irrelevant' alternatives.[12] On ordinality, the key idea is that the social ranking of any pair of alternatives must depend only on the relative rankings of the individuals – any cardinal information, for example on the strength of feeling underlying some individual's ranking, is to be dismissed as irrelevant. On the question of independence of other alternatives, the key idea is that the social ranking of any pair of alternatives must depend only on individuals' ranking of that pair of alternatives, with their rankings of other alternatives dismissed as irrelevant. These two aspects often intertwine, as in the case of the Borda count – a method of voting which assigns each alternative a score that is the sum of the rank order positions achieved by that alternative in each individual's ranking, and uses this score to construct the social ranking. The Borda count clearly breaches the independence requirement both

---

[11] See for example Goodin (1986), Elster (1979, 1983).
[12] The independence requirement is frequently given the title 'independence of irrelevant alternatives', which begs the real question of which alternatives are relevant.

because the social ranking of any two alternatives depends on individuals' rankings of all alternatives, and because the scoring method introduces a form of cardinality into the procedure.

The independence requirement is certainly normative in content – it sets sharp limits on the information deemed to be normatively relevant and on the allowable form of that information – but what is its normative justification? In fact, as with universal domain, most attempts at justifying the independence requirement are methodological rather than normative – concerned with analytical convenience and the wish to avoid the issues involved in the debate on the interpersonal comparability of welfare. But if, in practice, individual evaluations of alternatives are not ordinal, and individual evaluations of pairs of alternatives are not always independent of further options, such methodological points have no relevance to the normative justification of the independence requirement. Independence is a strong and essentially arbitrary normative requirement – arbitrary in the sense that it does not derive from consideration of the preferences of the individuals who constitute society.

Non-dictatorship and Pareto optimality

These two requirements are more obviously normative in intent, and do derive their normative force from consideration of the preferences of the individuals who constitute the society. This is not to say that the normative status of these conditions is incontestable, but simply to grant them rather firmer normative foundations than could be granted to the universal domain and independence requirements.

The Paretian requirement essentially demands that any acceptable social ranking should respect unanimity – if all individuals agree that X is better than Y, then society should not rank Y above X. As Sen and others have emphasised, the Paretian requirement is not as innocuous as it is sometimes taken to be (it is, for example, capable of contradicting other seemingly desirable requirements), but in the context of the search for democratic procedures, it would seem that the Paretian requirement is particularly relevant and appropriate. One possible concern might relate to the admissibility of individual preference rankings: if all feasible preference rankings are to be admitted, this might undermine the normative status of unanimity. But this concern is better addressed to the universal domain requirement than to the Paretian requirement which simply holds that if all *admissible* individual preferences in society rank X above Y, then the social ordering should not reverse that ranking.

Similarly, the non-dictatorship requirement seems to reflect a well-founded aspect of the normative case for democracy. The essence of the non-dictatorship requirement is that there should not exist any single individual who determines the social ranking in the sense that the social ranking coincides with that individual's ranking whatever his ranking might be and whatever might be the rankings of all other individuals. Such absolute control over the social ranking is clearly incompatible with any notion of democracy as either government *for* the people or government *by* the people.

However, it is important to notice that this endorsement of the non-dictatorship requirement is rather limited in value by the extreme nature of the specification of dictatorship.[13] The non-dictatorship requirement rules out only the most absolute of rulers – a single individual with absolute power to determine the social ranking without reference to others. If dictatorship is construed more widely to include absolute rule by some small group of individuals, or the situation in which an individual or small group of individuals has control over most but not all aspects of society, then the formal Arrow requirement is satisfied. And this in part reflects a difficulty in determining precisely what is wrong with dictatorship. Assume for a moment that a social ranking exists (so that we are not in the world of the Arrow requirements), and suppose that the social ranking is identical to the ranking of some individual, B. It is clearly not necessarily the case that B is a dictator in any normatively relevant sense. B might have had no greater causal impact on the process of setting the social ranking than any other individual: it might, for example, be the case that B is just the median voter in a setting in which the median voter is decisive under majority voting. The mere fact of coincidence of an individual's ranking with the social ranking is not sufficient evidence for normatively significant dictatorship; but nor is the fact that changes in the individual's ranking correspond to identical changes in the social ranking over some range. There are several possible stories here. One might be that the individual in question adapts his preferences to the social ranking – a possibility not countenanced in the Arrow world where individual preferences are foundational. Another might be a modification of the median voter story in which the pivotal individual is free to change preferences within the range that preserves his status as the median voter, and induce equivalent changes in the social ranking. In this case the connection between the change in individual preference and social ranking is causal, but still falls well short of any normatively significant idea of dictatorship. We might conceive of an individual's dictatorial power as increasing with the range over which

---

[13] This is to repeat the general point concerning the formulation of the Arrow conditions in the specific context of non-dictatorship.

changes in his preferences are causally effective in determining the social ranking. But even this specification omits reference to the other members of society. Is an individual a dictator if his preferences are causally effective in the relevant way with all other individual preferences held constant – or do we require a dictator's preferences to be causally effective in the relevant way regardless of all possible changes in the preferences of others'. This last case gets us back to the Arrow idea of dictatorship, and shows how strong that formulation is.

Of course, if the idea of dictatorship employed by Arrow is very strong, the idea of non-dictatorship is correspondingly weak – and that has methodological advantages in the construction of an impossibility theorem. Clearly the impossibility theorem would be still stronger for any stronger idea of non-dictatorship. But strengthening the Arrow result seems, on its face, uninteresting unless we are prepared to loosen the hold of the other requirements. As we have seen, there may be good reason for loosening that hold because there seems to be good reason to doubt their normative credentials.

We have suggested that the normative foundations of the Arrow theorem are questionable, but that the most reliable of those foundations relate to the Pareto requirement and non-dictatorship. These two requirements formalise the concern to reflect the interests of the constituent individuals (Paretianism) and restrict the abuse of power (non-dictatorship). Seen in this way, the basic normative commitments of the Arrow approach do not differ from the commitments associated with the principal–agent conception of politics. Nor do we believe that the Arrow theorem and its elaboration establishes the priority of the aggregation conception of the problem of politics over the principal–agent conception. One way of seeing the connection between the two approaches is to suggest that the social-choice theoretic literature from Arrow onwards focuses attention on the ability of social rankings to reflect individual preferences, with non-dictatorship imposed as a side condition, while the principal–agent literature in the public choice tradition attempts to investigate the limitation and control of dictatorial power, in models which often abstract from at least some of the aggregation issues. In this way the two literatures might be seen as complementary.

Majoritarian cycles and spirals

It has long been recognised that, under plausible circumstances, simple majority rule can generate 'cycles': policy or candidate *A* can defeat policy or candidate B, B can defeat C, and C can defeat A.[14] There is a clear link between the intransitivity of majoritarian voting and the Arrow impossibility theorem which imposes transitivity as a requirement of any acceptable social choice procedure; but we do not believe that this link captures the basic issue involved in the cycling debate. The Arrow argument, we believe, is best seen as an exercise in 'moral mathematics'[15] concerned with the normative justification of social choice rules; by contrast the central issue in the cycling debate, as we see it, revolves around the identification of the implications of intransitivity, and of the appropriate institutional response to the threat of cycling. After all, intransitivity might not matter much in itself. Arguably, the imposition of a transitivity requirement on social or collective choice is just a mistake, a misguided attempt to 'psychologise' the collective and treat the citizenry as if it were an individual person with attributes like rationality. But the problem of majoritarian cycling is not merely a problem of intransitivity *per se*. The anxiety over cycling lies more in what the intransitivity implies – first, about stability; second, about manipulability; and third, about uncontrollability. And what is of concern here is not just majoritarian cycles but majoritarian (downward) spirals.

The stability point is clear enough. Many collective decisions have the nature of capital investments: their value depends, at least in part, on their being in place over an appropriately extended period of time. To face a situation in which a policy is made, reversed and reinstated repeatedly may be the worst of all worlds for all citizens. Furthermore, in such a situation, individuals with rival views on policy may nevertheless be able to agree on the value of stability and on putting in place institutional arrangements that promote stability. Of course, any stabilising institutions must themselves be stable – perhaps constitutionally entrenched – so as to offer a real and credible commitment to stability of policy making.[16] The fundamental point is just that majoritarian cycling can threaten costly policy instability, and that such instability may be countered – to at least some extent – by institutional means.

The manipulability issue is only slightly more complicated. An individual Z who prefers A to B, and B to C, and C to A is open to financial exploitation. By definition, Z will pay some positive amount to have C rather than A; a further positive amount to have B rather than C; and a further positive amount to have A rather than B. Unscrupulous (or

---

[14] Since Condorcet, at least. See McLean and Hewitt (1994), Black (1958).

[15] Hausman and McPherson (1996).

[16] Majoritarian cycling is just one possible source of policy instability, and this line of argument applies whatever the underlying source of instability.

merely egoistically rational) W can make money out of Z by confronting her with an appropriate sequence of options. In much the same way, a community that suffers from majoritarian cycling is vulnerable to exploitation by a strategic agenda setter; and McKelvey (1976, 1979) formulates his classic version of the majoritarian cycling problem in precisely these terms. The general theorem points out that majority voting is not just subject to narrow cycles, it is globally unstable, and this global instability allows manipulation. Global instability means that for any two points, J and K, in the relevant policy space, there exists a path from J to K such that each step along the path will be approved by a majority of the population. In other words, an agenda setter can, by appropriately constructing a sequence of pair-wise votes, lead the political community to any final policy choice, regardless of the inherited starting point.[17]

It is at this point that the threat of a majoritarian spiral becomes apparent. The real concern raised by the manipulability of majority voting is not that society will be trapped in a cycle, but that anyone with the power to set the political agenda can use that power to lead society to the agenda setter's own ideally preferred outcome – however bad that outcome is for other members of the community. In the extreme case, there is no limit to how far down this democratic spiral may go.

Even if the problem of manipulability by an agenda setter could be overcome, majoritarian spirals might still remain a source of concern. Even in the absence of any systematic exploitation by an agenda setter, society might still face the prospect of an essentially random walk through policy space, in which no outcome, however bad, could be entirely ruled out as a possibility. This is the uncontrollability issue – where the threat is that politics may simply run out of control.

It might seem that uncontrollability is the price that one pays for avoiding the excessive and manipulative control of the powerful agenda setter. Furthermore, this might or might not be a price worth paying. Depending on the exact nature of the potential agenda setter's own preferences, it might be better for all to submit to exploitation than to accept randomness.

These problems of majority cycling have lent a distinctive accent to the public choice analysis of politics. From an analytic point of view, the problem has robbed public choice theorists of a robust equilibrium concept on the basis of which to conduct comparative static analysis. If there is no generally stable equilibrium outcome under majority voting,

---

[17] Again, there is a clear link between the McKelvey theorem and the Arrow theorem – the McKelvey agenda setter is essentially a version of Arrow's dictator.

how can we investigate the impact on that equilibrium of changes in the underlying parameters? From a more empirical viewpoint, majoritarian cycling offers a prediction of radical policy shifts alongside a majority coalition of continuously shifting composition – a prediction that is not strikingly in tune with the everyday experience of democratic politics. Gordon Tullock's famous question of 'Why so much stability?' articulates the mismatch between the prediction and the reality.[18] There is a puzzle here to which public choice analysis is obliged to respond. Accordingly, from this analytic point of view as well as the normative, the quest is for institutional and other mechanisms that serve to suppress cycling and so steer a course between exploitation and uncontrollability. The broad response to that quest from within the rational actor tradition has been that relative stability is provided by the further institutional details of the political process. Some of these apparent 'details' serve to counteract the destabilising tendency of majority voting. For example, Shepsle and Weingast see the US Congressional Committee system as a mechanism for securing the separation of political issues, so that trading votes across issues is restricted and stability restored.[19]

Our object at this point is not to analyse this or that institutional device as a means of suppressing majoritarian cycling, but rather to emphasise the fact that public choice theorists are inclined to identify majority cycling as a (perhaps *the*) problem that institutional devices are needed to solve. Public choice theorists tend to carry with them a picture of democratic politics in which global instability lurks just below the surface, always ready to break out if majoritarianism escapes its institutional straitjacket. Whatever else, as public choice theory sees it, political institutions must solve this problem: they must constitute the relevant straitjacket. And this aspect of the public choice understanding of politics is, we think, distinctive. Normative political theorists from other traditions can be made to see the point, but they never seem to take it very seriously once they have seen it. To these others, majoritarian cycling is an irrelevant curiosity; to public choice scholars, it is a critical analytic idea.

But the distinctiveness of the emphasis on majority cycling should not be overemphasised. The issues of manipulability and uncontrollability that are crucial to the analysis of cycling are broadly compatible with the general principal–agent view of politics outlined above. The agenda setter may be seen as the political agent, and the McKelvey result points to the

---

[18] Tullock (1981).
[19] Shepsle and Weingast (1981). See also the discussion of bicameralism in chapter 12 below and the references given there.

fact that the simple institution of majority voting, taken by itself, may do nothing to constrain the power of the agent. It might be objected that the basic model ignores the role of electoral competition for the role of agenda setter, in focusing on the power of the agenda setter to manipulate voting on policies. But the point we would emphasise is that the issue of manipulability simply specifies a particular aspect of the power of the political agent over the collective principal, and adds further impetus to the study of the additional institutional details of any given political process. The trade off between exploitation and loss of control can also be captured in the principal–agent framework, where the equivalent to uncontrollability is provided by the extreme case in which no agent is appointed so that the principal is cast adrift. The search is then for intermediate possibilities which constrain the power of the agent without effectively abolishing the role of the agent; and to evaluate these intermediate possibilities by reference to their ability to serve the interests of the principal in ways that improve on both extreme cases.

Expressive voting

Expressive voting behaviour is not in itself necessarily a 'problem' of democratic politics – but the recognition of expressive behaviour casts an importantly different light on the operation of political process and therefore on the role of institutions in resolving problems. The principal–agent view of representative democracy is transformed once one recognises that the election of representatives will be expressive in nature. And a considerable part of our reason for being less anxious about both majoritarian cycling and Arrovian aggregation than many of our public choice colleagues lies in our view that voting is not generally instrumentally self-interested in the way that rational actor orthodoxy has standardly assumed.

Of course, the detailed nature of voting behaviour cannot overturn the logic either of majoritarian cycling or of the Arrow theorem, but it can colour our understanding of the practical and normative relevance of those logics. Both, we think, are connected to the self-interested conception of political behaviour, because the self-interest model naturally picks out potential conflict of interests as being of central importance. In the simple example of the division of a fixed sum among N self-interested citizens, the possibility of log-rolling and cycling seems self-evident and compelling: simply spelling out a list of the pay-offs to each individual is sufficient to make the point. But if, as we believe, voting in large number elections is distinctive in that rational citizens will have virtually no reason to vote their self-interest, it will not take more than a minor concern for some conception of distributive justice for an individual to support the allocation in which each citizen receives, say, $100 against the alternative allocation in which 90 per cent of citizens receive $110 with the remaining 10 per cent receiving $1 each, even if the relevant individual expects to belong to the favoured majority group. The private benefit on offer from voting for the unequal distribution is just 10q$ where q is the probability that your vote will be decisive, and in any plausible electoral setting, q is a very small number – however precisely it may be calculated.

In much the same way, we suspect, Arrow's universal domain requirement is grounded in the belief that no coherent distinction can be drawn between values and preferences. Since preferences can plausibly take on any content given their formal structure – *de gustibus non est disputandum*, after all – then values must be similarly unrestricted. But if preferences and values differ, and if it is values rather than preferences that provide the foundation for normative theory, then the idea that any values at all are acceptable seems unpersuasive to say the least.

It is not our objective here to defend the logic of the expressive voting argument. A gesture in that direction has already been provided in chapter 2, and we will pursue the implications of this logic in chapters 8 and 9.[20] Our aim here is briefly to review the normative status of expressive voting and to draw out some of the implications of the expressive account of voting behaviour for the nature of the problems of politics.

The broad normative conclusion offered by Brennan and Lomasky (1993) is that while expressive votes may reflect agents' values more accurately than do their market-revealed preferences, the opposite may also be true. Expressive support for this or that candidate or policy may arise from a variety of sources – some of which may be normatively irrelevant or even perverse. There can be no simple or general claim that expressive voting is either more or less moral, virtuous or value revealing than preference-based, instrumentally rational behaviour. The basic conclusion in that earlier book was that the 'veil of insignificance' will tend to increase the moral variance of both individual voting behaviour and the aggregative electoral outcome. That is, the expressive nature of voting creates within many voters, over many issues, a more moral response – one that considers the electoral choice in terms that are more public than private, more normatively defensible than privately advantageous. But for many voters, the ballot box may also become an arena for the voicing of

---

[20] As before, the reader is directed to Brennan and Lomasky (1993) for a fuller discussion.

prejudices and dogmas that would never see the light of day in the more accountable and narrowly responsible arena of instrumental, market-like choice. And the relative sizes of these two groups might be expected to vary over time and over issues, so that even if on average electoral choice were more moral – more ethically defensible – than the equivalent instrumental choices, there might still be occasions and issues on which democracy might go horribly awry.

The recognition of this possibility, even on issues that are in the proper domain of politics, should remind us not to identify the 'voice of the people' as some kind of moral authority. For even the most enthusiastic democrat, it is a mistake to identify democratic approval with moral justification.

The claim that expressive voting will increase the moral variance of electoral behaviour is made against the background assumption of a given set of institutional arrangements. However, one of the tasks of this book is to trace out some of the implications of the expressive view of voting for institutional design. And here, as we argue, a range of novel possibilities is opened up. The essential additional task of institutional design under the expressive conception of politics may be summed up as attempting to ensure that the more moral aspect of expressive concern is supported, selected and amplified. In this way, the broadly expressive account of democratic politics can provide distinctive lines of argument in justification of such institutional arrangements as a continuous opposition, a free and independent press, a bicameral legislature, and so on – of the institutional checks and balances that go with the recognition that the basic structure of electoral decision-making will predictably make moral mistakes.

Of course, a case for checks and balances of various kinds can be made on the basis of the more conventional instrumentally rational actor account of democratic process as well. But there are differences between the implications deriving from the two approaches. We will illustrate by reference to one central idea from the traditional public choice literature. In Buchanan and Tullock's classic discussion,[21] the primary risk in democratic politics is a version of manipulability: majorities are expected to exploit minorities in search of private gains, and the process of log-rolling to generate shifting majority coalition will exacerbate this problem. The solution that Buchanan and Tullock identify is an appropriate move towards unanimity (with 'appropriate' here recognising the increased decision-making costs associated with more inclusive voting rules) and the shift from the in-period level of choice to the constitutional

---

[21] Buchanan and Tullock (1962).

level of choice where conflicts of interest are sharply reduced by the 'veil of uncertainty'. All of this is very much in the Wicksellian spirit – the concern over fiscal exploitation, the identification of unanimity as the relevant normative benchmark, and the retreat to 'relative' unanimity in the interests of practicality.

Under the expressive view of political behaviour, however, the move towards unanimity is much less clear. Under a pure unanimity voting rule each individual has an effective veto and so becomes semi-decisive.[22] In this situation voting is consequential and anyone with a private interest in exercising her veto power may be expected to do so. It might be tempting to believe that as we move from simple majority voting towards a unanimity requirement, voting becomes increasingly consequential and increasingly instrumental, so that expressive voting is driven out by more restrictive voting rules. However, this is not the case. Whatever the voting rule, short of unanimity, the probability of being the decisive voter will be essentially similar to that in the case of simple majority voting. The point is simple enough: whatever the required majority might be, any single individual's vote will be decisive only if the votes of all others are distributed in a way that exactly mirrors the particular voting rule. And the probability of such an outcome is vanishingly small in all realistic cases.[23] More inclusive voting rules (short of perfect unanimity) will not reduce the relevance of expressive voting. And in some situations – where the majority of citizens adopt relatively moral expressive positions but a minority adopt amoral or immoral views – any move towards unanimity will have undesirable results by strengthening the hand of the minority.

The key institutional ideas in an expressive framework are those associated with supporting and encouraging virtue, and using electoral and other devices to select for and amplify virtue. Institutions associated with representation (see chapter 9) or political parties (chapter 10) may serve to screen or amplify virtue in one way or another; but the general presumption in favour of more inclusive decision rules at the level of in-period politics as serving the public interest involves a level of optimism about the informational content of the vote and its normative authority that is unsustainable within the expressive view of politics.

---

[22] Semi-decisive rather than decisive simply because the veto power is one sided: each voter can bring about the failure of a proposal, but cannot bring about its success.

[23] The same point holds true under more complex proportional voting rules, where again the probability that any single vote will decisively influence the overall outcome must be very small.

Rent seeking

Although the term 'rent seeking' could legitimately be applied to much that goes on in ordinary market economics, the term has tended to be reserved in public choice theory for a particular range of activities in the political setting. The central idea is that political power generates rents that are potentially available for distribution. The simple case of the power to grant a monopoly licence will act as an illustration. Potential beneficiaries face an incentive to engage in any activity which they believe will increase their probability of receiving the rent, up to the point where the individual's expenditure on rent seeking activity is equal to the expected rent to be received. This will be so even if the rent seeking activities are themselves of no real value. In this way rent seeking behaviour can absorb resources to no real purpose, so that a political system that allows or encourages rent seeking will be inefficient, and institutional reforms which reduce the scope for rent seeking will be seen as efficiency enhancing.[24]

But in what sort of political environment is this rent seeking story located? First, it is clear that politicians must have discretionary power. Without such power (to allocate monopoly licences, or whatever) there could be no rents to seek. This implies that the process by which the politician is elected or appointed does not serve to fully constrain policy. In short, we are in a principal–agent world in which the agent is imperfectly constrained. Second, it must be the case that the powerful politician cannot simply retain the whole of the relevant rent (in this example, by running the monopoly himself). If political rents were simply the prize that goes with winning the election, there would be no prospect of others sharing in those rents, and no incentive to engage in post election rent seeking.[25] Third, in order for the rent seeking activity to have any effect on the allocation of the rent, the seekers must be offering something which the politician values – for example, campaign contributions which improve the chance of re-election or, in the limit, straightforward bribes.

In this way, it is clear that the rent seeking problem can be seen as a particular aspect of the general political principal–agent problem. The distinctive nature of the rent seeking issue arises not out of a distinctive conception of politics, but out of the particular analysis of the incentive

---

[24] See the papers collected in Buchanan, Tollison and Tullock (1980).

[25] Of course, this view of a rent as a reward for election means that the election itself might be seen as a rent seeking activity with candidates willing to invest in whatever activities improve their probability of election.

structures facing rent seekers. Attention has focused on two issues. First, given that there is at stake a rent of given size (the value of the monopoly profits), what amount of resources will be absorbed in the competition to win access to it? And second, what is the efficiency loss involved in this process?

The answer to the first question is interesting in that, in plausible circumstances (essentially where the probability of winning the rent increases with the size of resource expenditure and where resource expenditures are sunk costs), the total resources expended by those seeking rent can exceed the value of rent. The second question, however, is the real focus of normative concern: after all, if the resources spent in rent seeking are spent productively, there will be few grounds for concern. Often it is simply assumed that the resources employed in rent seeking are a total waste, so that the efficiency cost associated with rent seeking is the whole value of the expenditure. Sometimes this assumption might be justified – for example, if the rent seeking expenditures were made in terms of campaign contributions and the political equilibrium was such that the contributions made to each candidate had no impact on any candidate's probability of election. In this case each rent seeker is contributing to a purely positional good and the overall pattern of contributions leaves overall positions unchanged. But in most cases it seems plausible to suppose that the expenditures made by rent seekers offer real benefits to someone (even if only to campaign workers), so that at least some of the expenditure is in the nature of a transfer rather than a deadweight loss (the case of simple bribery seems like a clear example of a transfer payment with no direct implications for efficiency). At the opposite extreme, of course, lies the possibility that rent seeking expenditures are genuinely productive – generating value above their cost so that the whole enterprise might be a net contributor to the appropriate concept of social welfare. This, after all, is the case with instances of 'rent seeking' behaviour in the market economy where, for example, profit seeking behaviour by rival firms generates benefits for consumers.

In the normative evaluation of rent seeking, therefore, everything depends on the details. If we are to select a design for a new opera house, we might be inclined to announce a competition, inviting architects to submit designs with the winning design being awarded the contract. Such a competition has the formal structure of a case of rent seeking. In competing for the prize, the various architects will face incentives to invest in their design projects and in any other activity which might enhance their prospect of winning; and the aggregate sum invested may exceed the value of the rent associated with winning the contract. But whether the competition is a 'problem' or, instead, a good piece of institutional design depends upon what we believe about the likely outcome of the competition. If, for example, we believe that public rivalry will stimulate better designs, and that the opportunity for 'wasteful' expenditures is not too great, and that the judge of the competition will indeed select the best design, so that the final opera house is better than it would have been if the contract had been awarded by some other means, then the costs borne by the unsuccessful competitors may be socially worthwhile. If we believe the opposite, the competition will offer few benefits and may be worse than useless.

So while rent seeking is clearly a phenomenon of interest in the political arena, it is by no means obvious that it is a fundamental problem of politics. Rather, the lesson we take is that there is a relatively fine divide between institutional arrangements that provide examples of productive and beneficial competition, and institutional arrangements that provide examples of inefficient and wasteful rent seeking.

We would also note a suggestive connection between the idea of political rent seeking and the expressive nature of electoral politics. Clearly the model of rent seeking is one that is very much in the *homo economicus* tradition. The rent seeking paradigm paints a picture of individuals and small pressure groups seeking their own advancement through attempts to influence politicians by means other than the ballot box. But how does this influence work in a model in which all political activity is self-interested? Of course there will be *some* scope for interest group activity simply as a result of the logic of collective action[26] – a small group which is intensely interested in a particular policy may well be able to influence a politician into supporting its cause if rival groups (who bear the costs of the policy) are large, diffuse and unorganised. But the scope for interested behaviour of this type will be limited by the electoral constraint – if each individual has one vote and casts it in a self-interested way the rational politician will not wish to impose costs on too many individuals.

By contrast, a model in which the electoral process is expressive in nature may offer greater scope for interested rent seeking and pressure group activity. The idea is simple enough. If voting is not directly linked to individual interests, pressure groups may be able to enlist the support of politicians if they can present their (interested) policy proposals in ways that are expressively salient. In other words, if pressure groups can provide a rhetorical defence of the policy that will stand up to public scrutiny, they will be offering the politician something real in return for his support – a political platform with expressive appeal. In this way,

[26] Olson (1965).

pressure groups are seen to create political ideas that may turn out to be expressively supported. Of course, the motivation of the pressure groups is broadly self-interested, but to the extent that expressive support may be correlated with underlying moral value, their action may be of more general benefit. So while expressive voting and instrumental rent seeking seem to fit well together in the sense that each might seem to complement the other, the normative implications of this interaction are by no means clear.

Beyond public choice

The various conceptions of the problems of politics canvassed in the foregoing sections are all grounded in the public choice or rational actor approach. Although the approach we develop in this book departs from the rational actor orthodoxy in several significant ways, we nevertheless take that orthodoxy as the appropriate point of departure. An essential point underlying all rational actor theories of political behaviour is the recognition of a compliance problem. Agents will not routinely act as they ought to (even when they can recognise how they ought to act). A basic quest is for institutional solutions to this compliance problem. And a characteristic of the institutions that may be brought to bear is that they take agents as they are – at least in the short run. Institutional designers accept the structure of individual motivation and work with the grain of that structure. Even where motivations may, to some extent, be endogenous in the longer term, the institution design problem is heavily constrained in the extent to which it can change the people to fit the institutions. In particular, in our conception of politics as the interaction among individuals who are both rational and moral, and where rationality may apply to the choice of dispositions and not just the choice of actions, there is *some* scope for moral debate – for 'preaching' and virtue production. Nevertheless, the primary impact of political institutions will operate via incentives, selection, and virtue enhancing mechanisms.

We emphasise this point because, outside of the rational actor tradition, the picture of politics – and therefore of the fundamental problems of politics – is very different. In much traditional political philosophy, the 'preaching' aspect of politics becomes almost the whole picture. Politics is idealised as an exercise in moral debate and moral suasion in which well-meaning persons come together to discover (or create) moral truths: the essential *political* problem is that of discerning which values are right or appropriate; and what those values require of individual behaviour and collective policy. There are clear problems with this idealisation. It denies the relevance of the compliance problem. And once the compliance problem is denied, it is difficult to explain why we need the coercive force of government, or why we need policy at all. Or alternatively, if we admit the compliance problem as it relates to the governed in order to explain and justify government coercion, how can we explain why compliance is not also a problem for the governors?

If this traditional account overemphasises the moral element of politics and underemphasises the compliance problem, the opposite is true of the rational actor orthodoxy. Our attempt is to take a step beyond the public choice position to admit some aspects of the moral element of politics in a manner that we believe is consistent with a continued emphasis on compliance. In taking this step we are happy to acknowledge the relevance of the arguments concerning institutions deriving from traditional political theory. In particular, we have in mind three directly moral purposes of political/institutional arrangements: first, the capacity of those arrangements to accommodate and support ethical political argument; second, the extent to which moral motivations in individuals are supported and focused on political issues; and third, the way in which political institutions themselves become part of the content of moral rhetoric.

In relation to the first of these purposes, the issue is essentially one of providing an appropriate 'forum' within which ethical argument can proceed. This matter is one that dominates in the 'discursive democracy' tradition.[27] All that we would add at this point is that, in our view, it is not sufficient to assume that individuals (or their representatives), once placed in a forum, will be well motivated. It is a part of the task of designing such fora that the structure and operating rules are designed with a view both to the problem of selecting appropriate members, and of encouraging ethical rather than interested debate.

The second of these purposes is one on which our discussion of virtue-producing and screening mechanisms applies directly: if democratic elections do tend to select differentially those who are more virtuous and those who are better equipped to engage in moral argument, then the vision of politics as an exercise in moral debate may not be entirely infeasible even where only a minority of the population are virtuous. Even here, however, our approach would suggest that further issues of institutional design will arise. For example, if the parliament or representative assembly is to be seen as a forum for ethical debate, and we are to rely on appropriate electoral devices to ensure that members of the forum are, for the most part, virtuous, we should not focus on voting *within* the

---

[27] See, for example, Elster (1986), Cohen (1989), Bohman (1998) and the references they provide.

forum as a means of decision-making. It will be the process of debate that is important and the extent to which members can convince each other of the moral strength of this or that position. Persuasion is the key, and unanimity within the forum the ideal. Of course, some voting with less than unanimity criteria may be desirable as a means of reducing the cost of lengthy debate, but such voting is not to be thought of as voting on the mandates provided by the electorate. It is worth noting the link to the Wicksellian ideas of relative unanimity that are so strongly present in Buchanan and Tullock, but also noting the point that here the argument for near unanimity applies only within the forum.

The third and final institutional purpose – the idea that institutions themselves become part of the affective message, part of the language of moral argument – is one that sits oddly with the rational actor analysis of institutions and about which we ourselves are sceptical. The idea is this. A moral argument can persuade an agent that X, and not Y, is the right action to take. Because the agent has some desire to act as morality requires, this change in belief makes it more likely that the agent will choose X over Y. But what if the institutional fabric itself is like a moral argument here? What if institutions themselves serve to persuade agents? Take democratic politics as the relevant institution. The mere fact that an issue is being handled in the political sphere – rather than, say, the market – might cause citizens to highlight a public interest dimension, or sensitise citizens to a moral dimension of the issue that might otherwise have been obscured. In this way it is possible that citizens will react to the institutional setting in which an issue is presented, as well as to the issue itself. And even within the political sphere, it might be true that different institutional arrangements – relating to political parties or the procedures adopted in decision making perhaps – might have differential impacts of this kind. Some institutional arrangements might, for example, be associated in citizens' minds with the idea of equality, so that issues considered within that institution would tend to be viewed from the perspective of equality. On this account, it is not just the functional properties of an institution that matter, but also the connotation that the institution carries with it. If an institution connotes equality, it will render equality more salient as a value and so may influence social outcomes by a directly psychological route. We do not dismiss this argument, but nor do we discuss it further in this book. As should be clear by now, we have other reasons for thinking that collective, political decision making may induce behaviour different from that which would be induced under other institutional arrangements – reasons that are more closely related to the rational actor tradition.

Institutional robustness

This is the last point in this book at which the principles of institutional analysis will be discussed in abstraction from specific political institutions. For this reason it is important briefly to step back and try to see the whole project in perspective against the background of the standard rational actor approach to the design of political institutions.

There is, as we see it, nothing particularly new or startling about our general normative ambition – which is to consider political institutions from the perspective of their ability to secure social outcomes consistent with the interests and values of citizens. But our discussion of the motivational structure of individual agents, our interpretation of rationality as applying at the level of dispositions as well as at the level of actions, and our view concerning the implications of rationality in the context of voting, all point to a range of concerns that do not arise in the more traditional rational actor approach – concerns both about the ways in which institutions may influence social outcomes, and about the nature of the problems that well-designed political institutions should be designed to overcome. For example, we emphasise the normative worries associated with expressive voting – the problem, simply put, that voters may vote on expressive whims unrelated to either their self-interest or their moral beliefs – and the possible institutional responses to this concern. Or to take another example, we take seriously the *screening* aspect of political institutions, and specifically the role of democratic elections as selection rather than (or as well as) incentive devices. At the same time, our approach tends to diminish the weight placed on other concerns familiar from more orthodox economic approaches to politics. We are, for example, inclined to be relatively unconcerned about the Arrovian problems of preference aggregation, and rather less concerned than many of our public choice colleagues about majoritarian cycling.

Accepting all this, we try in what follows to keep an eye on a relatively wide range of considerations when appraising particular institutions. In principle each specific institution could be checked against each of the problems of politics identified in this chapter. In some cases, however, our checking is perfunctory. In some instances, we have nothing to add to existing debate; in others, we see no plausible reason to suppose that the particular institution under discussion can contribute to the resolution of a particular problem. We make no pretence of a complete analysis. Rather, in each chapter of part II of this book we offer a line of argument that stresses those more novel aspects of our approach, and the way in which these aspects interact with more standard lines of argument.

Concentrating on some aspects of the problem of the design of political institutions while ignoring others is both necessary and undesirable: necessary if any progress is to be made in understanding the detailed implications of institutional structures without being overwhelmed by the potential complexity of the problem, and undesirable because a key value of any institution's operation must make appeal to the idea of institutional 'robustness'. An institution may be robust in at least two important ways. First, it can operate well in a wide variety of situations (and very badly in very few – if any – situations). Second, it can operate well under a variety of different diagnoses of the underlying problem (and very badly under few – if any – diagnoses). Although both types of robustness are of considerable importance, it is the second type of robustness that is of special concern to us here. Arriving at the conclusion that institutions of type X are excellent at resolving problems of type x is, of course, valuable. But if institutions of type X are also very bad in the face of problems of type y, we may prefer to build more moderate institutions that offer more robust assurance of acceptable performance across the variety of problems that the democratic political process may present.

Our discussions of particular political institutions – representation, political parties, the separation of powers and so on – will be partial. We hope that they add to our understanding of these institutions, but they do not claim to be the type of all-things-considered evaluations of these institutions that would be necessary to satisfy the institutional robustness test. Nevertheless, we believe that our discussion does contribute to a more robust view of political institutions. By focusing on issues and problems that lie outside the range of the standard rational actor tradition, we are able to offer a discussion of familiar institutions couched in rather unfamiliar terms. What does expressive voting add to our understanding of representation? Are the benefits of electoral competition claimed under an incentive-focused analysis also available under a selection-based focus? Does standard rational actor analysis support the separation of powers? And if not, is that all there is to be said about the issue from within the rational actor tradition? These, and other similar questions, are the ones we will seek to engage in the remainder of this book. They are the kinds of question that go with the ambition to design institutions that are 'robust' – robust to the variety of problems that democracy might be seen to face, and to the variety of analyses of different institutions that intelligent and well-meaning scholars might proffer.

PART II

Democratic devices

8

Voting and elections

The process of election affords a moral certainty, that the office of President will never fall to the lot of any man who is not in an eminent degree endowed with the requisite qualifications ... It will not be too strong to say, that there will be a constant probability of seeing the station filled by characters pre-eminent for ability and virtue.

(*Federalist* papers, 68, Alexander Hamilton)

Introduction

In the chapters that make up part II of this book we turn our attention to the democratic devices of our title – the institutional structures that constitute democratic politics. Of course, institutional arrangements differ between democracies, but these relatively fine-grained differences will not be our primary concern. Rather we wish to discuss the broad institutional structures that we take to lie at the heart of almost all modern conceptions of democratic politics: voting and popular elections, representative elections, political parties, and variations on the themes of separating and dividing political powers.

Our aim in these chapters is to provide a discussion of each of these institutional devices in turn, drawing on the analysis of democratic desires provided in part I. Thus the bulk of this chapter will present an account of voting and elections that departs from the standard economic model of these topics precisely because it starts from our more moral and more expressive model of motivation and therefore allows discussion of a wider range of political mechanisms. Chapter 9 will then build on that discussion to give an account of the idea of political representation and the kind of work that representative institutions can do, and so on. These chapters, taken together, provide an outline account of the institutions of representative democracy that might serve as the framework for more detailed studies of particular institutions or institutional reforms. The discussion also provides evidence in support of the proposition that the motivational framework developed in part I offers an interestingly different perspective on the analysis of democratic political devices – a perspective that brings together some of the advantages of the more standard economic approach to politics with the insights more characteristic of traditional political theory.

Models of voting behaviour

As we have already noted, there are currently two rival accounts of voter behaviour within the rational actor tradition in political analysis – what we call the 'instrumental' and the 'expressive' accounts. Of these, the instrumental account is clearly predominant and is sometimes taken to be a defining feature of the rational actor approach to politics.[1] According to the instrumental account, voters are rational in the sense that they vote for the electoral outcome (or the candidate associated with that outcome) that they expect to leave them best off: that is, voters vote their preferences over electoral outcomes in a direct analogue to consumer choice in the marketplace.

On the rival expressive account, voters are also taken to be rational but the requirements of rationality are interpreted differently. The expressive account begins from the observation that, given the negligible probability of any particular voter being decisive, the act of voting is effectively decoupled from the causal consequences of voting seen in terms of electoral outcomes. Individually rational voting behaviour cannot therefore be explained primarily in terms of electoral outcomes: behaviour must be explained predominantly in terms of those considerations that are relevant to the voter's expressing a political position in and of itself. These considerations are termed expressive considerations. Voting is, on this account, much more like cheering at a football match than it is like purchasing an asset portfolio, and any direct analogy with market choice is inappropriate.

We shall not seek to engage in argument as to which model of voting best conforms to the tenets of rationality.[2] In this chapter our primary

---

[1] See for example, Mueller (1989), pp. 1–2.
[2] Although one of us has been active in that debate – Brennan and Lomasky (1985, 1993).

object is rather to explore the implications of the expressive account for certain key aspects of the electoral process – issues such as the size and composition of electoral turnout and the nature of political equilibrium. We shall then compare and contrast these implications with those that flow from the instrumental account of voting when participation is voluntary. In short, our aim is to provide the beginnings of a positive account of the expressive theory of voting that can be compared with the existing literature on the instrumental theory of voting, and to show how the expressive idea can contribute to our understanding of political arrangements. We shall argue that the expressive theory of voting offers an analysis of key features of representative democracy that carries distinctively different implications from those associated with the instrumental model, and that expressive voting provides a framework which supports certain powerful intuitions about political behaviour that are problematic in the instrumental setting.

In the ensuing section we briefly review the instrumental theory of voting. Our aim here is just to provide a summary and interpretation of the instrumental account of electoral equilibrium with endogenous participation, to act as an explicit basis for comparison with the expressive model. On this basis, we develop our account of the expressive voting model of electoral competition. Although, in this chapter particularly, our emphasis is on the contrast between the instrumental and expressive accounts of voting, we do not believe that the models are best viewed as global substitutes. Rather, the two models alert us to different aspects of politics. We will seek to identify and discuss the different views of the domain of electoral politics that we believe are properly associated with the instrumental and expressive views of voting respectively, and sketch a route to the possible integration of expressive and instrumental considerations in a more general account of rational electoral behaviour.

Instrumental voting with voluntary participation

The instrumental account of voting and of electoral competition is usually developed in the one-dimensional, two-candidate case, against the background assumption that every enfranchised person does actually vote. We will begin by briefly rehearsing this standard case.

The basic building block is the citizen's demand curve over political outcomes, built up from underlying preferences in a way essentially analogous to the market case. In an appropriately simplified formulation, the political outcome can be thought of as the level of supply of some publicly provided good, X, financed by an exogenously given tax

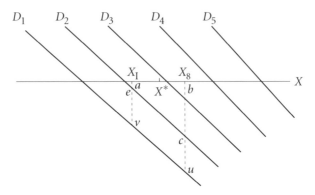

Figure 8.1 Instrumental demand curves

arrangement that will determine for each individual a tax price for X. A net demand curve for public activity can then be derived to show each individual's marginal valuation of X net of tax costs. Different individuals will in general have different net demand curves, D_i, and hence different ideally preferred levels of output X_i, determined where D_i cuts the horizontal axis. These net demand curves will be downward sloping; and in order to avoid spurious complication in what follows, we shall take it that all D_i are linear and have identical slopes. A family of such demand curves for a group of five citizens is depicted in figure 8.1.

The two political candidates, denoted I and II, offer as policy platforms X_I and X_{II} respectively ($X_I < X_{II}$). The instrumental benefit, B_i, for voter i of having X_{II} rather than X_I as the electoral outcome is given by the area under the citizen's demand curve, over the range X_I to X_{II}. This can be positive, as in the case of citizens 4 and 5 in Figure 8.1, in which case the citizen will prefer X_{II}; or negative, as in the case of citizens 1 and 2 in figure 8.1, in which case the citizen will prefer X_I. Each citizen will prefer the electoral option that is closer to her ideal point and, given compulsory or costless voting, each citizen will vote for her preferred candidate. If we endogenise the candidates' choice of platform on the assumption that each candidate attempts to maximise the probability of winning the election, we have the setting of the classic median voter theorem in which both candidates locate at the ideal position of the median voter.

This standard account of how the instrumental citizen votes can also throw light on whether she will vote when participation is both voluntary and costly. The relevant literature is surveyed in Aldrich (1993), but we follow, in particular, Ledyard (1984). The basic point to be emphasised here is that, in the setting where all citizens and both candidates take full account of the strategic incentive structures, all equilibria can be char-acterised by three simple facts:[3]

1. Both candidates choose the same platform.
2. The chosen platform is not necessarily that of the median citizen; rather it maximises a form of social welfare function – the sum of citizens' utilities.
3. No one votes.

Furthermore, such equilibria exist in a relatively wide variety of cases: existence does not depend upon the single-dimensionality of the relevant policy space, or on specific distributions of either preferences or costs of voting across citizens.[4] There will be cases where equilibria do not exist – particularly where the distribution of costs is far from uniform, or where the distribution of preferences is far from symmetric – but non-existence is not endemic.

In the remainder of this section we seek simply to draw out some of the implications of these fundamental propositions in the instrumental analysis of voting with voluntary participation. There are four general points we wish to emphasise. The first and most striking point is that, once the participation decision is endogenised in a manner fully consis-tent with the instrumental approach, failure to vote is to be understood as a desirable feature of electoral competition. Electoral competition has the effect of keeping citizens out of the polling booth. Electoral competition economises on costly voting. Low turnout is desirable. This interpretation of voting is one that follows necessarily from the instrumental model, but is at odds with the intuition (which we take to be standard) that relatively high turnout is generally to be preferred.

The second point also derives from consideration of the zero-turnout nature of equilibrium. Clearly, if both candidates adopt the same platform, B_i must be zero for all citizens and no one will vote. But this outcome is sustained as an equilibrium by balancing potential or marginal voters for each candidate against each other – so who are the marginal voters? Put most simply, those who are most likely to vote will be those who have most at stake – those for whom B_i is largest, *ceteris paribus*, or those with particularly low values of the cost of voting, *ceteris paribus*.[5]

Inspection of figure 8.1 is sufficient to establish that, when candidates adopt distinct positions, B_i is larger for those individuals whose ideal

[3] Ledyard (1984), pp. 23–9.   [4] *Ibid.*, pp. 30–4.
[5] Of course, it is the benefit net of costs that is crucial – in what follows we shall assume that costs and benefits are not correlated across individuals; extension to the correlated case raises no major new issues.

points are further from the mean of the platforms of the political candidates denoted as X^* in figure 8.1. Compare, for example, citizens 1 and 2. For any citizen, recall that B_i is the area between her net demand curve and the horizontal axis over the range X_I to X_{II}; this area measures the individual's utility gain from the more preferred candidate being elected. For citizen 2 (closer to X^*) this area is *abce*; the analogous area for citizen 1 (further from X^*) is the area *abuv*. Citizen 1 has more at stake and, therefore, more reason to vote. If these two individuals face similar costs of voting, 2 will never vote unless 1 does. Alternatively, if these two individuals face costs of voting that are drawn at random from a common distribution then, *ex ante*, citizen 1 is the more likely to vote. This fact simply reflects the convexity of demand: if instrumental demand curves slope downwards, voters whose ideal points are more removed from X^* will have more at stake in the election, *ceteris paribus*, and on the instrumentalist account, are therefore more likely to vote.

This result does, of course, depend strictly on the assumption of identical slopes of all demand curves (and the interpersonal comparability of utility). If different citizens have differing elasticities of net demand for X, then net demand curves may intersect in the range between X_I and X_{II} and no simple relation between the size of B_i and the distance of i's ideal point from X^* may exist. But to reverse the thrust of the result requires that voters with more extreme ideal points have systematically higher net-demand elasticities, and no plausible justification for this possibility seems available. Indeed, the opposite might seem more reasonable. We might distinguish between two possible senses of political extremism: one associated with an ideal point at an extreme of the distribution, the other with the idea that an extremist may be more reluctant to countenance any movement from her ideal point than a more 'moderate' person. This second sense of extremist is associated with an unwillingness to compromise and would be reflected in a more inelastic political demand curve. If these two forms of extremism are positively correlated – so that those who take extreme positions are also less willing to compromise – the result outlined above is reinforced. Only if there is a systematic negative relationship between the two forms of extremism would the result be threatened.

So while the instrumental account of voting predicts zero turnout in the equilibrium of the two-candidate model, it also predicts that, when participation is non-zero (i.e. when candidate positions are non-identical), voters will be disproportionately drawn from the extremes of the political distribution. So, for example, if candidates set policy platforms so as to deter the entry of a third candidate we might expect an equilibrium in which the policy platforms of the two candidates diverge so that turnout may be positive.[6] But in cases such as these, the instrumental account of voting carries with it strong predictions concerning the composition of the set of voters as compared with the set of non-voters.

The third point follows directly – there is no scope for the idea of citizen alienation in this model. Citizens do not abstain from voting because they do not see either candidate as representing them or because they do not identify with either candidates' position; they abstain from voting simply because there is not enough at stake – indifference rather than alienation is the key to non-participation. We do not deny that, in fact, citizens may abstain from voting because of alienation. On the contrary, we are inclined to the view that this is indeed a common motive for not voting. It is simply that the idea of political alienation does not belong in an instrumental account (Slutsky, 1975).

The fourth and final point we note here involves the failure of the Hotelling spatial equilibrium analogy to transfer to the voting case: electoral competition is not quite like ice-cream sellers choosing a location on the beach, it seems. Specifically, in the ice-cream sellers analogue, there is no suggestion that the sunbathers most distant from the ice-cream sellers are most likely to purchase ice-cream. But why is the voting case different? Simply put, the point is that citizen-voters do not 'buy' anything *except* the location of the candidate. In the ice-cream seller's case, location emerges as the incidental outcome of consumers buying ice-cream. In the electoral case, and on the instrumental account, the location of the candidate has to be seen as the object of voting: there is nothing that the voter gets for voting except the change in the policy position of the rival candidates – there is simply no analogue to the ice-cream. Of course, the ice-cream analogy could be supported if voters were identified as getting something out of voting of an intrinsic kind. But that 'something' is precisely what the expressive account of voting attempts to provide; and as has been argued elsewhere,[7] the expressive account, when most plausibly rendered, serves to undercut much of the instrumental voting story.

In summary, the instrumental account of voting, when applied in the case of voluntary and costly participation, yields a number of implications which are somewhat at odds with standard political intuitions and ideas. Turnout is predicted to be zero in the simple case of two-candidate competition. Lower turnout is normatively desirable. Where turnout is non-zero voters will be drawn from the extremes of the political

---

[6] See, for example, Palfrey (1984), Weber (1992).
[7] Brennan and Lomasky (1993).

distribution. With these implications in mind, we now turn to the expressive account of voting.

Expressive voting in one dimension

The expressive account of voting shifts attention away from electoral outcomes and focuses on the benefits and costs to the citizen of supporting electoral candidates. The basic argument derives from analysis of the role of the probability of i's vote actually bringing about the particular desired electoral outcome: if this is small, so the argument goes, then instrumental considerations cannot play the predominant role in explaining either voter participation or voter choice. Simply put, the citizen does not face an effective choice between alternative policy outcomes, but she does face an effective choice as to which candidate to support; and it is entirely rational for the citizen to concentrate attention on the effective choices faced.

Our purpose here, however, is to explicate and develop the expressive model of voting rather than defend it by *ex ante* theorising, and for that purpose we begin by directing attention to just two electoral phenomena – voter alienation and voter indifference. Once these phenomena are dealt with it will be possible to derive propositions about the nature of competitive electoral equilibria under expressive voting, and to contrast their implications with those associated with the instrumental voting account sketched in the previous section.

To alienation first. It should be clear that the expressive theory provides a natural account of voter alienation – of the idea, that is, that voters will be more likely to vote for parties/representatives/policies that are closer to their expressive ideal. Voter participation, in the sense of the voter actively showing support for something of which she approves, is analogous to the ice-cream purchased on the beach: voter participation just is the act of consumption that brings the voter to the poll. And just as sunbathers closer to the ice-cream stall are more likely to consume an ice-cream than sunbathers farther away, so expressive voters are more likely to vote if the option on offer is one with which they more closely identify. To be sure, the attributes with which the voter identifies (or which for some other reason induce the voter to show support) may not be specifically connected to the policies associated with particular electoral outcomes, still less with what the voter expects to gain from those policies. The voter may identify with the candidate's moral character, good looks or ethnic origin or with the candidate's or party's general ideology. In other words, the domain of politics under the expressive analysis of voting may be very different from the domain of politics under the instrumental analysis of voting (we shall return to consider this point more fully below). However, whatever the relevant expressive domain may be, citizens might be conceptualised as having notional ideal points in the relevant space, and it seems plausible to suppose that any given citizen will show support for an option if it is close enough to her ideal point, and not show support for options that are not close enough. We shall formulate this voter calculus in the most direct and straightforward way. Each citizen, i, is conceptualised as having some ideal point, Y_i, in the expressive domain Y; and i will vote for candidate I only if I occupies a point in the expressive domain no further from Y_i than some threshold distance,[8] k.

The second issue relates to indifference. Suppose that two candidates adopt positions within distance k of Y_i: then it seems natural within the expressive account to say that i will support the candidate closer to her ideal, and that candidates equidistant from Y_i will be supported with equal probability. There is no reason to suppose that voters who are indifferent between candidates within the support threshold will refrain from voting: they simply have equal reasons for supporting either candidate and will choose randomly, just as the sunbather who is equidistant from two ice-cream sellers but quite close to both will choose randomly, rather than – like Buridan's ass – fail to choose at all.

Note that this formulation carries some direct and striking implications. Most obviously, some citizens would vote for a candidate even if that candidate were unopposed. Indeed, a candidate's vote might well be larger when unopposed than if she were opposed by a 'similar' candidate (although the total number of votes cast might rise with two candidates). More generally, some citizens would be willing to vote in an election even when there was little or no doubt about the result. The act of expressing support for 'your' candidate is not necessarily influenced by the expected outcome of the contest, even though, of course, expressive votes will, in aggregate, determine the outcome of the contest. We find these impli-

---

[8] Our formulation focuses on what might be termed 'positive expressive voting' where citizens express approval. 'Negative expressive voting' might arise if citizens were motivated to express disapproval of certain positions/candidates. However, disapproval would presumably be directed at candidates adopting positions in the relevant expressive domain that were far removed from the citizen's ideal point and, under most electoral systems, the citizen would be required to express this disapproval by means of a vote for a rival candidate. If that rival has to be closer than some critical distance to the citizen's ideal point in order to be a suitable vehicle for disapproval voting, then it is straightforward to see that our formulation would also capture 'negative expressive voting'. More complex formulations which account for both positive and negative expressive voting are possible, but we do not pursue them here.

cations eminently reasonable; but more importantly, perhaps, they further underline the distinction between expressive and instrumental voting.

We are now in a position to make some initial progress with the expressive version of two-candidate electoral competition in a single expressive dimension. In any one-dimensional expressive domain, Y, a candidate located at Y_I will defeat a rival located at Y_{II}, if and only if the number of citizens with ideal points in the interval (Y_I-k, Y_I+k) is greater than the number in the interval $(Y_{II}-k, Y_{II}+k)$, whether these intervals overlap or not. This is so because, in the expressive account, it is precisely these citizens who will vote. It is therefore clear that, in the simplest case of a unimodal (but not necessarily symmetric) distribution of citizen ideal points, and with candidates motivated to win the election while being free to adopt any position in the expressive domain, competitive pressures will force candidates towards the mode of the distribution. However, co-location at the mode itself will only be the competitive equilibrium when the distribution is symmetric around the mode up to neighbourhood of $+k$. More generally, the competitive electoral equilibrium in the one-dimensional, two-candidate case with uni-modal (but not necessarily symmetric) distributions of citizens' ideal points under expressive voting involves a positive turnout, with both candidates locating at a point Y^E in a neighbourhood of the mode of the distribution of citizen ideal points such that the number of voters in the range (Y^E-k, Y^E) is equal to the number in the range (Y^E, Y^E+k).

To see that this is the equilibrium, consider the (asymmetric) case illustrated[9] in figure 8.2, and consider candidate I deviating from Y^E by moving towards the mode of the distribution to, say, Y'. Define Y^* as the mid point of the range (Y', Y^E). Relative to the situation in which the candidates co-located at Y^E, candidate II gains the voters in the range (Y^*, Y^E), and loses no votes, while candidate I gains the voters in the range $(Y'-k, Y^E-k)$, and loses the voters in the range (Y^*, Y^E). This must be a losing strategy for I. A similar argument shows that deviation to the right of Y^E (away from the mode) will cause the deviating candidate to lose.

Essentially, the problem here is that while deviation from co-location at Y^E increases the level of support for both candidates, it is bound to do so in a manner that benefits the candidate at Y^E more than the deviating candidate.[10] In the present expressive setting, the location of the median

[9] Here, and throughout, we use piecewise linear distributions to illustrate our arguments. This is entirely for ease of presentation – nothing in our argument depends on linearity.

[10] This argument is somewhat similar to the argument put by Comanor (1976) in the context of the instrumental account of voting where the median and mode

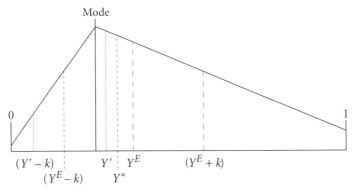

Figure 8.2 Expressive equilibrium – a unimodal case

citizen's ideal point is strictly irrelevant to the analysis. The point is that the basic idea underlying the median voter result relates to the median of those who actually vote – not the median of those who are enfranchised. The construction of the equilibrium at Y^E in the expressive case respects this basic idea – Y^E is pulled towards the mode of the distribution of citizens ideal points by the expressive nature of the decision to vote, but Y^E is also the median of the set of actual voters ideal points defined over the interval $(Y^E\text{-}k, Y^E\text{+}k)$.

At first sight it might seem that this quasi-modal result does little to undermine the standard, instrumental, median voter analysis – after all, one might suggest, the difference between median and mode is likely to be minor. We think that this response is inappropriate for several reasons. First, we would re-emphasise the shift in domain involved in the move from the instrumental to the expressive account of voting – to be discussed in more detail below. Second, we would repeat that the instrumental account of voting – when extended to incorporate the participation decision – does not actually give rise to the median voter result but rather predicts a zero turnout with co-location at the point that maximises the sum of citizens' utility. It is this set of predictions that should most properly be compared with the predictions of the expressive argument developed here. And this comparison provides sharp contrasts – most obviously in the matter of turnout. The expressive analysis predicts positive participation, with the exact scale of participation determined by k and the distribution of citizen ideal points. But the difference in the matter of turnout is not just a quantitative one. In the instrumental case non-voting results from indifference; while in the

do not coincide. The differences from Comanor are, however, more significant than the similarities.

expressive case non-voting results from alienation. The instrumental
account predicts that the non-voters will be those whose ideal points are
relatively close to the candidate positions, while the expressive account
predicts that the non-voters will be those whose ideal points are most
distant from the candidates' positions.[11]

Third, even leaving questions of participation and domain on one side,
there is still a wide variety of cases in which the predictions based on our
expressive analysis may differ significantly from those derived from
instrumental analysis either in the standard median voter variant or the
more relevant endogenous participation model. The most obvious
example relates to the uniform distribution of citizen ideal points. In the
uniform distribution case both instrumental results predict the same
unique equilibrium outcome, which has a strong claim to normative
desirability. However, the expressive argument outlined above predicts no
unique equilibrium in this case – any pair of candidate locations such
that each party locates at least k from either extreme of the distribution
will be an equilibrium. In this case, then, there is no implication of
candidate convergence under expressive voting, and no strongly centrist
predicted outcome.[12]

We might also note, in passing, a possible ambiguity in the interpretation of the scale of voter turnout that is particularly clear in the case of
the uniform distribution, but is of much more general relevance. While
the expressive model predicts positive turnout in equilibrium, it does not
maximise turnout. Nor can it be argued that larger turnouts are always to
be preferred in the sense that larger turnouts are associated with more
efficient outcomes. The extent of turnout will depend, *inter alia*, on the
degree of differentiation between candidate platforms, with maximum
turnout in the uniform distribution case requiring that the two intervals
$(Y_I -k, Y_I+k)$, $(Y_{II} -k, Y_{II}+k)$ do not intersect.

Similar analytic points to those developed for the case of the uniform
distribution can be made in the contexts of other multimodal distributions of citizens' ideal points, where the predictions of our expressive
argument may differ quite sharply from those of the instrumental theory.
For example, in the symmetric, bimodal case the instrumental voting
model will predict convergence to co-location at the position of the
median citizen's ideal point if full participation is assumed, and co-
location at the sum-of-utilities maximising position if participation is

---

[11] This difference provides the conceptual basis for a relatively simple empirical test
     to distinguish between the two models, though we shall not pursue this empirical
     issue here.
[12] Again, the threat of entry of a third candidate will affect the analysis, and again
     we leave this complication on one side.

endogenous. Given symmetry, these two predictions will be substantively identical except in the matter of participation. By contrast, the expressive argument outlined here will predict that no equilibrium may exist. To see why, recall that, in figure 8.2, the point Y^E did not maximise the number of voters within a k-neighbourhood. Label the point that does maximise the number of voters within a k-neighbourhood Y^M. In the symmetric, bimodal case illustrated in figure 8.3 we will find an equivalent to Y^E and to Y^M in the neighbourhood of each mode – label them Y^E_1 Y^E_2 Y^M_1 Y^M_2 respectively. Now, it is clear that a candidate locating at, say, Y^M_1 can be defeated by a rival locating at Y^E_1; but equally that a candidate locating at Y^E_1 can be defeated by a rival locating at Y^M_2. In short, no location is secure against both local competition and competition close to the other mode – except in the special case where we have sufficient local symmetry around each mode, in which case equilibria will exist and involve each candidate locating at one or other mode. This argument generalises to the multimodal case. In order for an equilibrium to exist we will require *either* a dominant mode – in which case equilibrium will be unique and directly analogous to the unimodal case – *or* sufficient local symmetry around relevant modes, in which case there will be multiple equilibria similar to the case of the uniform distribution.

We do not take the potential non-existence of equilibrium to be a major problem here since we see no reason to suppose that multimodal distributions lacking a dominant mode (or local symmetry) are particularly plausible in this context. Our point is rather that both the analytic structure and the empirical location of equilibrium under the expressive argument differ sharply from those derived under instrumental voting, and that these differences become particularly marked once we depart from the unimodal case.

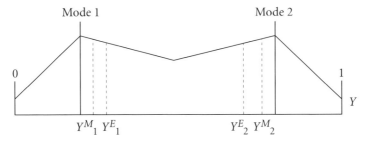

Figure 8.3 Expressive equilibrium – a bimodal case

Expressive voting in two dimensions

We now turn to the expressive account of voting in the two-dimensional case. Again, we would stress that the distinction between the instrumental and expressive cases operates at two distinct levels: at the level of the specification of the political domain, and at the level of the more detailed analysis of voting and equilibrium within a domain. Although the expressive domain will, in general, differ from the instrumental domain, there is nothing in the expressive account that makes the one-dimensional case particularly salient, so that the move to multidimensionality is just as important to the expressive argument as it is for the instrumental. Figure 8.4 presents the basic structure of the two-dimensional, three-citizen, two-candidate model; we identify the circles marked as d_k, e_k and f_k as signifying the range of expressive support associated with citizens D, E and F respectively. Thus, in a natural generalisation of the discussion of the one-dimensional case, a citizen will support a candidate only if that candidate's position lies within a radius of k from the citizen's ideal point. If both candidates locate within the relevant radius, the citizen will vote for the candidate closer to her ideal point.

One immediate implication of this formulation is that *global* cycling is not a possible outcome. Global cycling involves the idea that a sequence of majority votes between pairs of candidates can lead to any point in the relevant policy space being majority preferred in the final vote. But in the expressive case it is clear that no location which lies outside the union of the citizens' k-regions can ever gain the support of even one voter. To put the same point more positively, the only candidate locations that can ever receive positive support, and so be potentially electable, lie within the union of the k-regions: so, no location outside of this union will ever be adopted by a candidate seeking election.

In figure 8.4a we illustrate the possibility of equilibrium. Here citizen D plays a pivotal role since no coalition of two (or more) voters can form unless she is included. This special role grants D the effective power to ensure an equilibrium. To see this, first simply observe that a candidate located at D cannot be defeated (since a rival can, at best, secure one vote against D by locating within either e_k or f_k). The best response to D is therefore one that ensures a tie against D, and cannot itself be beaten by any location. One such possibility is for the second candidate also to locate at D – so that co-location at D is an equilibrium. But further possibilities exist. In the case illustrated, F is closer to D than is E. Consider the point P as a possible best response to D, where P is defined as the intersection of FD and f_k. A candidate locating at P against a rival at D will tie, since she will attract the vote of F.

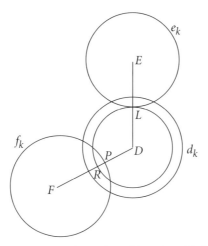

Figure 8.4a Expressive voting with a pivotal individual

Furthermore, P cannot be beaten by any other location since it is impossible to choose a point that will attract the votes of both D and F against a rival located at P, and it is also impossible to build a coalition of D and E against the point P, since any point that will gain the support of E must be further from D than is P. Thus P is a best response to D. This argument can be extended to show that all points on the line segment PR (defined as the segment of PF that lies closer to D than does L) are best responses to D and to each other. Location at any point in this line segment provides an unbeatable platform and one that ties against D. Thus equilibria exist in this case whenever the two candidates adopt a pair of locations drawn from the point D and the line segment PR.

But this is very much a special case. A somewhat more general perspective can be gained from figure 8.4b, in which no individual citizen holds a distinctive pivotal position. Here we would argue that while in general there may be no unbeatable location, and hence no equilibrium, cycling will be limited to the set of locations defined as the union of the intersections between k-regions. The argument here is only slightly more involved. First, it is clear that any point outside of this set can be majority defeated by a suitably chosen point within the set – for example the point F can be majority defeated by any point in the intersection of e_k and d_k (such as S). Second, consider any point in the intersection of any two k-regions – say e_k and d_k. It is clear that any point in this intersection that does not lie on the line ED will be majority dominated by appropriately chosen points within the same intersection and lying on the line ED. Third, any such point – say S – will either be unbeatable (and hence a

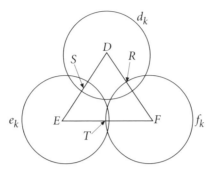

Figure 8.4b Expressive voting without a pivotal individual

potential co-location equilibrium) or it will be majority defeated by points which create a new coalition – for example, S may be defeated by at least one of T and R. The circumstance in which S is unbeatable is that S is both closer to D than is R, and closer to E than is T. This circumstance essentially identifies D and E as a pivotal coalition in a manner analogous to the pivotal position of D in figure 8.4a. What is certainly true is that no point within the union of intersections of k-regions can be majority defeated by any point outside that set, and this is sufficient to place a limit on the extent of cycling.

This three-citizen example may be of rather limited interest – but the general idea that expressive voting might be expected to result in what might be termed 'limited stability', with candidates constrained by the process of electoral competition to adopt positions within a defined neighbourhood, is suggestive of a more general result. Figure 8.5 depicts a multicitizen, two-dimensional, two-candidate case.

We depict the distribution of ideal points by means of contour lines which trace out the locus of points with identical numbers of citizen ideal points. The case illustrated involves a unimodal distribution, with the mode located at M. Now, any candidate position such as Y_I will define a circle of radius k such that all citizens within that circle will vote, and will vote for candidate I unless the rival candidate offers a position closer to their ideal point. There exists some point T such that the k-circle centred at T contains more citizen ideal points than any other k-circle. If the distribution is locally symmetric around the mode, T will be located at M; more generally, T will simply lie in a relevant neighbourhood of M.

In the case of symmetry around the mode, co-location at the mode will represent a unique and stable political equilibrium. In the asymmetric case, the existence of equilibrium is more problematic. The question is whether there exists some point (analogous to Y^E in figure 8.2) between

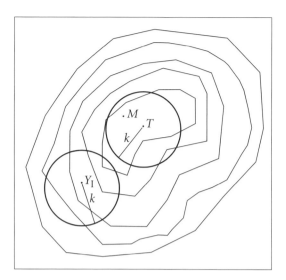

Figure 8.5 Expressive voting in two dimensions with many voters

M and T which resists entry on all sides. This is very demanding – requiring as it does that the k-circle centred at the relevant point be such that each diameter of the circle partitions the set of citizen-voters included in the circle into two equal subsets. Indeed, the condition is strongly reminiscent of the condition required for the existence of equilibrium in the standard treatment of the multidimensional case with compulsory instrumental voters.[13] And this is not surprising since, as we noted in the one-dimensional case, any equilibrium must lie at the ideal point of the voter who is the median voter within the set of citizens who actually vote. However, there is a crucial difference here. Although no equilibrium may exist, the range of locations which may be adopted by rational candidates is severely limited. Any point too far removed from the mode (where 'too far' is defined in terms of k) is ruled out. 'Limited stability' – that is convergence on a neighbourhood with instability within that neighbourhood – seems to characterise the expressive account of electoral competition in at least many cases of interest.

The domain of politics

As we have stressed, the most basic difference between the expressive and instrumental accounts of voting is that the domains of the models differ. In the instrumental model the political domain reflects the policy output

[13] See Enelow and Hinich (1990), Mueller (1989).

of the political process: politics is conceived as operating within a space that is defined by policy parameters. In the expressive model the political domain may not be directly related to the policy outcomes of the political process, and certainly will not be restricted to policy matters. Citizen-voters may express their support for any observable characteristic (say, general ideology or moral character) and may be very much influenced by a candidate's rhetorical or presentational skills.

While it is easy to see that the expressive domain is less restrictive than the instrumental domain, and relatively easy to outline the general idea of an expressive consideration as one that engages the individual citizen in an act of identifying with a particular cause or characteristic, it is much more difficult to be precise about the nature of expressive considerations.[14] This difficulty is particularly acute for economists who are used to thinking of individuals in terms of their interests modelled via a standard utility function, since expressive considerations engage with an individual in ways that need not bear on their interests.[15] And even where expressive concerns do bear on interests, the relationship may be neither direct nor harmonious. For example, imagine a citizen facing an election in which the most prominent issue raises nationalistic passions – as might be in the case of the independence of Scotland from Great Britain, or the political integration of Great Britain into Europe. Any particular citizen may be able to form a view about the impact of alternative policies on their instrumental interests, but may also identify expressively with one or other side of the debate. In such cases, there seems no reason to suppose that instrumental and expressive concerns will pull in the same direction.[16] In any case, we would argue that it would be entirely rational for individuals to vote on the basis of their expressive concerns, regardless of their instrumental interests.

The possible mismatch between expressive concerns and interests raises obvious normative concern. If voting is driven by expressive considerations, can there be any assurance that political outcomes will serve the interests of citizens? For the moment we will stress just one relevant point. The normative properties of a political decision-making system are a function of both the structure of that system and the political inputs. Recognising that at least some of the inputs to the democratic

---

[14] For a discussion, see Brennan and Lomasky (1993) chapter 3.

[15] Of course, it will be possible to incorporate expressive concerns into a formal utility function, but the distinction between instrumental and expressive concerns is not lessened by such a formalism.

[16] For a discussion that extends this argument and applies it to the question of the relationship between constitutional design and peace, see Brennan and Hamlin (forthcoming).

process are expressive provides an alternative basis for analysing and understanding the role of political structures. Structures that work well in normative terms on the assumption of instrumental voting might perform poorly in the context of expressive voting, and vice versa. An important example, to be taken up in the next chapter, involves the comparison of direct and representative democracy. The recognition of expressive voting, and of the expressive domain of politics, changes the lens through which we see questions of normative political theory and, in particular, questions of institutional design.

The equilibration process

In the discussion so far we have followed the spirit of the standard instrumental account in one important respect. We have assumed that competing candidates/parties seek to relocate themselves so as to max-imise voter support without any major constraint. Political candidates/parties are in this sense to be seen as firms that supply services – let us say dentistry services – and the critical process of competition is to give customers/voters the kind of service they most prefer. A dental firm that gives up the use of novocaine in favour of some superior painkiller, or that takes up the new high-speed drill in preference to the earlier pedal-driven alternative, simply provides a better service to its customers and so should be expected to attract more customers. This is just evidence of the market at work. So, in the political analogue to market competition, it is natural to make a similar assumption. And the adjustment of candidate/party position in the relevant domain (whether expressive or instru-mental) becomes a prime element in the account of electoral competition and the primary engine of equilibration.

However, the expressive account of voting introduces an important proviso into this picture. If we think of candidates or, more particularly, political parties as accumulating not customers but *loyalty* – if we think of political parties as offering packages of attributes with which voters can *identify* – then party positions may be more stable and less open to opportunistic adjustment than in the instrumental account. In an important sense parties both represent and articulate the ideological and policy commitments that become the language of political contest. If a party is seen to desire nothing other than to occupy power, so that all its statements on matters of policy are merely massaged versions of popular opinion, then that party will be seen to be whoring after votes. A voter cannot plausibly use party positions to express where she stands if the party itself 'stands for nothing' or is *seen* to stand for nothing. Put another way, if qualities like 'leadership' and 'integrity' are qualities that voters look for in some measure in their favoured party/candidate, then a party revealing that it is simply a cipher reflecting what current opinion polls say is unlikely to be maximally effective in garnering votes. This fact introduces an element of paradox into the quest for political popularity: that is, that the explicit search for political popularity is to some extent self-defeating. Political popularity has some of the character of Elster's 'necessarily incidental consequences'.[17] That is unsurprising, perhaps, since being liked or admired more generally has similar attributes: the person who is seen to be motivated predominantly by the desire for admiration and/or affection is inclined to appear slightly pathetic rather than particularly admirable or likeable.

The critical point to follow from this set of observations is that a party/candidate's capacity to change its position at will in the way that the standard account presumes is very much at risk. A party, on this reading, accumulates a kind of locational capital that makes significant shifts to quite different positions in policy space counterproductive. Parties may have a desire to move within the relevant domain, but find it electorally costly to move too far too fast. Positions become sticky. And the equilibration process is inhibited.

If the option of moving in policy space is unduly costly, then parties/candidates will find it correspondingly more attractive to expend resources in expressively defending the position that they currently occupy. Political advertising – and more generally the invention of novel rhetorical defences of positions with which the party/candidate has long been identified – come thereby to occupy a larger role in the whole competitive process.

Further development of the idea of the role of political parties in an expressive framework will be presented in chapter 10 below. For the moment we simply note that political competition between parties is likely to be characterised by a very considerable element of path-dependency. For this reason alone we would not expect the expressive account of voter behaviour to be consistent with wild swings in policy outcomes, or even necessarily with full co-location equilibria. Being faithful to party traditions and loyal to traditional party ideology will inhibit the operation of forces for co-location in the expressive context, though as the foregoing discussion indicates, those forces will remain in a weaker form.

A more general perspective

We have, so far, emphasised various dimensions of the contrast between the expressive and instrumental accounts of voting. But this strategy runs

[17] See Elster (1983).

the risk of being too successful – of giving the impression that the two approaches are best seen as pure substitutes offering mutually exclusive accounts of voting behaviour. But things need not be viewed this way. The expressive and instrumental accounts can be seen to offer different but fundamentally compatible perspectives on voting behaviour – each picking out a potentially important aspect of electoral politics. In this section we try to be a little more precise about this compatibility and the way in which we would see instrumental and expressive considerations working together to determine voting behaviour and electoral outcomes in a more general model.

In sketching an approach to such a model, the first and most basic point to stress is that voters are rational: whether they vote instrumentally or expressively in any particular situation, they do so as a rational response to that situation. There is no *a priori* categorisation into 'expressives' and 'instrumentals'[18] – these categories emerge as a part of the overall political equilibrium. We might think of citizens as endogenously dividing into two sets – those voters who are most appropriately viewed as 'instrumentals', and those voters who are most appropriately viewed as 'expressives'. Political parties or individual candidates are faced with the prospect of competing both in the domain of instrumental outcomes and in the domain of expressive concerns. Our earlier discussion allows us to speculate a little on what such a structure might look like. In what follows, we shall limit attention to the two candidate case.

The basic problems to be confronted in constructing a more general model may be conceived in terms of the relationship between the instrumental and expressive domains. This relationship has two basic components – one relating to citizens and the other relating to candidates. As far as individual citizens are concerned the relationship may be roughly conceived as the degree of (positive or negative) correlation between instrumental preferences and expressive considerations. There are two ways in which such a correlation may arise. The first, and most direct, is the case in which 'policies' are not only the subject of instrumental evaluation, but also an important subject of expressive concern. In this case the possibility of correlation is clear – in the limit (where policies are the *only* subject of expressive concern) an individual citizen's expressive concerns might mesh perfectly with her instrumental interests. If this were true for all citizens, not only would the instrumental

---

[18] We use these terms rather than 'expressive voters' and 'instrumental voters' since not all citizens in either set will actually vote. 'Expressives' are those citizens whose electoral behaviour is expressive in character, whether they actually vote or not; and similarly for 'instrumentals'.

and expressive domains be identical, but the distribution of instrumentally ideal points would exactly match the distribution of expressively ideal points.

The second manner in which a correlation between instrumental and expressive concerns might arise operates indirectly via candidates. In expressing support for a candidate I might be motivated by a specific characteristic or attribute of that individual, but that characteristic or attribute might be correlated with that candidate's support for a particular policy. To the extent that my expressive calculus picks out candidates who tend to support my instrumentally preferred policies, the relevant (positive) correlation may arise.

This indirect route to a correlation between instrumental and expressive concerns at the individual level points to the second component of the relationship between the expressive and the instrumental – that associated with political candidates. If electoral politics operates in both instrumental and expressive domains, it is clear that politicians must be seen as holding positions in both. The question then is the extent to which candidates are able to adjust a position in one domain given a position in the other. In one extreme case, there is a one to one relationship between the instrumental and expressive domains – so that either position in one is a perfect indicator of the position in the other. At the opposite extreme, the two domains are entirely unrelated in the sense that a candidate committed to any particular position in one is still free to commit to any position in the other. More generally, there will be some trade off between expressive and instrumental positions, so that a position adopted in one domain will restrict the choice of position in the other, and any shift of position in one domain may carry implications in the other. With these ideas in mind, we offer a discussion of two relatively straightforward special cases: the limiting case in which the expressive and instrumental domains are identical with strong links between domains for both citizens and candidates; and the opposite extreme case in which the expressive and instrumental domains are essentially independent of each other.

The 'perfect correlation' case

We begin with the simplest case of a single policy dimension which is both instrumentally and expressively salient. We further assume that each citizen's instrumentally ideal point is also her expressively ideal point, and that all candidates are fully defined by their policy position. In this framework, an obvious starting point for discussion is provided by the idea that while there will always be expressive voters, there may be no instrumental voters in equilibrium. If candidates position themselves centrally, those citizens with the most extreme (instrumental) ideal points will be the most likely to endogenously adopt instrumental criteria in their voting decisions, while those citizens with more moderate (expressive) ideal points will adopt expressive criteria. On the one hand the extremists have most at stake in the instrumental dimension, while on the other hand they have less opportunity to vote expressively. The opposite is true of the centrist citizen. This raises the possibility that the purely expressive equilibrium may carry over as the equilibrium of the more general model.

Recall that under purely expressive voting co-location equilibria are almost always available, and that such an outcome ensures that there are no instrumental voters. When will a co-location expressive equilibrium be an equilibrium of the more general model? The answer to this question seems to depend, *inter alia*, on symmetry. In unimodal and symmetric cases, the co-location equilibrium at the mode of the distribution persists when instrumental and expressive considerations are both relevant. To see why, consider the possibility of one candidate departing from the modal policy – imagine a move to the right, for example. Such a move must lead to a loss of expressive voters relative to the rival candidate but, in opening up a gap between the candidates, it also makes possible the entry of instrumental voters. However, given symmetry, any instrumental voters will be drawn mostly from the left of the distribution and so will support the modal candidate. Instrumental and expressive considerations work together to support the co-location equilibrium in this case.

Now consider the case of the uniform distribution of ideal points, and recall that in this case there are many co-location equilibria under purely expressive voting, as well as many which do not involve co-location. When instrumental considerations are added in, most of these potential equilibria are deleted and co-location at the mid-point, or symmetric location around the midpoint, is rendered more salient. To see why, consider first co-location at a point to the right of the midpoint. This cannot be an equilibrium since each candidate will face an instrumental incentive to move toward the midpoint. Such a move would leave the two candidates level in terms of expressive voters (this would be a non-co-location equilibrium under purely expressive voting) but would encourage the entry of instrumental voters, and such instrumental voters would be predominantly on the left and so would support the moving candidate. The same logic rules out asymmetric equilibria involving distinct candidate positions. The point is that since any potential equilibrium involving distinct candidate positions will involve equal expressive support for

each candidate, it must also involve equal instrumental support for each
candidate: and this will only be the case if the midpoint between the
candidate positions is sufficiently close to the midpoint of the distribution. In this way, the introduction of instrumental voters in this case
acts as a sort of equilibrium selection device, ruling out the possibility of
almost all asymmetric equilibria.

But the argument changes substantially when we consider an asymmetric, unimodal distribution of ideal points, as illustrated in figure 8.6.
Let E^* indicate the unique co-location equilibrium under purely expressive voting. Now, consider the best response to E^* when both instrumental and expressive considerations are relevant. Clearly, co-location at
E^* would ensure a tie with no 'instrumentals' voting, and this may be the
best available option – and if it is, E^* remains an equilibrium. But it may
now be possible for the candidate to do better by locating at a point such
as S, to the right of E^*. To see why, notice that the asymmetry in the
distribution of ideal points is such that, in this case, the opening up of the
gap between candidates located at E^* and S will generate more instrumental votes on the right (and therefore for the candidate at S) than on
the left. So, although positioning at S will cause the candidate to gain
fewer expressive votes than her rival, it will also cause that candidate to
gain more instrumental votes than her rival. The net effect may go either
way depending on the details of the distribution of ideal points and of
instrumental demands. But of course, if S is a winning strategy against E^*,
the choice of E^* by either candidate cannot be part of an equilibrium.
Clearly, co-location at E^* will not be an equilibrium in such a case. Here,
then, instrumental and expressive considerations pull in opposite directions.[19]

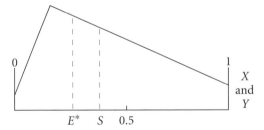

Figure 8.6 Mixed expressive and instrumental voting

[19] This line of argument does not depend on the identical distribution of
   instrumental and expressive ideal points – indeed the circumstances in which
   no co-location equilibrium exists will be easier to achieve with different
   distributions.

Indeed, there may be no pure strategy equilibria at all in such a case. Since any co-location equilibrium must involve only expressive voting, and E^* was the unique purely expressive co-location equilibrium, there can be no co-location equilibrium in the mixed instrumental/expressive model. To see that there may be no equilibrium involving distinct candidate positions, consider the best response to S in figure 8.6. It will always be possible to locate to the left of S by an arbitrarily small distance, and such a location will always imply a majority of the expressive voters. Since it will also imply a vanishingly small number of instrumental voters, this will be a winning strategy. This essentially expressive argument pushes both parties toward E^* but, as we have seen, E^* may be beaten by S. In this case the tension between instrumental and expressive considerations induces a form of instability.[20]

The 'independence' case

We now turn briefly to what might be thought of as the opposite extreme case – the case in which the instrumental and expressive domains are essentially unrelated. For all citizens the dimensions of instrumental and expressive concern are distinct, with no direct or indirect correlation between their ideal points in each domain; and for political candidates there are no cross-domain restrictions in the positions that they may adopt. In this extreme case, the two models of political process might be seen to operate side by side. Policies would be determined in the instrumental domain as analysed by the standard model. While there would also be competition for votes in the expressive domain, this competition would have no implications for policies. Essentially, candidates could adopt the equilibrium expressive position while simultaneously adopting the equilibrium instrumental position. Of course, in the simple case in which this involves co-location in the instrumental domain, all voters will, once again, be expressives, but this will not affect the outcome in the instrumental domain. In this case, policy choice will be explicable solely in instrumental terms, and although there will be much else going on in electoral politics, none of that extra activity will bear on the central question that has concerned traditional public choice theory – the question of policy determination.

---

[20] As noted above, equilibrium may not exist in the purely instrumental model with endogenous participation if the distribution is sufficiently asymmetric. The argument here is different, since it makes essential use of expressive voting, but the general flavour of the result is similar.

The middle ground

Both of these extreme cases are implausible. A major thrust of our discussion has been to emphasise the differences in the conception of the political domain as between the expressive and instrumental accounts, as well as the differences in the more detailed analysis of voting within those domains. But it is surely implausible to suggest that the expressive domain is completely unrelated to matters of policy. Both from the perspective of the citizen-voter and from the perspective of the political candidate, links and trade-offs between expressive and instrumental considerations must be taken as the normal case. We have done no more than sketch some of the ingredients required in a more general model of electoral competition that takes seriously both the expressive and the instrumental aspects of voting behaviour. But we hope that we have done enough to suggest that mixed models of this type offer an interesting and rich set of possibilities. In the more complex world of mixed models, we might imagine political equilibria in which some citizens' electoral behaviour is instrumental, while other citizens vote on expressive grounds; in which candidates attempt to adopt positions in policy space which may not wholly correspond to their expressive image; in which individual candidates may have an important expressive effect on the electoral success of their party even when they offer no distinctive policy position.[21] These, and other, eminently realistic possibilities are available to rational choice theorists who adopt an account of voting which incorporates an expressive element, while they are denied to rational choice theorists who maintain the strict instrumental line. We see this fact as providing a strong argument for the more detailed exploration of mixed models incorporating an expressive account of voting. It is surely not implausible to suggest that the tension within political parties between expressive and instrumental considerations, and the implications of these tensions for electoral competition are a significant element in, and conceivably the very core of, democratic political process.

---

[21] A recent paper by Harrington and Hess (1996) utilises a framework that we would see as related to that suggested here. They use a two-dimensional spatial model in which one dimension relates to the personal attributes of the candidate while the other relates to a policy variable. Voters are modelled instrumentally (and assumed to vote) but are given preferences such that they care about the candidates personal attributes. Each voter is therefore balancing what we might term an expressive consideration (personal attributes of the candidates) against an instrumental consideration.

Overview

We have argued that the standard analysis of instrumental voting with voluntary participation generates implications that jar with relatively standard political intuitions, and specifically with intuitions that are often invoked in connection with the simple median voter theorem. In particular, turnout is predicted to be zero in the equilibrium of a two-candidate election; and even when the policy packages of candidates diverge so that some citizens will vote, voters will tend to be drawn disproportionately from the political extremes. This is so because, under a thoroughgoing instrumentalism, it will be the most extreme citizens who have most reason to vote. Voting is evidence not of a sense of civic responsibility, but of electoral disequilibrium. Accordingly, the intuition that a reasonably high level of turnout is both reasonable and desirable is severely undermined.

However, this intuition does find a natural home in the expressive account of rational voting where citizens vote to identify themselves with particular positions and to register support for those positions rather than to bring certain policies about. We argue that equilibrium under an expressive account of voting generates predictions of positive turnout with those voting being those most closely associated with the positions adopted by candidates. Equilibrium tends to converge on a defined neighbourhood of the mode of the distribution of citizens' ideal points while simultaneously satisfying the requirement that it is at the ideal point of the median of those who actually vote. Although equilibrium may not be stable, the threat of *global* instability is removed: political platforms are restricted to a significantly constrained region of the relevant space.

Seen as rivals, the instrumental and expressive accounts of rational voting generate testably different predictions, fit with very different intuitions, and offer different perspectives on questions of institutional design. However, the two accounts do not have to be seen as natural antagonists: they can be seen rather as distinct aspects of a more complex whole. Although we have emphasised how and in what ways the aspects are distinct, we have also tried to suggest how they might be brought together.

9

Political representation

The effect of [representation] is, on the one hand, to refine and enlarge
the public views, by passing them through the medium of a chosen body
of citizens, whose wisdom may best discern the true interest of their
country, and whose patriotism and love of justice will be least likely to
sacrifice it to temporary or partial considerations. Under such a regulation, it may well happen that the public voice, pronounced by the
representatives of the people, will be more consonant to the public good
than if pronounced by the people themselves, convened for the purpose.
On the other hand, the effect may be inverted. Men of factious tempers, of
local prejudices, or of sinister designs, may, by intrigue, by corruption, or
by other means, first obtain the suffrages, and then betray the interests, of
the people.

(*Federalist* papers, 10, James Madison)

Representation and political agency

Ideas of representation in political theory are notoriously diffuse and
recalcitrant.[1] We shall not here be concerned with the full array of these
ideas. Our attention in this chapter will be focused on the issue of
political agency – on the simple fact of representation, rather than its
detailed form. The essential feature of representation, as we shall
understand it, is that a mediating assembly of some kind is set between
the citizenry and political decision making. Representative democracy, in
this structural sense, stands in contrast with direct democracy: citizens do

---

[1] For more wide ranging discussions, see Pitkin (1967), Birch (1972), Manin (1997).
For classic texts see Hobbes (1651/1968), Mill (1861/1946) and Burke (1975).

not make decisions on political outcomes directly – rather, political outcomes are decided by some group of 'representatives'. We shall be interested in exploring and justifying this kind of indirect decision making structure.

If this is a somewhat restricted approach to questions of representation, it is at least focused on what we think is a foundational concern. Within the principal–agent perspective that we have already identified as a key aspect of the rational actor conception of politics, the basic issue of democratic politics is seen to be the design of institutional arrangements so that political agents, with their own identifiable interests, can be induced to act in the interests of their principals, the citizenry at large. This view clearly presupposes that politics is representative in our structural sense. In principle, it would be possible to avoid the principal–agent problem altogether by the simple expedient of adopting direct procedures – that is, by removing the agents and the mediating assembly and allowing the citizens themselves to choose directly among policy options. In other words, viewing politics through the principal–agent lens simply *assumes* that political representation is an unavoidable fact of life. It seems important to understand why this is so, if indeed it is so, before designing institutional arrangements intended to solve the agency problems that political representation creates.

In the same way, occasional complaints about the non-representativeness of putatively 'representative' bodies presuppose a particular idea of 'representation' within which the further question of the 'representativeness' of a particular set of agents may be addressed. But it would seem that an understanding of the logic leading to the structure of agency must be an important ingredient in any satisfactory discussion of the detailed composition of the relevant assembly. The structural idea of representation is logically prior to any specific understanding of the 'representativeness' of any particular group of agents.

More generally, it is difficult to see how the various detailed issues associated with representative institutions can properly be broached without a clear notion of the work that representation as such is supposed to do, and of how representation is useful in doing that work. It is in this sense that the structural aspect of the idea of representation strikes us as being foundational.

Our object in this chapter is to develop an argument for representation in our sense of indirect decision making – an argument based on our interpretation of the rational actor approach to political theory. In fact, we will distinguish between two classes of arguments for representation, which we term second-best and first-best arguments for representation. Second-best arguments share the characteristic that they accept direct democracy as the relevant ideal but see direct decision making as somehow impractical and see indirect or representative democracy as a practicable means of achieving an approximation to the direct ideal. First-best arguments, by contrast, see direct democracy as imperfect in one way or another, and see indirect or representative institutions as a politically superior alternative. While second-best arguments have dominated in the rational actor approach to politics, we will discuss such second-best arguments mainly in order that they may stand in contrast to the first-best argument we advance. Our emphasis on a first-best argument for representation connects with two aspects of our particular account of democratic political process: the expressive element in voting behaviour; and the possibility of selection as an important aspect of institutional design.

The novelty of our argument lies in its re-interpretation of the rational actor model as it applies in political settings, and in the structure of the argument deployed; not in its conclusion, which might seem relatively familiar outside of the modern, rational choice framework. In particular, a first-best argument for representation was an important part of the political vision of many of those who are often seen as influential precursors of modern public choice theory. For example, Condorcet, Madison and Schumpeter all presented positive, first-best arguments in support of representative democracy relative to direct democracy, and each of these different arguments has something in common with our own.[2] In more contemporary debate, our argument contrasts with James Fishkin's discussion of democratic institutions.[3] Fishkin's argument for a 'deliberative opinion poll' or 'national caucus' addresses the issue of the relative merits of direct and representative democracy from a perspective of deliberative democracy in which individuals are assumed to be motivated to seek the public interest if only the institutional arrangements offer them an opportunity to participate meaningfully. In our terminology, his argument might be construed as a second-best argument for a form of representation – as a means of approximating the ideal of direct deliberative democracy in the face of costs of mass deliberation. We would suggest that by grounding our analysis in the rational choice tradition and by building on the analysis of expressive voting, we can go beyond Fishkin's account of essentially statistical representation to provide a more positive account of Madison's claim that an effect of

[2] For discussion of Condorcet's argument, and relevant translations, see McLean and Hewitt (1994), Baker (1975). Madison's argument is laid out in *The Federalist* (particularly paper no. 10) and discussed in Elkin (1996). Schumpeter's argument is presented in chapter 22 of Schumpeter (1950).

[3] Fishkin (1991).

political representation is 'to refine and enlarge the public views, by
passing them through the medium of a chosen body of citizens, whose
wisdom may best discern the true interest of their country'.[4]

Our argument proceeds in several steps. First, we provide an account
of the second-best theories of representation that derive from the more
traditional rational actor perspective. We then proceed to offer a sketch
of a first-best theory of representation based on a critique of direct
democracy. This sketch is further developed in the ensuing two sections
which build from the familiar idea of rational ignorance to the idea of
expressive behaviour.

Second-best theories of representation

As already indicated, 'second-best theories of representation' in our
classification are those that hold direct democracy to be the conceptual
ideal, but see direct democracy as somehow infeasible or too costly: the
basic idea of representation on these accounts is that it achieves a
reasonable approximation to the outcome that direct democracy would
produce but does so at lower cost. The relevant trade offs here can be
depicted by appeal to a diagram redolent of a familiar construction used
for a different purpose in *The Calculus of Consent*. Along the horizontal
axis, we depict the degree of representation. A variety of measures of the
degree of representation or indirectness are possible. The measure we
shall use is the simplest available: the complement of the proportion of
the total citizenry that acts in the decision-making assembly – a 0 degree
of representation corresponding to the case of direct democracy, and a
degree of representation approaching 1 corresponding to the opposite
extreme of a single decision maker. The vertical axis represents (total)
costs, which consist of two elements – first, agency costs, which reflect the
expected loss involved in the departure from direct democracy including
the costs associated with establishing and maintaining the relevant
assembly, and second, the decision-making costs arising within assemblies
of different size. By definition, agency costs are zero in the case of direct
democracy and would be expected to rise as the degree of representation
or agency rises (the size of the assembly falls). Of course, a much more
detailed account would be necessary to give the agency-cost curve any
particular shape, but this is a matter of detail and can be put to one side.
The decision-making costs reflect the costs of operating any particular
decision-making procedure within the relevant assembly and can be
presumed to rise from a minimum in the case of a single decision maker

[4] Madison, *Federalist* paper 10.

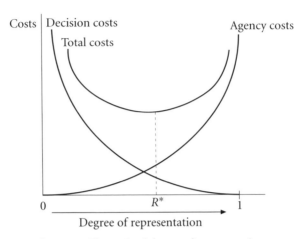

Figure 9.1 The optimal degree of representation

to a maximum where all citizens are enrolled in the business of collective decision making. On this basis, the general shapes of the two underlying cost curves are given in figure 9.1. The total cost curve is the vertical sum of agency costs and decision-making costs and has its minimum at $R^\star$ – which specifies the optimal degree of representation.

This model can be cashed out in a number of ways depending on the details of the way in which the assembly is conceived and according to the nature of the agency and decision costs involved. To be more specific, we will briefly consider four cases which, taken together, offer a variety of possible second-best arguments for representation: a statistical sampling model; a transactions cost model; a competitive agenda–setter model; and a monitoring/enforcement model.

A statistical sampling model

Statistical sampling models exploit the familiar idea that the differences between the properties of a sample and those of the underlying population are insignificant provided that the sample is 'representative' and sufficiently large. Consequently, if taking a complete census of all views is costly, then using an appropriate sample will be efficient.

Consider a particular case. A community with an adult population of, say, one million is to decide on the level of expenditure on some given public good, to be financed according to some fixed cost-sharing arrangement. Assume further that everyone will vote and vote instrumentally. There is, in other words, sufficient structure imposed on the decision to render the standard median voter theorem relevant. There seems to be no reason to believe that voting will operate differently within a representative assembly from the way in which it will operate in the full polity, unless the assembly is small enough to permit log-rolling of a kind that would be ruled out in the total population. We will consider the log-rolling case below. At this point, however, we assume that vote trading is impossible. Each person will vote her individual preference in the same way whether voting as a citizen under direct democracy or as a representative under representative democracy.

There is no real principal–agent problem in play in this model. Representatives here are not conceived as acting in accord with the wishes of principals, but rather as acting totally in their own self-interest, without any consideration for the interests of other citizens as such. It is the statistical representativeness of the sample that is doing the work, and not any attempt to encourage representatives to act as dutiful agents. Statistical representativeness dissolves the principal–agent problem.

In this setting, the electoral outcome in the representative assembly – by assumption, the median of the assembly members – will be expected to differ from the electoral outcome under direct democracy – the median of the population – by an amount that will be smaller the larger is the assembly and the more statistically representative is the sample. On purely statistical grounds, the assembly need not be particularly large. The expected deviation of the assembly median from the total population median will be small with a 0.1 per cent sample and negligible with a 1 per cent sample – provided of course that the sample is statistically representative. Whether appropriate representativeness is best secured by purely random sampling or by some other form of stratified sampling is an issue that we will set aside here (though within the statistical conception of representation it is clearly a major issue).

This statistical sampling model may be interpreted as a claim about the shape of the agency cost curve in figure 9.1. The essential point is that the marginal agency cost of an increased degree of representation will be very small over a range which extends from very low degrees of representation up to degrees of representation close to 1. The agency cost curve will be essentially horizontal over this range,[5] so that the optimal degree of representation will be close to 1.

A critical point to emphasise here is that there is no case for elections in securing the desired representativeness. Voting will play a crucial role *within* the assembly, presumably, in securing the median outcome – but it is voting *within* the assembly, not voting *for* assembly members, that is

[5] There may be some fixed cost associated with any departure from direct democracy, and the level of the curve will reflect such fixed costs.

crucial. Indeed, it is critical that representatives not be elected, at least on every occasion, if the statistical case for representation is to be coherent. The gains from representation here take the form of the decision-making costs of voting avoided. And if representation is indeed to economise on these costs, it must be the case either that:

1. representatives once selected make decisions on more than one issue; or
2. representatives are selected in some other (cheaper) way than voting; or
3. voting on representatives must somehow be less informationally demanding or otherwise less costly than voting on issues.

For clearly, if representatives are elected for each issue separately, then representation *increases* the total amount of voting: each citizen votes to select the assembly representatives and then the representatives vote to select the policy outcome. So unless not all voting is equally costly (point 3, above) then either representatives must be selected by means other than voting or they must sit over an extended sequence of decisions or both. And since both strategies seem to be mechanisms for reducing decision-making costs, both would seem to be appropriate. In particular, even if universal voting on representatives turned out to generate an appropriately random sample of the population, voting would seem to be a remarkably profligate way of securing such a sample.

It is also worth emphasising that the logic of the argument for representation here is antipathetic to the spirit of the general argument in favour of popular participation. The argument is based on the desirability of minimising participation costs. It is predicated on the idea that political participation (at least at the level of conscientiousness appropriate to the nature of the decision to be made) is a costly business and that increased political participation can be justified only to the extent that it changes (improves) political outcomes.[6] There is a contrary tradition in some political theory to the effect that a more engaged and politically active citizenry is an end desirable in itself. Public choice theorists are inclined to think that this tradition is inappropriately attentive to the opportunity cost of serious political engagement.[7] Those who believe, for example, that higher electoral turnout is intrinsically a good thing – that is, a good thing even if there are no implications for electoral outcomes or if effects on outcomes are undesirable – will naturally be unimpressed with the argument for representation advanced here. But, of course, the premise that higher electoral turnout is an

---

[6] This is essentially an alternative version of the point made in chapter 8 that, on the instrumental account, low turnout is desirable since it economises on costly voting.

[7] See Brennan and Lomasky (1997).

intrinsic good is not one that can be endorsed within the traditional model of the instrumentally rational political actor.

It may also be complained that the statistical sampling model outlined here, by assuming the conditions under which the median voter theorem applies, sweeps away too much about which public choice theorists have traditionally been anxious – and specifically, problems of global cycling. However, this charge is to miss the point. Whatever difficulties of this kind arise in the representative assembly are no less likely to arise in the larger polity, and vice versa. Unless problems associated with a method of decision making can be shown to be related to the size of the group of decision makers (over the range relevant for the discussion here) then they are irrelevant to the main point. In other words, the median voter theorem is an essentially irrelevant feature of the model of representation sketched here. Whatever decision-making process is employed, it would still pay to choose a degree of representation that secures those decisions at lowest possible cost, and that will almost always imply at least some degree of representation. The basic structure of the statistical sampling model involves holding everything constant except the size of the assembly: the gains from agency are the reduction in decision-making costs associated with a reduced number of decision makers, while the losses relate to the direct costs of operating an assembly and the departure from the direct democracy outcome, however good or bad that outcome might be. The next two subsections consider the decision-making costs aspect of the model more explicitly.

The transactions cost model

In the statistical sampling model, the benefits from agency take the form of reduced costs of voting by citizens. As we have seen, a key assumption is that the decision-making procedures involved are essentially independent of the number of decision makers. This assumption is one that the transactions-cost model, as we denote it here, specifically seeks to relax. The central point can be captured by reference to the case of a jury. It is a trivial observation that the size of the jury affects the feasibility of more demanding decision rules: it is one thing to require unanimity among a body of 12, another entirely to require unanimity among a body of 100 or 1,000. As the degree of representation rises, more restrictive decision rules become feasible. This observation connects the issue of representation with the classic concerns of Buchanan and Tullock (1962), and their original use of a diagram similar to our figure 9.1. In Buchanan and Tullock's analysis the choice is over the restrictiveness of the decision-making rule, and the trade off is between larger decision-making costs and larger 'external costs' as coalitions foist on others the costs of special interest legislation. Presumably, however, the decision-making costs are a function of the number of persons required to be party to the decision, and accordingly fall as the degree of representation increases. This observation suggests an additional dimension to the Buchanan–Tullock analysis: agency costs can substitute for decision-making costs over the entire range of decision rules.

To focus specifically on this issue let us suppose that the decision-rule is settled at, say, 90 per cent of the decision-making agents. It seems clear that any process of discovering policy packages options that meet this extremely stringent test of support will involve a considerable amount of negotiating, trading, log-rolling and the like. The transactions (or decision-making) cost of such a process will be high – but more particularly it will be higher the greater is the size of the assembly. This fact represents an argument for a smaller assembly – for a greater degree of representation, other things including specifically the decision rule being equal. These points may be illustrated in figure 9.2, which repeats the basic structure of figure 9.1. Let D_1 depict the decision-making costs associated with a simple majority voting rule, and D_2 depict the decision-making costs associated with the more restrictive 90 per cent rule. D_2 lies above D_1 by an amount that varies with the degree of representation, the additional cost being particularly large in larger assemblies. Clearly, the optimal degree of representation conditional on the use of the more restrictive voting rule will be greater (the optimal assembly smaller) than would be the case if the less restrictive voting rule were in use.

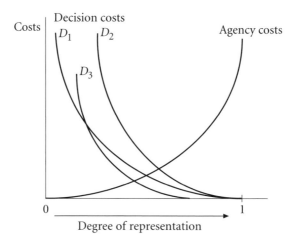

Figure 9.2 Representation and decision rules

It is equally clear that the total costs are higher in the case of the more restrictive rule, and this may appear to support the idea that societies should always select the less inclusive rule (and the lower degree of representation); but this would be to ignore Buchanan and Tullock's 'external costs'. These external cost could be modelled in our figure 9.2 as shifting D_2 down relative to D_1 – to D_3, say, since the more restrictive rule involves lower external costs. In the case illustrated (with D_2 and D_3 differing by a simple vertical shift) the optimal degree of representation under the more restrictive rule will be unaffected, but the total costs associated with the more restrictive rule are reduced, so that it may be optimal to choose the more restrictive/more representative structure summarised by D_3 over the less restrictive/less representative structure summarised by D_1. More generally, the point is that the optimal decision-making rule and the optimal degree of representation are simultaneously determined by the interaction of agency costs, decision-making costs and external costs.

Further complications might be expected. As transaction costs within the assembly are reduced, so presumably are transactions costs between assembly members and other interested groups – lobby groups, special interest groups and the like. If representatives are randomly selected for assembly duty, many of the traditional ways in which lobby groups can influence assembly members – by campaign contributions, public endorsement, assistance in electioneering, etc. – would not apply. Influence would have to be secured by direct bribery, and we can imagine further institutions in place to restrict such bribery. Nevertheless, it may be a cost of increased representation that scope for external influence of assembly members is increased. What such external influence does is to imperil the statistical representativeness of the assembly. The transactions-cost argument, then, alerts us to the possibility that effective representativeness in the statistical sense may decline as simple representation increases (assembly size decreases). Again, there are several trade-offs in play here. But the central point is that, at least over a considerable range, greater representativeness (i.e. smaller assemblies) makes more inclusive decision rules increasingly feasible. And for those in the tradition of Buchanan and Tullock (1962) (and earlier, Wicksell), who see external costs as an essential problem of simple majority rule, this aspect of representation must have considerable appeal.

The competitive agenda setter model

The transactions-cost model provides a rather thin view of the political decision-making process, and so it is worthwhile to pursue the ideas sketched above in a rather more concrete setting. The familiar account of spatial equilibrium in the one dimensional case, offers a plausible and explicit process to consider. In the standard version of this model, the purpose is to show how in idealised circumstances rival candidates for political office will be led to co-locate at the median voter's ideal point. This is a model that takes representation as a fact and attempts to show how electoral competition may work in that context. But suppose we interpret the model in a rather different way as giving an account of how representation might solve a problem of equilibration that might otherwise dog non-representative processes. If we imagine a process of direct democracy, there has to be a question of how issues come before the citizenry. Who determines what options are before the citizens to vote on? And how quickly might we expect the polity to settle on some suitable equilibrium outcome? The institutional structure embodied in the median voter model answers both those questions. Rather than a process of iteration over randomly emerging options, the electoral race between two candidates serves to establish equilibration to the median outcome relatively quickly. It does so by giving the candidates an incentive to put up as a policy package their best estimate of the median voter's ideal and rewards the candidate who is most successful in doing so. That reward takes the form of holding office and receiving the attendant 'rents'. So there is put in place an incentive structure that encourages candidates to attempt to read the 'public mind'; and a selection device that tends to select those with the best capacity to manage this delicate task. By establishing an institutional regime in which there are two rival agenda setters (candidates for a presidential office, say) offering specific proposals for collective action, and in which there are rewards to each agenda setter from having her agenda chosen, an equilibration mechanism is created that seems well suited to achieving the median voter outcome quite quickly. Whatever the details of the competitive agenda setter model, and however effective such a regime might be in operationalising the median outcome, or any other normatively relevant outcome, the question we wish to ask concerns the relationship between this general account of the process of decision making and the idea of representation.

Conceived as a model of political representation, the competitive agenda setter model is fairly minimalist. In the pure case, there is no representation as such. There is, in particular, no real attempt to place some mediating institution with a decision-making role between electoral options and citizens' preferences over those options: the role that the competitive agenda setter arrangement plays is simply to accelerate the process of equilibration within an essentially direct system. Voters vote on policy packages, and rewards flow to the candidate who offers the policy package that is actually chosen – chosen, in the standard case, by direct democracy. To underline this point, it would be no less possible to see the competitive agenda setter arrangement operating in association with an assembly of the statistically representative kind. In this case, the competitive agenda setter would offer proposals not to the citizenry at large, but rather to the representative assembly – and it would be the electoral process within the assembly that would be equilibrated via the agenda setter process. The successful agenda setter (president) and the associated policy package would then be selected by the assembly, not by the people as a whole.

Of course, in impure cases, there may be some degree of 'representation'. Where the chosen president retains some discretion, she may be thought of as the limiting case of a representative assembly – an assembly of one person. But this will not be seen as a desirable feature of the agenda setter model; on the contrary, it is precisely the possibility of discretionary action by chosen agenda setters that gives rise to the standard principal–agent problem. The fundamental idea of the agenda setter model is to use the process of competition to restrict or, if possible, abolish agency or representation. To the extent that this object is not fully realised, the agency or representation that remains is a problem.

This view of the trade off between decision-making costs and agency costs can again be illustrated in terms of our standard diagram – figure 9.3. Recall that agency costs relate to the expected costs of relying on an assembly of any particular size relative to the case of direct democracy.

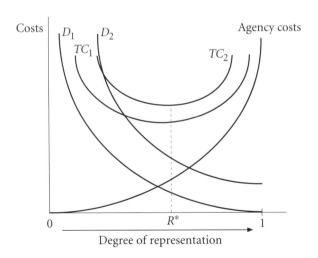

Figure 9.3   Representation and agenda setting

The decision-making cost curve D_1 may in this case be taken to indicate the decision-making costs associated with a pure agenda-setting process which fully constrains the agenda setter. If this technology were available the resulting optimal degree of representation would be R^*, as before. Now consider an impure agenda-setting process, which gives rise to a principal–agent problem by allowing the winning president some residual presidential discretion. Such a technology might be depicted by a curve such as D_2, which lies everywhere above D_1 to reflect the additional cost of presidential discretion. Clearly, relative to the situation in which the pure process was available, the optimal degree of representation will be increased, decreased or remain constant depending on the precise nature of the cost shift from D_1 to D_2. We have illustrated the case in which the size of the additional cost is independent of the size of the assembly, and this is obviously the case in which the optimal degree of representation is unaffected. In this way the competitive agenda setter model is shown to be formally very similar to the transactions-cost model.

This simple story again focuses attention on our separation of decision-making process from the degree of representation. Only if the shift from one decision-making process to another carries costs which vary with the degree of representation will there be an interaction between the choice of decision-making process and the optimal degree of representation.

The monitor/enforcer model

Whatever collective decision is made, and whatever process is used to make it, there remains the further issue of implementation. Who is to act as the collective's 'representative' in ensuring that the policies that have been decided on are put in place conscientiously? Suppose, for example, that a society decides by due process to build a dam (under specified cost-sharing arrangements). There is now the further question of implementing this decision by putting the contract out to tender, negotiating with prospective contractors, monitoring the performance of the contractor and so on. In short, there is a further principal–agent relationship involved at the implementation stage. And however the collective decision was made – whether under direct or representative democracy, whether with the aid of competitive agenda setters or not – there is the further possibility that the collective may have good reason to appoint a 'representative' to act on its behalf in implementing the decision. This role of 'implementation agent' is clearly distinct from the role of 'decision-making representative', as we have discussed it. And this distinction seems to capture a central part of the classic distinction between the legislature and the executive. One immediate question is then whether or not it is desirable to combine the roles of decision-making representatives and implementation agents in the same person – that is, whether to separate or combine the powers of the legislature and the powers of the executive. This is a question we will pursue in later chapters and we leave it on one side here.

What are the arguments for appointing an implementation agent? The essential point seems to be the public good nature of the work to be done, and the consequent lack of incentives for individuals to contribute to the task of monitoring and enforcement. But this is not a line of argument that sits well with the general approach of second-best theories of representation. For once we accept that considerations of this type apply, it is a short step to argue that they apply equally at the level of decision making, and that the public good nature of political decision making undermines individual incentives and so renders direct democracy problematic. This is the stuff of first-best theories of representation, to which we now turn.

A first-best theory of representation: an intuitive account

A first-best theory of representation, as we define it here, involves two propositions: first, that direct democracy is identified as a fundamentally flawed mechanism for producing political outcomes in the public interest; and second, that representative or indirect democracy offers the prospect of improved political performance. It is useful to begin our discussion with a simple intuitive claim about direct democracy, and then to seek to interrogate that claim from a rational actor perspective.

One reason for concern about direct democracy is that it seems to offer a kind of 'lowest common denominator' view of politics – that it does not yield the prospect of the best government of which a society is capable. Clearly, the typical voter cannot bring to policy issues the attention that a minister or president would bring to them as a matter of course. And it is no response to this concern to point out that the attention of all citizens, when added up, exceeds that of the specialist, because 'attention' just does not aggregate in this way. The line of thought would suggest that, rather than relying on direct democracy to aggregate political preference, we would do better to appoint an 'average' individual (or, more plausibly, a statistically representative group of individuals) as our full-time political agent and allow her the opportunity and resources required to decide what would be the best policy in some particular area: we would clearly do better to take the fully considered view of a group of average citizens, rather than the average of the less than fully considered views of all citizens. This seems to be the central point of Fishkin's deliberative polling proposal mentioned earlier. But, equally clearly, we could do even better. We could select, if not the ablest and the most conscientious and public spirited, at least those who are more able and more conscientious and more public spirited than average. And all of this will ensure that a tolerably well-designed representative democracy may outperform even an idealised direct democracy – where 'tolerably well-designed' incorporates the need to provide institutional structures to ensure both that the selected representatives have the right character and that they do not exploit their positions excessively.

The orthodox rational actor theoretic response to this intuitive claim would be in three parts. First, it would insist that the final proviso about the exploitation of power is crucial, and that the institutional structure required to guard against such exploitation is by far the most important aspect of the design of political institutions. Perhaps all that is at stake here is a difference of emphasis. The rational choice critic is not denying anything in the intuitive account, but merely arguing that the opportunities for exploitation under a representative system may be large relative to the opportunities for improved performance, so that the primary focus of attention should be on resolving the principal–agent problem. However, unless we can isolate major benefits associated with representation, such a rational choice theorist would seem to be committed to direct democracy.

The second aspect of the response is to argue that the intuitive account mistakes the nature of the expertise involved in political representation. On the intuitive account, the political expertise required of the representative lies first in the capacity to discern the public interest, and second in coming to understand the consequences of alternative policies in terms of their contribution to that public interest. But the intuitive view supposes that there is a relatively clearly identifiable concept of the public interest, so that the first element of political expertise is de-emphasised relative to the second. On this view, then, the most important aspect of political expertise is the ability to analyse policy options. The rational actor critique, by contrast, would argue that it is the identification of the public interest that is both the more important and the essentially political aspect of the problem. The delicate trade offs and compromises between opposing interests and values are what political process is all about. The public interest, on this view, is revealed only through the political process itself, and the criteria against which the design of political institutions should be judged should include the ability of institutions to process information on political preferences. Compared with this fundamental task of identifying some approximate idea of the *content* of the public interest, the task of analysing the consequences of different policies is really a technical matter – politically essential but not essentially political.

The third aspect of the critique argues that the genuinely political issue concerning representation relates to incentives, not capacities. That is, it is not important for politicians to have relevant expertise: the relevant expertise can be bought from consultants who specialise in such matters. Economic consultants, for example, can forecast the consequences of this or that interest rate policy for employment/inflation/growth, etc. To be sure, there will be a principal–agent problem inherent in the purchase of such expert advice, but this problem is no different in kind from that involved in hiring a contractor to construct a dam, and no one would suggest that expertise in dam building is an important prerequisite for political office. Issues may arise as to whether it is desirable to privilege particular sources of advice (say, from within the bureaucracy) over others (say, from academics or private consultancies), and/or whether institutional regimes should encourage the competitive use of alternative sources of advice; but none of this is really central to the issue of political representation. What is important, on the rational actor account, is that politicians face incentives to obtain appropriate advice, and to act appropriately on that advice. And this is the focus of the principal–agent conception of the political problem.

To summarise, then, the rational actor critique of the intuitive argument for representation comes down to three basic propositions: first, that the incentive problem is crucial; second, that the public interest has no independent existence from the expression of voter preferences within an appropriate set of institutional structures; and third, that expertise of a technical kind about the consequences of policies is not essential in a politician – the use of expert advice raises a principal–agent problem, but not the *political* principal–agent problem.

To state our own position here, we believe that the first and third propositions of the rational actor critique are broadly correct, but that the second proposition is wrong. And, more to the point, we believe that the mistake involved in this second proposition creates the space for a first-best theory of representation. To see how, consider the following simple example. Citizens are, we assume, largely ignorant of what policies are required to promote their interests and, indeed, not entirely sure *ex ante* what exactly their interests consist in. One possible response to such radical uncertainty under a system of representative democracy is to vote for the incumbent if you feel better off now than you did at the time of the last election, and vote for the opposition otherwise. Such a situation makes possible an activity we might term political entrepreneurship. That is, agents with a distinctive capacity to discern what would make voters feel better off, can enter the political arena as candidates. And where their vision actually gives rise to outcomes that citizens do indeed value, these candidates will be successful – and successful precisely because they are able to imagine citizens' interests in this way. Just as a market entrepreneur imagines products that she believes consumers would buy if only they were available, so the political entrepreneur imagines policies that voters will applaud if (and only if) they are introduced ('truths you love, but know not' as Thomas Traherne puts it). The political entrepreneur might be viewed as simply speeding the process of politics – helping the process to reach an outcome that would be reached more slowly in the entrepreneur's absence (under direct democracy, say) – but we believe that the role of the political entrepreneur is more substantive than this. The political entrepreneur is essentially proactive, identifying and promoting policies that she believes will be appreciated *ex post* rather than preferred *ex ante*. The political entrepreneur influences the nature of the political outcome and not just the efficiency with which it is reached. The institution of representation establishes a place in the division of labour for the political entrepreneur. Under direct democracy it is impossible to create such a role: representation is a necessary condition for political entrepreneurship.

Of course, this simple example does no more than identify a possibility. Many questions and doubts arise immediately. Are the assumptions of citizen ignorance and uncertainty reasonable? What is the rational voting rule for such a citizen? Under what circumstances might we expect the presence of political entrepreneurs to operate in a normatively desirable manner? In the ensuing sections we explore some of these issues in more detail. We begin with the well established idea of the rational ignorance of citizen-voters.

Rational ignorance

As public choice theorists since Downs[8] have recognised, we have good reason for doubting that citizens will have a very clear idea of what policies are available, which of these policies best promote their interests, or precisely what their preferences for particular public goods might be – and this even where relevant information is available at modest cost. Citizens are rationally ignorant.[9] A simple story makes the point. When *A*

[8] Downs (1957).

[9] Empirical evidence on this point is plentiful and generally supports the claim that voters are ignorant. Some of this evidence is reviewed in Fishkin (1991) though, since Fishkin does not work within the rational actor paradigm, he does not discuss *rational* ignorance specifically. For further discussion of the evidence Brennan and Lomasky (1993), chapter 7.

considers buying a video recorder, she is inclined to read consumer reports and ask her friends in order to find out which brand and model best suits her needs; and she will shop around to find the best price. She is, after all, planning to lay out a fair amount of money and she wants to be reasonably sure that she is getting a good deal. Yet this same person will almost certainly pay much more than the price of a video recorder each year in taxes without any clear idea of how that money is spent. She will know, in a general way, the sorts of things that the government does – defence, law and order, health and so on – and she may hold general views to the effect that too much (or too little) is spent on this or that service; but she is unlikely to be able to say, within an order of magnitude, the amount of public money actually devoted to each service. Nor would it be rational for her to acquire such information. Unlike the case of the video recorder, she is not in a position to choose tax rates or levels of expenditure on the various public services. At most (under direct democracy) she merely votes on such things. More probably, she merely votes for a representative who in turn votes on such things. The return to gathering information in such a setting is very low. It is not that she will make a careful calculation of the optimal amount and type of information to acquire; it is rather that she is unlikely to spend much time thinking about issues that do not present themselves as real, active choices. We will have more to say about this line of reasoning in the next section, but the basic point should be clear enough.

Proponents of direct democracy might argue that the reason why citizens have an inadequate incentive to be informed is that the real decisions are taken by remote politicians, and that a move to direct democracy would help to restore incentives to acquire information and participate actively in the political process. The Downsian argument (rightly, in our view) reverses that argument. Representation is required precisely *because* citizens have inadequate incentives to be informed. Thus interpreted, the Downsian argument is the starting point for a first-best theory of representation. But the argument, interpreted as an argument for representation, is seriously incomplete. Downs's original formulation, and the standard public choice reading of it, is directed at a comparison between collective and individual decision making, between politics and the market. The question in the context of an argument for political representation is why we should think that representative democracy will fare any better than direct democracy in the face of rationally ignorant citizens. More specifically, if citizens are not sufficiently well informed to choose among policies, how can they choose representatives or monitor the choices made by their representatives?

There are three possible responses to this question. The first is to reiterate the characteristic features of the intuitive argument sketched above: if citizens can tell *ex post* whether things are going well or not, that may be sufficient to encourage rival candidates to undertake actions that are more likely to make things go well *ceteris paribus*. Of course, *ceteris* may not be *paribus*: the candidates/parties will have some stake in the gains available, and are likely to appropriate some rents. Electoral competition in the face of rational ignorance will not necessarily drive candidate/party surpluses to zero. Moreover, whether things go well for citizens depends on many things apart from the choices of politicians. Politicians may just be lucky (or unlucky). More to the point, as is standard in the economic analysis of regulation, if much depends on luck, the incentive for politicians to choose policies with high expected returns to citizens will be blunted. Nevertheless, and despite all of these caveats, the basic idea of *ex post* voting provides at least a partial answer to our question.

A second part of the answer derives from the simple idea that the incentive to become informed is a function of the probability of being decisive. A representative assembly will provide more informed and more effective monitoring than the citizenry at large. This idea may seem odd. If the assembly is monitoring the decision makers, then who are the decision makers? And if the assembly constitutes the decision makers, who are the monitors? But this oddity can be resolved in a number of ways. One possibility is that a representative assembly elects a government – so that there is two-stage agency, with the assembly acting as both electors and monitors on behalf of the wider citizenry, and those individuals competing for government office acting as political entrepreneurs.[10] Another possibility is that the assembly itself takes on both roles within a more structured setting: if parties compete for seats in the assembly with the party winning the most seats forming the government, and other parties forming the opposition, we might have good reason to expect the opposition members of the assembly to have good incentives to monitor and provide information on the performance of the government – a system more reminiscent of the Westminster tradition of parliamentary government. Whatever the details, it is at least possible to imagine a representative assembly acting to monitor a representative government, whether that government is located within the assembly or as a separate entity.

Third, and quite distinct from anything said so far, there may be an

[10] Such a system is somewhat reminiscent of the ideas underlying the electoral college system for electing presidential candidates in the USA.

argument for representation even if the representatives do appropriate the rents. In the extreme case, this argument would point out that even if representative institutions did nothing to improve political outcomes, it is better that someone should appropriate the rents than that no one does. If direct democracy with rationally ignorant citizens produces inefficient outcomes, and representative democracy leaves citizens at large no better and no worse off, but gives significant benefits to the chosen politicians, then representative democracy is presumably to be preferred. Indeed, if the relevant normative criterion is broadly utilitarian, we might even approve of representative institutions which made citizens worse off, provided that these losses were more than compensated by the gains to the representatives. This argument, in this extreme form, is unlikely to be viewed favourably by democrats – but it is consistent with the normative principles that economists are disposed to use elsewhere and points to an important lesson: attention should be focused not on the rents appropriated by political agents, but on the effects of representation on the well-being of citizens. Exploitation is a danger to the extent that it threatens to reduce the well-being of citizens relative to some feasible alternative, and not simply because it grants a few political agents access to rents.

Taken together, these three considerations suggest to us that the idea of rational ignorance establishes a basis for a positive, first-best argument for representation. But it is still a rather insubstantial argument. We need more.

Expressive voting

As we have made clear in earlier chapters, it is our view that the Downsian rational ignorance argument does not go anything like far enough in exposing the problem that non-decisiveness poses for rational voting behaviour. The picture offered by Downs is one in which individuals will vote according to their perceived self-interest, but their *perception* of their self-interest will be systematically under-informed and faulty. However, we believe that the Downsian logic actually reinforces the view that citizens will have virtually no reason to vote their self-interest at all – that voting will be expressive in nature.

As we have seen, the picture of political process that springs from the idea of expressive voting is very different from that associated with more orthodox rational actor models. We do not wish to engage with the large literature concerned with the empirical investigation of the question of why voters vote in the way that they do or, indeed, why they vote at all – beyond noting that this literature seems to us to throw considerable doubt on any purely instrumental account of voting.[11] Rather, we shall attend specifically to the implications of expressive voting for representation. There are two relevant lines of argument, the first relating to the informational content of the vote and the standing of direct democracy, the second bearing more directly on the possibility for selection opened up by representation. We will consider each in turn.

Expressive voting raises considerable doubts about the ability of direct democracy to realise outcomes that are in the interests of the citizens. It is implausible to suggest that voting directly on policies will operate as an invisible hand mechanism under expressive voting. The inputs are simply of the wrong kind. Individual votes do not reflect the interests of the voters – even in the rough and ready way that might be true in the rational ignorance formulation. Accordingly, the informational content of individual votes does not allow of the standard interpretation of the aggregating effects of voting: we can place no clear normative interpretation on the outcome of such a system. However, if expressive voting cannot operate as an *in*visible hand it could, at least in principle, operate as a *visible* hand. That is, voters might systematically vote their views of the public interest. The direct democratic mechanism could then be interpreted as responding to the range of views of the public interest rather than constructing a sense of the public interest out of information on private interests. We consider this possibility a thin reed. Expressive voting seems at least as likely to pick out particular enthusiasms and prejudices as the key to individual voting. And the aggregation of such votes will yield no reliable information about either private or public interests. Indeed, the obvious concern is that expressive voting on policies will prove reckless and irresponsible. Some enthusiasm – a minor war in some distant country, for example – might seize the popular imagination. We might do very much better if someone had the incentive to calculate more carefully the consequences of such a policy and take responsibility for policy choice.

In this way, expressive voting undermines the normative credibility of direct democracy in a manner much more radical than that threatened by the more standard idea of rational ignorance. Rational ignorance might be conceived as adding statistical noise to an otherwise essentially deterministic system. In this interpretation, although the vote is not a perfect reflection of voter interests, it is at least still correlated with interests; and this correlation might be sufficient to ground the normative status of direct democracy. The expressive voting idea, when applied to

---

[11] See Brennan and Lomasky (1993), chapter 7, and Mueller (1989), chapter 18, for overviews of this literature.

direct democracy, removes the prospect of any reliable, consistent relation between voting behaviour and either private or public interest.

As well as strengthening the critique of direct democracy, the idea of expressive voting adds an extra dimension to the *positive* argument for representation, relating specifically to the selection of representatives. The basic idea is simply that the process of electing representatives may systematically select for certain more desirable types of representatives, so that the representative assembly will outperform any merely statistically representative sample of the population. This possibility is one that is familiar in much political writing, but it has been hitherto unavailable to the rational actor tradition because of that tradition's assumptions both about the motivation of individuals, and about the nature of the decision to vote. The argument proceeds via three propositions.

> *Proposition 1.* Individuals are morally heterogeneous. They differ, *inter alia*, in their capacity to discern the public interest and their inclination to pursue it – in short, in terms of their civic virtue.
>
> *Proposition 2.* The extent to which persons are virtuous is detectable by others, but imperfectly – motivational dispositions are 'translucent' in this sense.
>
> *Proposition 3.* Voters have a systematic tendency to express support for candidates who are perceived as having more rather than less civic virtue.

Propositions 1 and 2 have been defended at some length in earlier chapters, and so we focus our attention here on proposition 3. Clearly, we cannot simply assume that citizens will themselves be motivated by the public interest in choosing their representatives, because if citizens *were* so motivated in their electoral behaviour then direct democracy would be significantly rehabilitated, and our argument for representation would be correspondingly weakened. Equally, we cannot assume that voters will vote for virtuous candidates on any instrumental basis, since that too would undermine our own argument. What we need to show is that expressive voting is likely to lead to 'voting for virtue' given our characterisation of voter motivation.

The expressive voting story we advocate offers an alternative account of voting. This account begins from the observation that rationality requires attention to be focused on the intrinsic benefits of voting, and argues that those intrinsic benefits are likely to be expressive in nature. That is, votes are like 'speech acts' in which the content relates to the available political options, but which are irrelevant to any causal chain which brings about one or other of the options. Those aspects of the political options that are relevant to voting are, on this reading, the aspects that would 'occasion comment'.

Now consider representative as opposed to direct democracy. To restate the obvious, representation substitutes persons for policy options as the proximate objects of electoral attention and comment. Whereas direct democracy calls for voters to comment on policy options, representative democracy calls for voters to comment on potential representatives. It is important to stress this simple point precisely because so much of rational actor political theory serves to suppress it, by rendering candidates or political parties as mere ciphers for their policy platforms. And, of course, one can understand this tendency given the underlying (and we believe mistaken) conception of what rationality requires of voters. But in the expressive account of rational voting, the precise nature of the particular options presented to citizens for electoral comment will make a difference. Of course, individual candidates, political parties and policy platforms will not be totally disconnected in voters' minds; but nor are these categories identical.

For example, within the expressive account, the *ad hominem* aspect of politics makes perfect sense: it would be perfectly rational (in the strict sense) to vote on the basis of a candidate's appearance or speaking voice if those are the characteristics the voter identifies with. But most voters, we believe, do not see good looks or speaking voice as central: in making electoral comment, voters are more likely to consider the candidate's character and competencies – at least in so far as these can be discerned. Perceived characteristics and competencies combine to establish a candidate's political attractiveness. Other things equal, candidates who plagiarise their speeches, or break the law, or are involved in sexual scandals, signal aspects of their character that might be expected to reduce the probability of their getting elected, whatever their policy platform, and likewise for candidates who fail to impress with their professionalism. Perceived competence is no less important than perceived character in determining political attractiveness.[12]

We focus on the idea of the personal candidate – whether that candidate be seen as a potential president, a potential party leader, or a potential assembly member – and the idea of political attractiveness. It

---

[12] The precise set of characteristics and competencies perceived as relevant, and the trade offs between elements of this set may be expected to vary from voter to voter and from time to time. The saga of President Clinton's sexual behaviour, and the American public's apparent lack of concern over this aspect of his character, are consistent with the view that most Americans currently view sexual behaviour as a poor indicator of political attractiveness – at least where perceptions of political competence are generally positive.

seems clear that, *ceteris paribus*, candidates with relatively attractive characteristics will receive more favourable electoral comment, and therefore more votes, than others. Indeed, our notion of what characteristics are politically attractive makes it almost definitionally true that such characteristics will be supported in the ballot box. It is hardly a rash conjecture to suppose – again *ceteris paribus* – that voters will comment favourably on, and therefore vote for, candidates they believe to be decent, honourable, sincere, morally serious, publicly concerned, competent, careful and conscientious. This does not collapse to the simple question of whether one likes a candidate; there is also the question of whether one respects the candidate, believes that she has politically relevant qualities, and so on.[13] And notice that voters' behaviour here is not instrumental. My vote for a particular candidate is an expression of favourable comment; I do not vote for that candidate because of any perceived connection between my vote and any particular desired policy outcome. To the extent that policy has a role, it may well be as much because the policies a candidate supports tell voters something about the character of the candidate as because the voter seeks to secure particular outcomes directly.

There remains the important question of the strength of the *ceteris paribus* clause. We might all agree that voters have rational grounds for supporting candidates whom they perceive to possess relevant civic virtues, *ceteris paribus*, but still disagree as to whether there will be any systematic tendency for the electoral process to select for civic virtue *all things considered*. We suggest that the electoral process will so select – at least under helpful institutional arrangements – and we offer two arguments in support of this view. The first simply observes that rational ignorance tends to deflect the force of many other considerations. Voters can only base their voting behaviour on information that is available to them. The rational ignorance argument works to exclude much normatively relevant information. The expressive voting argument is especially salient, in our view, because it works with the grain of the rational ignorance argument rather than against it. Citizens can hardly avoid forming some opinion of the general competence and political attractiveness of candidates even where their understanding of particular issues and policy options is (rationally) poor. Our second argument depends on the claim that the attributes making up the idea of civic virtue may be expected to be particularly widely attractive to the population. Other

[13] For a discussion of the selection of politicians by moral character which stresses the possibility that the relevant characters may not always be likeable, see Williams (1978).

attributes may be considered attractive by some voters, but the aggregative effect of majority voting will tend to amplify only those attributes
that are widely agreed to be attractive.

All of these considerations taken together lead us to conclude that
there is a clear, first-best argument for representation that is grounded in
the expressive account of voting. This expressive account involves a
radical attack on direct democracy as the relevant ideal – in the limit,
direct expressive voting on policies yields normatively arbitrary outcomes.
The expressive account of representation also departs from the idea of
statistical representativeness – indeed, a basic theme in the account is the
attempt to create an assembly that *overrepresents* characteristics that are
both politically attractive and politically productive. The political attractiveness of these characteristics explains why individuals express support
for them, whereas their political productivity provides the basis for the
normative appeal of the system of representation. The expressive theory
of representation sees elections primarily as selection devices, which
function to create what might be thought of as a democratically elite
assembly – democratic in its mode of selection but elite in its civic virtue
and in its competence. This approach seems to us to be Madisonian in
spirit. As Madison claimed, there is good reason to think that representatives will be more public spirited, conscientious and competent than
those whom they represent. The major point may be illustrated by the
case of a referendum on a particular major issue – Britain's membership
of the European monetary union, for example. In such a referendum, we
might expect at least many citizens to vote expressively – that is to use
their vote to express their Europeanness, or their Britishness, or their
sentimental attachment to the queen's head on bank notes. It would be
difficult to believe that in the face of the complexity of the issue, and of
the incentives facing citizens, a referendum would achieve the status of a
reliable indicator of the balance of interests within society. By contrast, it
might be relatively straightforward for citizens to come to an expressively
relevant view as to which of the various candidates for the office of prime
minister is better able to command the respect of citizens as a trustworthy
and reliable person to charge with such an important decision, particularly given the incentives that the chosen politician will face when
making a choice between the policy options. In such a case, it seems
entirely reasonable to argue that the representative route to decision
making is more likely than the directly democratic route to yield a
decision based on a careful analysis of the issues and a careful balancing
of arguments and interests.[14]

---

[14] Of course, a referendum, in practice, would operate within a representative

In addition to this major line of defence of representation, our expressive account of voting allows a further, minor line of argument associated with incentives and responsibility that returns to our earlier discussion of political entrepreneurship. We have already noted as a criticism of direct democracy the fact that literally no one is responsible for policy choice. Under representative democracy it is candidates who adopt policies and who are responsible for the policies they adopt. Clearly, candidates face incentives to adopt policies that they believe will increase their electoral support. This much would be standard in any instrumental account of voting behaviour. But in our expressive voting setting, this incentive effect takes on a rather different character. Policies may have expressive appeal in two distinct ways – directly as policies that excite popular enthusiasm, and indirectly as policies that contribute to the political reputations of candidates associated with them. We have already addressed the concern that expressive voting may select policies with only direct expressive appeal – indeed, this concern would be well founded if expressive voting operated directly on policies. But we have argued that representation focuses attention on candidates rather than on policies; and when candidates select policies, they will be particularly keen to choose policies that enhance their own reputations – policies with indirect expressive appeal. In the limit, candidates stake their reputations on the policies they espouse, and this fact suggests that they will espouse only those policies which they expect to be able to defend *ex post* rather than those that may carry only *direct* expressive appeal. Representation creates an environment in which candidates take responsibility for policies as political entrepreneurs, and this creates incentives with regard to policy choice. Under expressive voting, we argue, these incentives will tend to reinforce the selection effect to promote relatively virtuous representation.

Two notes of warning should be sounded at this point – in case our argument is taken too far. First, our expressive argument for representation does not imply that there is no place for direct democracy in practice. Rather our aim has been to redress what seems to us to be an inappropriately overwhelming presumption in favour of direct democracy within rational actor political theory. We emphasise that direct democracy is at least capable of seriously misrepresenting the interests of citizens; but this does not imply that direct democracy will always perform poorly. In particular, if other institutional arrangements are

system, so that citizens might vote in the referendum depending on the recommendation of their favoured politician. This might be thought of as a form of representation by the back door.

designed in such a way as to support direct democratic procedures over some range of issues – by decentralising decisions to relatively small electorates, by providing relevant information and so on – direct democracy may play an important role in some constitutional designs. An obvious case in point is Switzerland. But even here we would suggest that our argument is important in identifying the fundamental trade off that underlies the choice of an appropriate combination of direct and representative institutions.

The second point is that the expressive argument for representation also points to a potential danger, which might be termed the extreme politics of personality. If the expressive nature of mass democracy picks out not civic virtue but some other and less desirable personal characteristic, democratic politics may descend into elective demagoguery. The fact that such outcomes are not totally unknown seems to us to offer some support for our generally expressive line of argument, but it equally points to the need for the idea of representation to be set within a further institutional context so as to ensure to the greatest possible degree that the expressive factors pull in an appropriate normative direction. We offer no support for the simple idea that representation *per se* offers a reliable route to desirable political outcomes regardless of all other aspects of political life. Rather we see our argument as providing the basis for the inclusion of some degree of representation in a political constitution – not as a necessary evil, but as a potentially valuable means of harnessing what at first sight appears to be a problem in the nature of democratic decision making.

The libertarian spirit of much of public choice theory may not much admire the view of representative, democratic politics outlined here. The better politics works, the more the balance in the relative domains of politics and the market is likely to shift towards politics; and the more we can rely on political representatives to be virtuous, the more we might be inclined to leave them to get on with the business of government, free of costly constraints on their discretion. Our view is that government by the relatively good and the relatively wise is good if you can get it. The major issue is one of feasibility. And we believe that representative democracy on the model sketched here *is* feasible. But it would be wrong to think that such representative democracy demands little in the way of further institutional support. On the contrary, much institutional scaffolding is required to ensure that the electoral system works as well as possible as a selection device. We have pointed to some aspects of that scaffolding above, and we will extend this discussion in later chapters. There is also a fine balance to be struck between the scope for discretion that appropriately selected representatives are allowed, and the institutionalisation of guards against abuse of that discretion.

Overview

In this chapter we have laid out a first-best argument for political representation within the framework provided by our more moral, more expressive account of the rational political actor. On a traditional interpretation of the rational actor framework, characterised by instrumentalist, self-interested voting, the arguments for representation are typically weak and involve appeal to a second-best mode of reasoning. Direct democracy is the relevant ideal, and representation simply a useful device to render democracy less costly. While these second-best arguments for representation are useful, they seem to us to miss an important aspect of what is at stake. And they miss the point precisely because of the assumption of instrumental, self-interested voting. That assumption can, and in our view should, be relaxed while staying within the general rational actor tradition. We have argued here and elsewhere that, alongside the shift to an expressive account of voting, there should be a shift to a more general and heterogeneous account of individual motivation.

More specifically, the expressive account of voting builds on the idea of rational ignorance to provide a first-best argument for representation – that is, an argument which provides both a critique of direct democracy, and a positive account of the potential benefits of representation. The idea of representation developed in terms of the creation of an assembly that is 'representative' not in a statistical sense but in the sense that it is composed of 'representatives' who exhibit particular competence and virtue – characteristics that are both attractive to voters, and productive of more public-interested political outcomes.

We will make no attempt to review the various steps in the argument. Instead, we will end by returning to a point suggested in our introduction. Just as we believe that the account of agent motivation and expressive voting explored here provides a distinctive line of support for the general institution of representative democracy, so we believe that this conclusion will appear distinctive only to those who are immersed in modern public choice or rational actor political theory. The idea of selecting the relatively virtuous and conscientious for public office is hardly a novel one in political theory more generally. And we are inclined to see this fact as a merit of our discussion. We believe that our relaxation of the standard rational actor assumptions on motivation and voter behaviour opens up avenues of thought and topics of analysis which have been closed to modern rational actor theorists. Pursuit of these avenues allows rational actor theory to be reconnected with some of the central ideas of traditional political theory and with ideas concerning institutional design that traditional political theory supports. In the process, this reconnection also allows the undoubted power of rational actor theory to be deployed in analysing such ideas.

10

Political parties

By a faction, I understand a number of citizens, whether amounting to a majority or a minority of the whole, who are united and actuated by some common impulse of passion, or of interest, adverse to the rights of other citizens, or to the permanent and aggregate interests of the community.

(*Federalist* papers, 10, James Madison)

Political parties in public choice and political theory

Any satisfactory analysis of the practice of Western democracy – and any discussion of how it might be made to work better – must recognise and account for the role of political parties. That much seems self-evident. Indeed, for many people, to be political is to be party political. So, for example, much of the discussion, both popular and academic, of matters like alternative voting procedures – proportional representation, preferential (transferable) voting, compulsory voting and so on – is preoccupied with an investigation of how existing and potential political parties would fare under the various procedures. On this general view, to conceive of politics without parties is rather like conceiving of football without teams. Whatever such an activity would be exactly, it would certainly not be politics (or football) as we know it.

Yet parties as such have not received much attention in public choice analysis. It is generally noted that electoral candidates will have a party affiliation; and often, as in the early work by Downs, parties are identified as the contestants in the electoral process. But, as we noted in the previous chapter, the precise description of electoral options in terms of candidates and parties, tends to be seen as an issue of second-order significance: parties and political candidates are treated as mere proxies for the policy platforms that are the central object of voter choice. The practice in most public choice literature of treating 'party', 'candidate' and 'policy platform' as essentially interchangeable suggests clearly enough that the political party as such is not an object of central concern.

There are two reasons, we think, for that backgrounding. The first is connected with the practice of using the simple median voter equilibrium model as the point of departure for further analysis. In that model, electoral competition serves to constrain rival candidates fully, just as perfect competition fully constrains rival firms in a market. Accordingly, it is acceptable to proceed by treating political parties in the same generally cavalier way that economists traditionally treated perfectly competitive firms. There is, one might argue, no particularly urgent intellectual problem in failing to disaggregate competitive firms to the level of the individuals who compose them: one can simply acknowledge that these firms constitute islands of non-market organisational structure in a sea of market relations, and then proceed by treating the firms as profit maximisers on the grounds that competitive market constraints will be binding. In the political case, this translates into treating political parties as individual candidates on the grounds that the forces of electoral competition will produce the median voter outcome regardless. There is an element of irony in the public choice literature accepting, albeit implicitly, this benign view of politics, given the general presumption in public choice theory that 'political failure' is a genuine problem. In any event, the structure of the political party must become an issue of substance once we move away from the fully constrained setting of the median voter result – just as the analysis of the internal structure of the firm becomes highly significant once we move away from the idealised case of perfect competition. The structure and operation of political parties determines how political rents are distributed and this distribution will influence political behaviour, just as the structure and operation of oligopolistic firms determines how profits are distributed and thereby influences commercial behaviour. Recently there has been some attempt to apply insights from the theory of firms' organisation to the study of democratic process, but this 'transaction-cost' approach to politics is still in its infancy.[1]

The second, somewhat related, reason for the relative lack of concern

---

[1] See, for example, Jones and Hudson (1998), following in the style of Coase (1937, 1988a, 1988b, 1988c), Williamson (1964, 1985) and others. For a general discussion of the transaction cost approach to policy making, see Dixit (1996).

about political parties relates to the instrumental account of voting that orthodox public choice theory offers. If citizens vote in such a way as to maximise their self-interested benefits (defined to include the benefits derived from publicly provided goods and services, as well as the effects of government activity on private incomes and prices), then the way in which electoral options are described – whether in terms of parties, candidates or whatever – will be epiphenomenal. The labelling of candidate or party will be seen as merely a veil that the rational voter will pierce with the calculus of self-interest. Of course, a party label may provide information to voters, and this may help to overcome certain sorts of problems, but in the standard models in which voters are already assumed to be fully informed, party labels must be redundant.

Under the expressive account of voting, as we have stressed, the precise nature of the options and their descriptions matters. Whether the voter is enrolled to cheer or boo for particular candidates or for particular policy packages or for particular parties is likely to make a difference to how the boos and cheers fall out. Of course, in any particular case, all three elements may be relevant. Candidates will appear not only with their array of personal characteristics but also with a party identification and a policy platform. But the details of voting procedure and electoral tradition may serve to background or foreground these different elements in securing voter support. In some systems, voters can vote for a *party* without any identifiable candidate: in other contexts (mostly local settings whose candidates can be presumed to be well known) individual candidates may not have clear party labels. Institutional arrangements may serve to assist in backgrounding or foregrounding these various elements, and in the expressive voting account such effects may make a substantial difference.[2]

One question of particular concern to us in this chapter will be how the essentially expressive case for representative institutions set out in the previous chapter is affected by the presence of political parties: does the fact that candidates appear with a party label, and the related fact that many voters routinely vote according to party label, undermine or in any significant way moderate our earlier case for representation?

If most public choice scholars have treated the topic of political parties with relative indifference, the prevailing attitude within other traditions of political theory has been fairly uniformly hostile. Consider, for

---

[2] An honourable and major exception to the general lack of interest in political parties within rational actor politics is provided by Aldrich (1995), who provides a mainly historical and empirical account of the origin, growth and current state of political parties in the USA from a rational actor perspective, arguing that political parties are essential to the operation of democracy.

example, the discursive democracy tradition,[3] mentioned in chapter 7. Within that tradition, the key normative feature of democratic politics is political debate concerning the nature of the public interest as it bears on collective action. The chief object of political institutions, accordingly, is to provide a forum congenial to discussion of the right kind, a discursive arena within which the business of discerning the public interest can be collectively engaged. Within this arena, every relevant consideration, every plausible perspective, every purported fact that bears should, in principle, be given voice and (more important perhaps) given ear. Practical considerations, and in particular the need to come to a decision in time for the required action to be taken, will necessarily obtrude and will require some rationing of time and attention, but the restriction of representation and debate along specifically *party* lines seems entirely antipathetic to the desired spirit of free enquiry. Indeed, the practice of 'parliamentary debate' in actual democratic systems in which parties are at all strong must lead any enthusiast for discursive democracy to total despair. Two spectacles are routine. On the one hand, there is the familiar phenomenon of someone reading a speech to an almost deserted chamber, where even those present seem to be asleep or reading the daily newspaper. On the other hand, there are occasions where the chamber is full and everyone alert, but all are engaged in shouting invective at the other side, as someone gives a set speech the primary object of which seems to be not to give too much away, while delivering appropriate 'sound bites' for the media. And nothing else should be expected: in strong party systems: parliamentary debate is either a ritual or a continuation of campaigning by other means. No one much listens; no one is expected to change her vote in response to arguments offered; voting is largely a forgone conclusion. The discursive democracy ideal requires a discussion rather like an idealised academic seminar, in which all participants maintain an independent stance, keep an open mind, listen with equal attentiveness to all points of view and then exercise their judgement. Party politics limits the terms of debate where it does not render debate essentially pointless, and predisposes participants to listen sympathetically only to the arguments of their own party.

Equally, the mainstream view of parliamentary democracy in terms of the model of responsible and representative government is generally critical of the role of political parties.[4] The ideal form here is of a

---

[3] Cohen and Rogers (1983), Cohen (1989), Bohman (1998) provide relevant discussion.

[4] Pomper (1992) provides a useful overview of alternative concepts of political parties. Our discussion here relates to the idea of party as governing caucus associated with Wilson (1973) and others.

government that is held responsible by its accountability to a parliament that is itself representative of the general population. If a strong and disciplined party structure offers government almost guaranteed control of parliament, the idea of accountability as an institutional safeguard for responsible government is reduced to vanishing point. At the same time, the party-based structure of parliament will tend to restrict the degree of representation of a statistical kind. Parties may represent the dominant or most salient interests or ideological positions, but they seem an unlikely vehicle for representing the full political range. Arguably, within a party-driven assembly, many citizens will lack a voice (and, more particularly, lack a vote) that reflects their particular view or interest. In this way, much traditional political theory charges strong political parties with undermining both the representation of the electorate, and the responsibility of the government.

Political parties have had a similarly poor reception in a third intellectual tradition – perhaps closer to the public choice tradition than either the discursive democracy or the representative, responsible government strands. We have in mind here the broad Anglo-American tradition associated with Hume, Mill and the authors of the *Federalist* papers. It is not entirely clear whether the modern political party quite corresponds to the category of 'faction' or 'party' so cordially deplored by David Hume and the writers of *The Federalist*; but it *is* clear that factions/parties as they understood them were, in their view, central corrupting features of representative democracy. To be sure, the *Federalist* papers offer a kind of 'countervailing power' argument to defend the use of rival parties to control each other – but it is clear that this involves making a virtue of necessity. If parties are ineluctable, then the best *feasible* political arrangement is, like the amateur's golf swing, a mass of compensating errors. Affairs must be so arranged that faction offsets faction, party neutralises party: but it would be better if parties/factions did not arise in the first place.

In summary, then, within normative political theory of a traditional stripe, political parties have generally been seen as a negative force, and within rational actor analysis to be a matter of second-order concern. 'Party' has received a poor press, where it has received any press at all. We ourselves are, by contrast, inclined to think that political parties are a 'good thing'; that much of the animus towards them is based either on confusion or on an implausibly romantic view of democratic politics; and that institutional arrangements that would diminish the influence of parties or undermine them altogether (arrangements that currently have some vogue in potentially influential circles) are generally moves in the wrong direction. In part, our view springs from our emphasis on a particular problem in large-scale collective decision making – that of 'diminished responsibility' and expressive behaviour – and our corresponding desire to bolster those institutional arrangements that support government that is 'responsible' in this sense. But our view also reflects a dissatisfaction with the coherence and/or practical relevance of anti-party arguments – with the failure of those arguments to specify a plausible counterfactual. In this spirit, the lines of argument we develop in this chapter are organised around the question: 'compared to what?' We shall, in other words, take seriously the general predilection in normative economics to think *comparatively*, and will do our best to make explicit the particular comparisons we have in mind.

Compared to what?

Two types of comparison seem particularly relevant, one concerned with the number and strength of political parties, the other concerned with the contrast between political parties and individual politicians. The nature of the first type of comparisons may be illustrated by reference to extreme examples. At one extreme, there is the one-party state, where a single highly disciplined party rules. This extreme challenges the idea of democracy – or at least, it points to the idea that any democratic forces that do operate in such an environment must operate *within* the party, rather than through any competition between parties within an assembly or any electoral choice between parties. At another extreme, each potential assembly member might be considered as a party in herself; or, alternatively, party discipline may be so lax that it fails to constrain individual politicians who vote atomistically on whatever issues come before the assembly. In this case, the idea of party itself fades to insignificance either through the sheer number of parties or through their weakness. Clearly, the middle ground between these extremes will attract most interest since it offers a spectrum in which both the number of parties and their strength can vary continuously over a substantial range. Alternatively put, what is at issue is the nature of the contracts that assembly members enter into with one another in the exercise of their votes. For example, such contracts may be more or less binding; they may be restricted to specific pieces of legislation (I will vote for bill *A* if you will vote for bill *B*), or cover a range of issues; they may involve larger or smaller numbers of assembly members; they may be limited to a specific period of time, or be of indefinite duration; they may be an explicit part of the candidate's identity as presented to electors at the time of the electoral race, or play no role in the specification of electoral options at all.

For our purposes here, we shall assume that parties extend over an indefinite time period and that a party label may form a significant part of a candidate's identity in the eyes of the electorate.[5] Against this background, we will focus on two fairly specific comparisons, one concerned with the number of parties and the other concerned with their disciplinary strength. We will compare a two-party system of the kind often offered as a relevant model of the current British or Australian arrangements with a multiparty system of the kind more characteristic of Italy, Germany and other European countries. In this first comparison, we will assume that all parties are strong in the sense that party commitments are binding constraints on the political behaviour of all representatives aligned with the party. But we will also make a second comparison between the strong two-party system and the weak two-party system that is more closely associated with the US system.

The second type of comparison to be considered reflects the distinction between the case in which political agency is exercised by a single individual and the case in which agency is exercised by a collective group, team or party. Unlike the previous comparison where we were considering alternative party structures within an electoral contest or political assembly, we shall here be concerned with the individual versus collective nature of political agency itself. Informing this comparison is the contrast between the idealised presidential system in which a single individual is elected to perform certain functions and hold certain powers, and an idealised parliamentary system in which those functions/powers are exercised by a *team* of agents – the majority party.[6] Of course, this is by no means the only, or necessarily the most important, difference between practical presidential and parliamentary systems such as those of the US and the UK, but we will focus on just this one aspect of the presidential/parliamentary divide for the time being. Our central claim will be that team agency – with teams taking form of long-lived and disciplined political parties – can be more reliable than individual agency because teams face at each point in time a discipline of continuous dealing that the individual does not necessarily face, or not to the same extent.[7] Political parties are in this sense more likely to prove trustworthy than individual presidents – more likely that is, to fulfil undertakings given,

[5] This requirement does not rule out the possibility of 'independent' candidates, but does imply that the independence of that candidate will be an explicit and distinctive part of the candidate's profile in the electoral contest.

[6] This contrast between the concentration of power in one pair of hands and the division of power is taken up again in chapter 12.

[7] The argument at stake here is an instance of a more general argument set out in Brennan and Kliemt (1994).

and/or to respond to changed circumstances in ways of which the electorate will approve. Arguing this proposition is the task of the penultimate section of this chapter. The final section then attempts to draw together some relevant conclusions.

Partitioning the assembly

As we have seen, the focus of attention within public choice orthodoxy has fallen on winner-takes-all electoral competition in which the winning party/candidate has both the right and the power to implement policy without reference to other parties/candidates – except in relation to the need to fight further elections in the future. The legislative assembly – which we have taken to be a defining feature of truly representative democracy – serves little purpose in this extreme vision of democratic politics, but becomes much more significant if the winner-takes-all nature of electoral competition is relaxed. One way in which it might be relaxed involves moving towards a model of proportional representation, and one way of characterising the basic idea of proportional representation is to think of the democratic political process in two stages: first the creation of a number of focal points around which political support congregates, and then the determination of policy in a manner which reflects the existence and variety of these focal points, and the sizes of their congregations. The standard link from proportional representation to representative democracy is then to interpret the 'focal points' as political parties, and their 'congregations' as their membership in an elected assembly. If parties are to be a central feature of the legislative assembly, the obvious questions are then how parties influence the determination of policy, and how this influence feeds back into the process of electing the assembly. In this section we focus mainly on the first of these two questions, before considering the implications for electoral competition in the next section (although the two questions are necessarily entwined to some extent).

In most treatments it is assumed that the logic of proportional representation requires strong party affiliation on the part of both individual candidates and individual voters. In short, parties are the key players. Parties carry policy commitments. Party identification (and therefore policy identification) is the major characteristic of individual candidates, and the major determinant of voter decisions. For example, in Austen-Smith and Banks (1988) the multistage political process is explicit, with parties bargaining over policy outcomes in the assembly. Individual candidates/members play no real role other than contributing to the bargaining strength of their party. A similar idea is approached from another perspective in Ortuno-Ortin (1997), where policy outcomes are modelled as the weighted averages of the policy platforms of the parties; here, there is no specific model of the behaviour of the assembly and proportional representation is seen as a policy implementation rule, rather than as an explicit model of the political process.

This view of strong parties both supports and is supported by some form of proportional representation. If voters vote essentially for parties (or, perhaps, party leaders) then single-member political constituencies seem to make little sense. Single-member constituencies present the well-known possibility that party A may gain a majority in the assembly against party B by receiving a bare majority of the votes in a bare majority of the electoral districts – that is, A can receive more seats with 26 per cent of the votes than B does with 74 per cent. And, of course, gerrymandering is a mechanism designed to exploit this possibility. Single-member districts seem intuitively to be an obfuscation in the electoral system, and the case for some form of proportional representation with multimember constituencies which explicitly recognises the party as the relevant object of voting seems clearcut. Similarly, a proportional representation system requires parties (or some such groupings of individual candidates) if the idea of proportionality is to be operationalised – the very idea of proportional representation is not well defined if all candidates are 'independent' or 'non-aligned'.

In fact, however, the choice between single-member districts and proportional representation involves more than the issue of what it is that voters are voting to secure. In practice, that choice also has important implications for a number of aspects of assembly operation, including the number of parties within the assembly, how majorities within the assembly might be constituted, the extent to which 'governments' constituted by such majorities can be held accountable to the electorate, the relation between electoral support and political power (as in, but more broadly than in, the gerrymander example) and so on. In our discussion, we seek to focus attention on the number of parties as such, and on the influence of the number of parties on the conduct of the assembly and democratic process more broadly. In order to secure that focus, we initially consider a rather stylised institutional arrangement in which the number of parties is the only relevant parameter. Specifically, we suppose that all voting is on the basis of one single nationwide constituency and that the seats in the assembly are allocated among the n parties receiving the highest number of popular votes in proportion to the number of votes received – where n is the parameter that can range from 2 to a possible maximum of S (the number of seats in the assembly, so that each individual representative is a separate party).

For example, suppose that there are six self-described parties in a given election and that these parties are labelled *A*, *B*, *C*, *D*, *E*, *F*. Suppose also that the allocation of the popular vote is: *A* 28 per cent; *B* 22 per cent; *C* 14 per cent; *D* 13 per cent; *E* 12 per cent; *F* 11 per cent. Taking this allocation of votes as given, if $n = 2$, party *A* would gain 56 per cent of the seats in the assembly and party *B* 44 per cent; if $n = 3$, party *A* would have 44 per cent of the seats, *B* 34 per cent and *C* 22 per cent; if $n = 4$, party *A* would have 36 per cent of the seats in the assembly, *B* 23 per cent, *C* 18 per cent and *D* 17 per cent. And so on.[8]

In this context questions arise about the way in which citizens' votes for parties actually reflect citizens' preferences over the composition of the assembly. Usually, it is taken for granted that a vote for party *A* implies that the voter prefers an assembly in which party *A* has a majority in the assembly, and hence constitutes 'the government'. But, in fact, as we have argued, the inference of voter preference from vote cast is a perilous exercise – and not only for expressive reasons of the kind canvassed in earlier chapters. The standard problem of strategic voting will arise whenever the number of parties exceeds two. Furthermore, citizens may care not only about which is the majority party but also the size of the majority, or the more detailed structure of the assembly. Such preferences may lead citizens to vote for parties other than 'their' party. Whether voting in order to secure a particular composition of the assembly is itself strictly rational is, of course, part of the challenge of the 'expressive voting' account. But even if that particular challenge fails, the fact that voters vote for parties as such and not for parliamentary composition can be an independent source of electoral 'noise'. Each voter would have to know how all other voters were going to vote in order to cast his vote in the way designed to bring about a composition as close to his desired one as possible – and clearly, his influence in securing his preferred composition will be negligibly small.

Within the familiar median voter model, such problems are finessed by means of particular assumptions about the value of *n*. These assumptions operate at two levels. First, electoral competition results in a 'winner-takes-all' outcome – that is, the policy package advanced by the party receiving the highest number of votes becomes the policy package that prevails, and all other parties have zero influence. Second, electoral competition itself is standardly taken to involve only two rival contenders. In other words, *n* is taken to be equal to one, with a further restriction

---

[8] The exact form of the citizens' votes – that is whether they are of a 'first preference' vote, or a Borda ranking, or a 'transferable vote' where the number of effective votes for a party is itself a function of *n* – will, of course, be important, but will not concern us here.

that the number of parties contending the election is two. Here, our attention focuses on the former aspect, with the latter aspect treated in the next section.

In fact, within the standard median voter construct, there is no scope for 'parliamentary process' or 'assembly politics' that might mediate between citizen choice at the ballot box and ultimate policy outcomes. To the extent that a president unilaterally determines policy outcomes, this median voter model might be conceived as applicable directly to the presidential case. If the majority party in a two-party race exercises an effective monopoly in the legislative assembly, then the median-voter model may also seem to be directly applicable to the parliamentary case. But then it would have to be explained what exactly the role of parliamentary process in a two-party assembly is. In short, what needs to be explained is the role of the formal 'opposition' in the assembly. Clearly, that role cannot involve any direct check on the exercise of majority party power because the majority party, by definition, 'has the numbers'. Parliamentary debate cannot be explained plausibly as an attempt to induce any members to change their minds or, more significantly, their votes – because in a tight party system all votes are committed.

Is parliamentary process simply a legacy from a time when there *were* no parties in the modern sense, when elected candidates exercised their judgements according to their own individual interests (as in the public choice view) or according to their particular judgements of the public interest (as in a more heroic, 'benevolent despots' view)? We are not inclined to think so. Acceptance of the proposition that the major constraint on government behaviour is electoral competition does not commit one to the view that electoral competition should be the *only* constraint. The presence of an institutionalised opposition can provide a further constraint, even if it would have to be accepted that it is likely to be a somewhat second-order one and essentially parasitic on electoral competition itself. What institutionalised opposition can provide is a check on the behaviour of the majority party to the extent that its presence ensures that day-to-day politics is subject to explicit public attention; parliamentary process involves, on this reading, the continuation of electioneering by other means. There will be a continuous rhetorical appeal to the electorate, with the government forced to advocate and defend its actions in public. And note that the institution of an official opposition locates the role of scrutinising and criticising government action precisely in that body which has the greatest incentive to scrutinise and criticise. This role is, to be sure, one that is shared in an effective democracy with an independent press – understanding that the press's role here must also include that of scrutinising the opposition for specious criticism or plain bloody-mindedness. But parliamentary process and the role of the opposition does seem capable of influencing and constraining government by means that are not available in a one-party assembly (or in the case of an elected president with substantial independent powers). An institutionalised opposition also maintains the salience of the alternative government and in that sense diminishes the incumbency advantages of name recognition.[9]

Of course, granting the opposition a role in government, and a position in the public eye, may carry costs as well as benefits. At the level of electoral competition itself, the fact that both contending parties play some role in the elected assembly may somewhat blunt the parties' incentives. There is more at stake in a winner-takes-all race than in a winner-takes-most race. The cost to a losing party is not so great if members of the losing-party establishment are nevertheless provided with jobs as assembly members, and a stage thereby on which to enjoy the benefits of public attention. A party is, arguably, more likely to trade off the probability of victory for ideological purity and/or be more resistant to changes in the light of prevailing electoral views if the cost of electoral defeat is *not* total obscurity. Nevertheless, it seems reasonable to ascribe to the politicians that constitute parties a desire to hold political power, both for its own sake and for the sake of the public attention and other benefits that attach to it.[10] Accordingly, it seems self-evident that parties will want to *win* the electoral contests in which they are engaged, and we take it that that will normally be so. However, it is worth noting that the trade offs between probability of victory and other ends (e.g. adherence to morally or ideologically derived policy ambitions) are influenced by the number of parties admitted to the assembly, and their roles in that assembly.

In the case where the number of parties so admitted (n in our formulation) is three or more, it becomes necessary to say something about the outcome determination process at two levels – both within the assembly and at the level of popular elections. We will take it that simple majority rule applies on policy initiatives within the assembly, while the

---

[9] In the US system, for example, the need for explicit limits on presidential terms might be modified if the most successful rival candidate were institutionalised as a 'shadow president', with some scope to put rival proposals to Congress and to argue the inadequacies of presidential initiatives on a systematic basis.

[10] We are not, incidentally inclined to the view that income as such – whether in cash or kind – is a particularly important motivator in this setting. Politics tends to select for persons who value relatively highly the rewards that politics distinctly provides – public attention and the power to influence significant events. Politics is probably more attractive to actors and moralists than to the merely venal.

form of proportional representation described above applies at the popular level. We shall focus our remarks here on the case of $n = 3$: the points to be made generalise to larger n. The special case where $n = S$ we shall reserve for brief treatment below.

As is familiar from the 'voting power' literature,[11] the mapping from electoral support (as reflected here in number of assembly seats) into policy determining influence in the assembly when there are more than two parties is problematic and potentially perverse. Simple examples make the point. Consider the case in which the three parties A, B and C receive 48 per cent, 48 per cent and 4 per cent of the popular votes respectively – we will depict that outcome as the triplet (48, 48, 4) for convenience. It is clear that these three parties hold *equal* power in the assembly, in the sense that no one of them can determine policy (i.e. form a majority coalition) without the support of one of the others, but that *any* coalition of two parties will do. For example, the (A, C) coalition is just as powerful as the (A, B) coalition, in that either coalition is sufficient to secure a majority on the floor of the assembly. In this example C has as much policy determination power as either A or B despite the fact that A and B each receive twelve times as many votes as C. Moreover, C could improve its popular support and see its power diminish. This would happen, for example, if (48, 48, 4) were transformed by a new election into (52, 40, 8). In the first case, C would have a good chance of being in a ruling coalition, and has as much power as A or B, whereas in the second case, A has a simple majority in the assembly, so that C's power has evaporated despite the doubling of its electoral support. And obversely, a party's power can increase despite reduced electoral support – as, for example, in a four-party case, where (46, 46, 3, 5) gives way to (49, 49, 2, 0), in which party C goes from having *no* power (it cannot make or break a majority coalition) to having as much power as A and B, despite having reduced electoral support and losing one seat in the assembly.

In summary, then, for $n \geq 3$, it is neither the case that electoral support translates directly into policy-making power, nor the case that changes in electoral support necessarily result in changes in policy-making power in the same direction. There is, in this sense, something special about the two-party assembly: only in the two-party case does the party with the larger electoral support necessarily have the larger amount of political decision-making power.

This ambiguity about the relation between electoral support and

---

[11] For discussion, see Barry (1980), Holler (1982, 1983, 1998), Brams and Fishburn (1995).

decision-making power within the assembly in the multiparty (n > 2) case is, of course, a source of the possibility of strategic voting. However, still more significant than this possibility, we believe, is the difficulty in holding parties *accountable* to the electorate – and the consequent erosion of electoral incentives. If a party can actually gain policy-making power while losing electoral support, the incentive for parties to choose policies that appeal to voters is surely moderated. Moreover, the lines of responsibility for policy outcomes are themselves blurred. And, as we have implied in a preceding chapter, under plausible assumptions about voter behaviour, responsibility for policy outcomes is precisely what is at risk in large-number collective decision settings. It is the fact that no individual voter is, in general, causally efficacious in bringing about collective outcomes that severs the link between individual action at the ballot box and responsibility for what emerges. Not only does the absence of this link imply that individuals who vote irresponsibly will do no less well than individuals who vote responsibly (one interpretation of what 'rationality' requires at the dispositional level) – not only is the moral force of considerations of individual prudence blunted – but so is the moral force of considerations of public interest. *Any* directly consequenti-alist argument for voting in a particular way must be moderated by the observation that it is extremely unlikely that my vote will make any difference. In the voting context, this diminished responsibility is an inevitable and potentially destructive feature.

What we seek, therefore, is a set of institutional arrangements that will support a sense of responsibility. Such a consideration is, for example, the basis of the argument for the open as opposed to the secret ballot advanced by the later Mill (and more recently by Brennan and Pettit (1990)). It is also the basis of our argument for representative democracy (and against direct democracy) advanced in the previous chapter. An important element in that argument is that representatives are obliged to stand for – to take responsibility for – the policies with which they are associated. Policies do not simply 'emerge' from an essentially invisible and impersonal plebiscite process: they are, rather, attached to political candidates whose future electoral success or failure depends in significant part on the success or failure of the policies in question. This fact mobilises several constraints on the policies with which political candi-dates will seek attachment. One of these constraints is a rhetorical one. Suppose there exists a widespread prejudice within the electorate for particular policies which could not endure explicit scrutiny or could not be supported in public debate. (Suppose this popular prejudice is against particular races, or in favour of particular, vindictive, forms of punish-ment for convicted criminals.) If the articulation of policies based on such prejudices is to identify oneself as a racist or a peculiarly vindictive person, or if public adversarial debate on the issue is likely to reveal the flimsiness of the evidence in support of the policy in question, then the institutions of representative democracy as we know them – the require-ments of structured debate and the explicit identification of candidates with the positions they take in the policy debate – will tend to filter out such policies that might otherwise be implemented under a more direct democracy. Whether or not the unexamined life is worth living, the unexamined policy is surely not worth implementing – and this is a special problem because ordinary forces of individual prudence do not necessarily make policy examination a profitable task. What political representation secures is a connection between individual prudence and policy defensibility for at least *some* members of the polity – namely, those electoral candidates whose electoral fortunes are attached to policies and the case they can make for those policies.

Representation also imposes a temporal constraint. There is the possibility that a popular enthusiasm may arise that is not expected to stand the test of time. The requirement that candidates must not only advance particular policies at the time of the current election but also be held accountable for those policies at the next election modifies the incentive for representatives to respond with total enthusiasm to every transient electoral whim. Suppose, for example, that a nation has been afflicted by some huge natural disaster – say, a once-in-a-century flood that has caused huge damage to persons and property. Because the issue of flood damage is so salient to citizens and because salience (as distinct from prudential calculation) is disproportionately influential in electoral politics, there is considerable electoral support for implementing elabor-ate and expensive flood protection measures. These measures, let us suppose, will indeed assist in the amelioration of the effects of once-a-century floods, but would not pass the test of even the most generously disposed cost–benefit analysis. It will surely be some discipline on the actual policy response that those who most vigorously defend such policies now must also be held accountable for the lavish expense three or four years later when memory of the floods has faded and where the citizenry is preoccupied with a new calamity – drought, forest fires, or whatever – the effects of which are manifestly worse by virtue of the natural-disaster budget having been swallowed up in flood management activities. We accept that even representative democracy will be influ-enced to some extent by the salience of particular policy areas: we could hardly expect, and would not want, a policy regime that was totally insensitive to electoral views. But representative democracy differs from direct democracy in that representatives must look to the question of electoral support over a horizon that encompasses the candidate's expected political career – and this within an environment where rival candidates have an incentive to remember and advertise to the electorate any past extravagances in which the candidate in question may have been implicated. We would not want to deny the claim that these 'representation' constraints are imperfect: we do (both here and, in a slightly different way in the previous chapter) deny that democracy would work better without them.

The relevant question in this chapter, however, is less whether representation imposes these responsibility constraints and more whether such constraints are made more or less effective under a party-based structure of representation. As we see it, parties are a positive force here and are the more so the fewer of them there are over the range $n \geq 2$. Take, as a limit, the case of S parties or 'independent' representatives. In this case, no candidate can plausibly promise to deliver particular policy outcomes if elected, and hence cannot plausibly be held to account if those policy outcomes do not eventuate. All the candidate can reasonably promise is to pursue certain policies to the best of her ability – and establishing *ex post* whether she has been faithful to that promise will be no simple business. Conscientious pursuit of her task will involve her in doing various trades with other 'representatives' and voting for policies that were no part of her originally avowed platform. She will be *more* responsible for assembly decisions than would an ordinary voter be for decisions of the citizenry at large, but she can still plausibly claim that most policy decisions are not her responsibility – either because she did not vote for them at all, or because she only voted for them to secure support for something else. She certainly cannot specify *ex ante* what vote-trading she will engage in if elected because she cannot know *ex ante* what other candidates will be elected. And *ex post*, her record will be ambiguous and difficult to interpret.

Even in the case of a reasonably small number of parties, say five or six, the same problems arise – and not obviously in significantly reduced measure. Voters cannot know *ex ante* what coalitions among parties will form; and *ex post* the extent to which political expediency actually required the degree of compromise of originally specified policy goals must be a matter of interpretation and judgement. If a stable coalition forms, and transcends the life of a particular parliament, then the effective number of independent parties falls to a point where rival coalitions can contest the electoral race as rival governments, and be held accountable accordingly. If on the other hand, parties form a coalition that lasts only the life of the current parliament, then only *ex post* accountability is possible. And if we have separate coalitions on every issue, then familiar problems of global cycling loom – in which 'responsibility' for the sequence of policy decisions falls to the elected parties precisely because and to the extent that they failed to secure a stable majority coalition.

Only, it seems, in the two-party case, where one party constitutes the 'government' and holds a decisive majority on policy decisions, or in a single candidate presidential race – only in other words where the electoral contest is bound to produce a determinate winner, which has the power to implement campaign promises – can voters confidently vote for the party with its attendant policy commitments that they would prefer as government – and only then can successful parties/candidates be held fully accountable for the policies actually implemented. Alternatively put, the rhetorical and temporal constraints that representation involves are maximally operative when the successful candidate/party gets to determine policy. Perhaps there are other considerations that weigh in favour of larger numbers of parties (we shall examine and basically reject one set below). But in our view the central logic of political agency set out in the previous chapters is generally most strongly supportive of a two-party system.

The attentive reader might well claim that there is an important difference between the argument developed here and that set out in the previous chapters. In the earlier version, the case for representation was that it shifts the focus of voter concern away from policy evaluation (for which 'rational ignorance' is a particular problem) towards questions of candidate character and political attractiveness. There, the picture of political agency was based on electoral choice as a selection device rather than a direct constraint on policy choice. Here, we seem to be resurrecting the idea of voter choice over policies, albeit in an indirect form mediated by the additional rhetorical and temporal constraints imposed by full electoral responsibility/accountability. Are these lines of reasoning actually compatible?

We think they are – and indeed that they are mutually supportive. The issue of assessing candidates' character, candidates' inclination to pursue and capacity to secure the broad public interest, can hardly be divorced from candidates' performance in doing so. Candidates must in this sense be accountable – their performance must be as accessible to scrutiny as is possible. What direct democracy requires is that citizens make a determination on policy questions one by one; what representative democracy allows in the presence of decisive parties is that citizens make an assessment of the broad policy performance of the government of the day, both in terms of its record and its projected future *vis-à-vis* the future 'offered' by the salient rival(s). Our claim is that both accountability and predictability are greater under an institutional order in which popular elections directly select governments than under an order in which popular election merely selects an assembly of independent members, or a multitude of parties which will form unpredictable coalitions to secure a decisive majority. As Madison emphasises (the *Federalist* papers 51 and 62), agents can only be held responsible for that which they have power to determine. This fact argues not only for political parties, but for an essentially two-party order in which popular electoral contests are indeed contests for government.

As we remarked earlier, whether this two-party order is better achieved by proportional representation, single-member districts, or some other electoral arrangement is a separate issue. However, experience certainly suggests that single-member districts are more effective in securing a two-party arrangement than are standard forms of proportional representation, and we regard this fact as constituting a strong argument for the single-member district scheme. However, we do not deny that forms of proportional representation can be devised that can secure a two-party outcome, and in the foregoing discussion we have indicated a simple example. It may nevertheless seem as if the single-member district is the arrangement that most foregrounds candidates' personal characteristics: that the role of party label, with its typical ideological connotation, serves to background personal characteristics; and that there remains a tension between popular-candidate selection and party dominance. The tension can, however, be overstated. Electoral politics tends to personalise parties, even when party affiliation predominates. The personal characteristics of leaders and the senior members of the major parties become critical features of electoral party politics. Voters vote in part on the basis of whether they have confidence in the various leaders (more than on the basis of candidates' characteristics in single-member districts in all but special cases). And it is not unreasonable that this should be the case, since the government party leader is almost certainly more significant in determining the citizen's fortunes than is the local member.

Moreover, parties will have an incentive to select candidates with the relevant characteristics of public interestedness, party loyalty and competence, so as to improve the party's overall electoral prospects. There can be a degree of division of labour and specialisation in the business of discerning candidates' characters: parties are arguably better placed to assess candidates' personal characteristics than are voters, and will certainly want to avoid candidates whose personal ambitions, unscrupulousness and rank incompetence are likely to reflect poorly on the party's reputation.

To summarise, we consider that electoral arrangements that result in the partitioning of the representative assembly into a small number of parties (especially two) have much to be said for them. If, as we believe, the chief argument for representative institutions lies in doubts about incentives and responsibilities at the level of individual voter choice, then the logic of that argument is also supportive of party rather than individualistic politics. Structuring elections so that voters choose explicitly to empower a government makes for clear lines of political responsibility. Elections with this character more effectively constrain the actions of rival parties, both when in office and when making promises as to what they will do if in office. And, as we see it, such elections do not undermine the effectiveness of the selection element in democratic process: there can still be some confidence that the system will favour candidates with politically attractive qualities – not merely charm, but some measure of honesty, integrity, public interestedness, intelligence and competence.

Partitioning the contest

As we have already noted, there is a distinction to be drawn between the number of parties present within the assembly and the number of parties who figure in the electoral contest. In a simple 'winner-takes-all' presidential contest, for example, only one person/party is elected, but in principle any number may stand. But, as those familiar with the median-voter model know, the number of contestants matters even in the winner-takes-all (or winner-takes-most) settings. As we demonstrated in chapter 7, a presidential race between two contestants operating in one political dimension will tend to produce a 'co-location' equilibrium, whether voters vote expressively or instrumentally. As the number of candidates expands to three or more, the co-location equilibrium is at risk. Threat of entry of a third electoral option, in the standard Hotelling median voter model, leads to an equilibrium in which two parties/candidates/policy packages locate at different points.[12]

The number of contestants does, however, depend on the number of parties present in the assembly, because the number of contestants is itself a function of the potential gains from winning (a share of) the prize and the probability of doing so. In the winner-takes-all election, for example, it is presumed that candidates will stand only if the expected return from standing is high enough. Candidates are assumed to be rational, and the costs of contesting an election can be taken to be positive and non-negligible. The endogenous decision to enter an election race as a

---

[12] See, for example, Palfrey (1984) and Weber (1992). Similar effects of additional options would emerge in the probabilistic voting models of Coughlin (1982) and others.

candidate is the focus of several recent papers which otherwise adopt the standard framework of instrumentally rational voters.[13] The basic idea in all of these papers is to model the decision to stand by individual citizens, so that there is no party structure to politics. One of the issues explored in this emerging literature is the question of the equilibrium number of candidates, where the models reported to date provide some support for the idea that two-candidate equilibria are of particular significance – even in the case of proportional representation.

One relevant difference between equilibria in the winner-takes-all and winner-takes-most cases is that in the winner-takes-all case the only key parameter is the probability of being the winner, whereas in the case where the most successful non-winner gets some (smaller) share of the total rents – as for example in being *the* 'official opposition' party – then it may pay parties to enter even if the probability of actually winning is zero, provided the probability of gaining sufficient support is high enough. For example, in the uniform distribution case of the standard median voter model illustrated in figure 10.1, the pair of candidates (X_I, X_{II}) (where $X_I = \frac{2}{3}M$; and $X_{II} = \frac{4}{3}M$) is sufficient to deter entry from any potential third candidate if the winner takes all, and is therefore a potential equilibrium. But if the benefits from being the 'opposition' within parliament are high enough, then a third party can enter, at say $X_{III} = \frac{4}{3}M + \varepsilon$, and obtain the benefits of coming second and being the parliamentary opposition – even though it cannot win. To deter entry by a third party when there is a pay-off to coming second would require a two-party equilibrium such as (X_I', X_{II}') where $X_I' = \frac{1}{2}M$, $X_{II}' = \frac{3}{2}M$, where no third party entering could ensure second place.

So, a wider dispersal of political rents among contenders seems likely to lead to a greater dispersion in the political positions adopted, even if it does not lead to an increase in the number of parties. It would require analysis of a considerable number and range of models to establish this

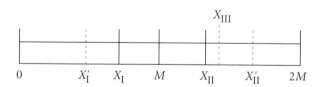

Figure 10.1 Winner takes all and winner takes most

[13] Osborne and Slivinski (1996), Besley and Coate (1997) both study the case of winner-takes-all election structures, while Hamlin and Hjortlund (1999) view the case of proportional representation.

proposition with any degree of generality, and we do not intend to engage that task here. We seek, rather, to make some general normative points about co-location, and the notion of 'electoral choice', partly because there seems to be some confusion on such matters in some of the political science and public choice literature. The confusion hovers around the normative status of (centrist) co-location. Misgivings seem to surround co-location because it is claimed to diminish electoral 'choice': if both parties in a winner-takes-all contest occupy the same position, this fact is often seen to undermine the reality of voter choice. Better, so the intuition goes, if there really *is* a difference between parties, some suitable ideological or policy divide, so that voters have a proper opportunity genuinely to declare their views. It is not clear where this intuition comes from, or on what it is grounded. It may well spring from a tendency to value electoral participation as such (and independently of the policy outcome to which voting gives rise), for it seems difficult to deny that, *ceteris paribus*, a greater dispersion of contestant positions generates more voting, under whichever of the models of voting behaviour one adopts (expressive or instrumental). Perhaps the perception is that voters become committed to the political outcome by participating in the election (even those who vote against the successful option) and that the increased perceived legitimacy increases compliance to governmental edicts (e.g. more regulatory compliance, higher taxpayer morality, etc.).[14] It is not clear, however, that any legitimacy effects involved here are not entirely spurious, dependent as they seem to be on what are essentially voter illusions. Unless the increased participation affects the political outcome, it is difficult to see how additional participation can increase legitimacy except by sleight of hand – and if the increased participation arises from changes that make political outcomes *qua* outcomes less defensible, then the whole legitimacy argument seems to rest on very shallow foundations. In the same spirit, arguments for proportional representation on the grounds that it is likely to increase voter turnout, or give voters more 'choice', seem to us to demand sceptical scrutiny.

In this connection, it needs to be clearly stated that the kind of co-location arising in the standard median voter model is presumptively *desirable*. Comparing, for example, the outcome in figure 10.1 where both parties locate at M with the (X_I, X_{II}) equilibrium, which yields the policy outcome of either X_I or X_{II} with probability $\frac{1}{2}$, the co-location at M outcome is manifestly preferred by a majority of voters and, for reasons connected with considerations tabled in chapter 6, is also superior on

---

[14] Frey (1997a, 1997b) argues this way, for example, in defence of direct democracy on the basis of Swiss evidence.

utilitarian grounds. To be sure, in the expressive voting analogue there must be some query as to whether the spectrum across which votes lie maps directly into citizens' interests: but in the absence of any *a priori* evidence on that question, there is an independent risk aversion argument in favour of centrist outcomes.[15]

The prejudice against party co-location, the idea that greater voter 'choice' is better than less, springs in part perhaps from the familiar economic aphorism that more choice is better than less. This is an idea that draws its force from the context of market arrangements for private goods. In the political context, however, it is an idea that requires careful application in only limited circumstances. To a significant extent, the relevant limits are intrinsic to collective choice. It is of the essence that collective decision making involves choosing an option that will apply equally to all citizens. Whether political decision making involves a single dimension or many, whether voting is instrumental or expressive, the task is to find a single outcome which is the best (or at least, the most acceptable) compromise between the judgements/views/preferences/values of individual citizens. When voters 'choose' between M, X_I or X_{II} or whatever in figure 10.1, only one outcome emerges: voters cannot have both X_I and X_{II}, according to individual preference or expressive opinion. This is a simple and self-evident point. But once it is accepted, the idea of 'increasing' voter choice via a larger range of options to vote for becomes recognisably problematic: ultimately only one outcome is possible. Furthermore, there are many more or less familiar contexts in the economic theory of politics where less choice is preferable to more. It may be a useful reminder here to catalogue a few of these contexts:

1. In prisoner's dilemma interactions, removing the 'off-diagonal' elements – reducing the domain of choice for each player – is one route to securing the Pareto-efficient outcome. [16]
2. In two-dimensional voting contexts, suppressing the deals via which representatives agree to trade votes across issues reduces representative choice but is supportive of stable majoritarian equilibria. (The 'structure-induced equilibrium' literature is precisely about institutional devices designed to suppress such deals.)
3. Indeed, the whole conception of 'constitutional economics' as the

---

[15] In one sense this is a particularly clear example of the distinction between *ex ante* and *ex post* ideas of welfare. *Ex ante* both alternatives offer the same expected outcome. But *ex post*, the outcomes differ systematically. In situations of this type the *ex post* criterion seems clearly superior, since individuals have no intrinsic interest in expected outcomes.

[16] See Buchanan and Congleton (1998).

choice *among* constraints (as distinct from the choice *within* constraints), to use Buchanan's description, suggests that one should choose what options one wants to close off as well as which options one might wish to render more accessible.

In the voting context, we do not deny that voters derive some intrinsic utility from voting for the electoral option that is closest to their respective 'ideal' points: indeed, this is precisely what is at stake in the expressive voting story. There is then a second-order utility benefit involved in being able to fulfil that particular preference more effectively. But this *is* a second-order matter, normatively speaking, even if – as we claim – it may be of first-order significance in explaining voting behaviour. The normatively first-order aspect must be the political outcome that emerges: and in this respect the provision of many voting options is likely to subvert the mechanism by which a single most-approved electoral outcome is chosen. Restricting both the number of effective agents within the parliament and the number of options available at the election, which a simple two-party system does, is a further example, we believe, of a potentially utility enhancing restriction on the extent of choice. Put another way, it is not more choice that is necessarily desirable; it is more effective choice over the relevant thing. In electoral choice, the object of ultimate normative significance is the set of policy decisions the elected government makes. Choice on that matter counts normatively: arrangements that obscure such choice are presumptively undesirable.

Party versus president

We now turn to our second type of comparison – between individual and team agency. In this section, we suppose a winner-takes-all contest. The comparison we seek to make is between the case in which the 'winner' in question is a single person (a president) or a team (a party). The argument we shall present is in favour of the party, over the president. It is an argument that can serve two rather different roles – one, the obvious normative one, of establishing a justification for one kind of institutional arrangement over another; the other, of suggesting why it might be the case that parties emerged fairly quickly in parliamentary experience as quite robust features of assembly life.

The central claim here is simply put. It is that parties have a longer life than do individual politicians (and more particularly, at any point, an indefinite life). This means that the discipline of continuous dealings, the constraint imposed by the desire to be elected at the *next* election, on which much of the logic of electoral discipline depends, is more effective with parties than with single presidents. Indeed, it may not (for 'backward induction' reasons) be effective with single presidents *at all*.

The backward induction problem can be most simply illustrated by appeal to the example in which there is a term limit, say of three electoral periods. Consider a president in his/her final term. It is clear enough that the threat of not being elected next time cannot be a discipline on presidential action: other constraints – the desire to be well regarded, internal dispositions, etc. – may be operative as a discipline, but the upcoming election cannot be. This being so, no voter has reason to think that the electoral threat will be effective at the next to last election either. If everyone knows that the president will not be constrained by the electoral threat in the final term (and that grounds if any for re-electing for the final term must depend on other considerations), then either those other considerations constitute the reason for electing the president to the final term, or they do not – in which case the next-to-last term will be the final one, the president will know this and will be undisciplined by the electoral constraint applying at the end of the next-to-last period. And analogously in the first term. The idea is that the failure of electoral discipline to work in the final period operates via a domino effect through the whole sequence back to the first period.

Now, even if there are no formal term limits, the logic of the backward induction argument goes through if, at some point, the likelihood that the incumbent will retire at the end of the period (or die in office) is sufficiently high. That is, the discipline imposed by the threat of the next election will not have sufficient force to make the incumbent act in the voters' interests.

The critical difference between the single agent and the party is that, in a real sense, the party *does* (or can) live forever, even though none of its members does. Suppose, for example, that each individual politician has a term limit of three periods. Suppose further that each politician would rationally act to exploit his power in his final period, but that each would want to be elected in non-final periods. Then if the party maintains an age structure such that there are at all times a majority of politicians in the party that are not in their final terms, then a majority within the party will always be in favour of postponing full exploitation. For example, a three-person party consisting of agents I, II and III with I in her final term, II in her second term and III in her first term will have I voting within the party for immediate exploitation, and II and III (a majority) voting *against* immediate exploitation (and for future exploitation). Next period, I will have retired and the party will consist of II, III and IV – of whom II will be in her final term, III in his next-to-last term and a replacement for I, IV, in her first term. Again, a majority will be against immediate exploitation (and for future exploitation). The relevant fact about future exploitation is that, like tomorrow in the aphorism, the future never comes. The party is such that the term structure of its membership is always the same in each period. The discipline of future elections may constrain the behaviour of political parties, therefore, in a way and/or to an extent that it is unlikely to constrain the behaviour of independent individual candidates.

This fact not only provides reasons why a party arrangement of political agency is to be preferred. It also provides a reason why parties may form more or less spontaneously in an assembly of independent members. If such teams, in which individual candidates effectively *pool* their reputations under the party label, are known to be more trustworthy (because always more susceptible to electoral constraint) than would be those same individuals operating separately, then parties will have an electoral advantage *ceteris paribus*. Parties will, therefore, tend to drive 'independent' candidates out.[17]

Of course, there may well be other sources of electoral advantage to parties – there may, for example, be economies of scale in reputation pooling, or it may be that increasing the number of votes the party can deliver increases the party's coalitional power more than proportionally. But the reputation pooling argument is not set at risk by any of these further considerations: party members have an expanded incentive to monitor one another's behaviour and to protect the party's reputation because the party lives or always expects to live beyond the current election.

There is some evidence, we might note, that politicians behave differently in mandated final terms from the way they behave in non-ultimate terms.[18] In itself, this finding does not sit particularly happily with the strict logic of the backward induction argument, since that argument predicts uniform behaviour in all periods. However, the finding does suggest that in some ways final periods are different and specifically that political agents act in a less disciplined fashion where there is no immediate electoral constraint. Because there is no final period for parties, this evidence is relevant to our case.

Conclusion

Political parties, though a common feature of functioning democracies, are often not a welcome feature – at least in much political theory.

---

[17] See Tirole (1996) on the analysis of collective reputations.
[18] See Besley and Case (1995) for a study of US state governors that draws this conclusion.

Within our broad rational actor approach, however, we believe that they have much to recommend them. This is so because the rational actor tradition foregrounds popular election as the primary discipline encouraging political outcomes that correspond to the demands of the electorate. Parties, at least in our view, seem likely to make elections go better in this critical respect. Generally, for reasons set out above, we think parties are likely to be more sensitive to electoral constraints, and hence more trustworthy, than are independent candidates. Furthermore and more specifically, we reckon that there is much to be said in favour of the two-party system of government. This system maximises the extent of electoral accountability: it imposes clear constraints of 'responsibility' on those who propose and implement policy initiatives, and in that sense tends to wash out whim, prejudice and ephemeral enthusiasm from voter judgements on policy questions. Moreover, the two-party system ensures a direct association between popular support (as reflected in number of seats won) and effective political power understood as the capacity to make or break majorities on the floor of the assembly – an association that does not obtain in general with more than two parties. At the level of electoral contest, the number of contenders is also relevant: the situation in which there are two salient parties encourages more centrist political equilibria (with centrist here interpreted in terms of the expressed wishes of the electorate), and that centrism is itself commendable under most plausible normative criteria.

These arguments will not perhaps much impress those who support a more discursive conception of democracy, or who think of the 'representative' assembly as the analogue of a body of independent jurors. And it will probably be no comfort to such analysts that their conceptions of democracy seem remote from most democratic practice. But within the kind of democratic practice that is familiar, it is not necessary to think of parties as a kind of necessary evil: a small number of strong parties makes the system work better than it seems likely to do in their absence. Attacks on party structure, or arguments for institutional arrangements that will diminish the power of parties and/or increase their number (as standard proportional representation voting systems may do, for example) seem to us to be mistaken: such arguments fail because they are not set in the context of a reasonably complete account of how the democratic system is intended to work, and more particularly of why it is that a larger number of parties will help the system work better.

11

The separation of powers

The accumulation of all powers, legislative, executive, and judiciary, in the same hands, whether of one, a few, or many, and whether hereditary, self-appointed, or elective, may justly be pronounced the very definition of tyranny.

(*Federalist* papers, 47, James Madison)

Separations and divisions of power

In the last three chapters we have been concerned with what might be termed the basic structure of modern representative democracy – popular elections, the idea of representation itself, and political parties as the major vehicles of representation. In this chapter and the next, we turn our attention to a rather different class of constitutional and institutional structures that have as their shared theme the idea of the separation or division of powers – the idea, that is, that structuring the political process in a manner that divides and separates political power will serve the interests of citizens. The doctrine of the separation of powers is, of course, both old and almost universally supported.[1] But what exactly does it entail? What does the separation of powers require at the operational level, and how exactly are the benefits to citizens generated? And does the argument for the separation of powers depend upon a particular model of politics? These are the key questions we wish to engage in this chapter and the next. Our first objective, then, is to

[1] Sabine (1973) and Vile (1967) provide discussions of the history of the doctrine. The classic authors include Locke, Montesquieu and Madison.

interrogate the definition of the separation of powers in an attempt to tease out its key ingredients. We will suggest that there are several distinct senses in which the 'separation of powers' might be read and that these senses point to different analyses and different normative conclusions.

In particular, we distinguish two senses of the 'separation of powers', each of which gives rise to several subcases. The distinction may be conceived as one between the separation of powers and the division of power. What we have in mind here is that separating powers involves the pulling apart of distinct powers and allocating them to distinct agents, rather than bundling them together in the hands of a single agent. This sense of the separation of powers is exemplified by the functional division of powers between the executive, the legislature and the judiciary, with each set of powers separated from the others and placed in different hands. By contrast, the division of power is to take a particular power (or set of powers) and spread it across agents so that no one individual is uniquely powerful. This sense of the division of power is exemplified by the move from a single all-powerful president to a cabinet in which the same powers are collectively held by a group of individuals, so that the exercise of power requires agreement across agents. Other examples of the 'division' of power in this sense include bicameralism and coalitional government, where the structure implies that any decision has to be agreed by both houses of a bicameral legislature, or all parties to the coalition. In such cases, each house or party has a form of veto power, and no house or party can act independently. We will postpone discussion of the 'division of power', so understood, to the next chapter. The remainder of this chapter will focus on the separation of powers in the first sense.

There are two rather different intuitions which seem to underlie the normative appeal of the separation of powers – two different ways in which we might conceive of the separation of powers acting to provide checks or balances on the abuse of power and to promote the interests of citizens. It will be useful to spell these intuitions out in some detail. The first intuition relies on a form of strategic interaction between powerful agents. Consider the following simple example. The task to be performed is the allocation of a resource of fixed size among a population of N individuals. If the power to determine the allocation is wholly vested in a single individual, that individual will face an incentive to bias the allocation towards himself (subject to any other constraints on the process). If, on the other hand, the bundle of powers involved in allocating the resource are separated into, say, a power to split the resource into N parts and a further power to distribute these parts among individuals, with the power to split vested in one individual and the power to distribute vested in another individual, then the incentives and the expected outcome will be very different. When $N = 2$ this is simply the 'you-cut-and-I'll-choose' method of cake division, which will ensure equal division even when both agents are entirely selfish (assuming no other constraints apply).[2] The point we wish to emphasise for the moment is simply that the strategic separation of powers operates by creating a form of multilateral monopoly with each agent having a monopoly over a subpower. The interactive tension between the agents – all with their own objectives – is then argued to benefit citizens, if the interaction is appropriately structured.

The second intuitive model of the separation of powers relates to the notion of competition rather than multilateral monopoly. Government is characterised – and often defined – by its possession of a monopoly in the legitimate exercise of coercive power. Such a monopoly threatens the exploitation of citizens, and the intuition is simply that a reduction in monopoly power by means of a move in the direction of competition might serve to protect citizens from exploitation. But exactly what do we mean by 'competition' in this context? If monopoly is essential to the very definition of government, how can we design governmental institutions to incorporate competition?

One possibility that we will stress in what follows is the provision of exit options to citizens. The now-standard contrast between 'exit' and 'voice' as alternative means of influencing outcomes normally associates exit most closely with competitive markets and voice most closely with non-market processes; indeed, popular elections are a paradigmatic example of the voice mechanism. But it is clearly possible to think of the use of exit options – and the competition that goes with exit options – within at least some aspects of government. One familiar example is that of federalism and the exit option that is provided via the mobility of citizens between states.[3] State governments can be conceived as offering different and competing portfolios of tax and expenditure policies, with

---

[2] When $N > 2$ the outcome may depend on details that need not concern us here, but the general idea that so long as the individual who has the power to cut the cake is allocated the slice of cake that is least desired, we can expect the equal division outcome will continue to hold, since in these circumstances the cutter will face an incentive to maximise the size of the smallest slice of cake.

[3] The exit/voice distinction was introduced by Hirschman (1971). The classic reference on mobility between states as a mechanism for providing information on the demand for local public goods is Tiebout (1956). For a discussion of federal competition that emphasises the exit/voice contrast see Marlow (1992), for an overview of the political economy literature on federalism see Brennan and Hamlin (1998b).

at least some citizens choosing their locations on the basis of the policies set by different state governments. There are two advantages in this federal arrangement: any policy differences offer alternatives to citizens in any state and thereby limit the scope for citizen exploitation; and to the extent that governments of states prefer more citizens (or tax base) to fewer, those governments will have an incentive to offer citizens the policies those citizens prefer.[4] The point we wish to stress here is simply that the introduction of competition based on some sort of exit option seems to provide a rather different account of the separation of powers from that provided by the strategic interaction account outlined above. In the federal case, the power to tax and provide local services in different locations is separated and allocated to different bodies, in the expectation that the competition between these bodies will serve the interests of citizens. In the resource allocation problem outlined earlier, the various agencies do not compete with each other by offering alternative allocations, but rather determine an allocation as a result of the interplay of their monopoly powers.

These two apparently different accounts of the operation of the separation of powers should alert us to the fact that no single clear-cut argument in support of the separation of powers exists. In fact, there has been remarkably little analytic work addressing the limits of the intuitive arguments.[5] The doctrine of the separation of powers is, in our view, best seen as a cluster of propositions each of which draws on rather different intuitions and models. A major aim of this chapter is to examine some of these propositions in more detail. Our question throughout is whether the apparently widespread confidence in the separation of powers as a means of promoting and protecting citizens' interests is really justified. Our answer is that it all depends on the details of how powers are separated. There can be no presumption that separating powers will always act in the interests of citizens; indeed, some separations that seem to fit within the traditional doctrine may actually harm citizens. We attempt to isolate the considerations which pull in favour of the strategy of separation and those that pull against. We begin by investigating the strategic and competitive accounts of the separation of powers in turn, in

---

[4] Clearly, these are independent advantages. There could be differences between states offering choices to citizens with state governments being indifferent as to numbers of citizens. And equally, the competition for citizen numbers and/or the associated tax base could be present when all states are identical in equilibrium.

[5] Recent analytic papers which offer discussion of the separation of powers include Hammond and Miller (1987), Brennan and Hamlin (1994), Persson *et al.* (1997, 1998), Segal (1997). These papers typically offer specific models rather than discussion of the potential range and limits of the doctrine.

the context of the traditional economic model of rational politics. With that discussion in place, we will then extend the discussion to our more moralised, more expressive model of representative democracy.

Before we begin, there are two basic points that require emphasis. The first is that any separation or division of power must actually involve different agents in the political process if it is to be effective. A purely formal separation of division of power which locates this power in this office and that power in that office can have no real effect if the two offices are under common control. This point is most obviously relevant in the presence of strong political parties. If a single disciplined party holds all of the key offices, it is difficult to see how any separation or division of power with respect to those offices can provide additional constraints on that party. However, this point should not be overplayed; it is only in the limiting case of a perfectly disciplined party, or otherwise identical political agents that the separation or division of powers can have no effect. In all other cases, there may be some effect, even though it might be muted. Since this point applies to both separations and divisions of powers and points to a possible modification of arguments concerning parties presented in the previous chapter, we will defer further discussion until the end of the next chapter.

The second point to be emphasised concerns the normative criteria to be applied in judging the separation of powers. Whatever the details of the argument, the separation of powers operates via imposing some check on the abuse of power – by denying politicians access to rents or otherwise constraining their behaviour. But constraining politicians is not an end in itself, and there is no reason to suppose that there is a direct one to one relationship between limiting the pay-offs to politicians and improving the pay-offs to citizens. Indeed, we will draw attention to cases in which this relationship fails. It is the provision of benefits to citizens, rather than the imposition of checks on politicians, that provides the central normative criterion by which the separation of powers should ultimately be judged.

Strategic separation of powers

We will consider first the 'strategic interaction' interpretation of the separation of powers. Under this interpretation, functions are separated out so as to create strategic incentives between agents with different powers. Our initial aim here is to provide a relatively detailed account of the possible disadvantages of such a functional separation of powers – disadvantages that seem potentially relevant to a number of standard applications of the classical doctrine. Separating functions that might otherwise be integrated opens up the potential for adverse strategic interactions, or creates 'externalities' that a more integrated political structure would internalise. Initially, we will develop this idea in the context of a simple stylised model of the separation of powers between a legislature and an executive. In building up the model, for convenience, and to provide a benchmark, we will first sketch out the behaviour of an autocratic and all-powerful government that is not subject to any democratic constraint. We will then introduce popular elections in making a move towards a more democratic, but still monolithic, form of government. Finally we will impose a functional separation of powers on the model.

Autocratic government

Suppose that government is entrusted with the supply of a composite public good (G) that is produced under conditions of constant average cost. We will abstract from the issues concerned with the revelation of demand for public goods and assume that the aggregate demand curve for the public good is accurately perceived by all political actors. Political agents, we assume, are motivated by the surplus associated with holding office and, under autocracy, are unconstrained in their ability to appropriate this surplus. However, we assume that this surplus ultimately derives from the public good supplied. This has two immediate implications. First, it places a bound on government's ability to exploit its citizens – government can, at most, expropriate all the surplus generated by public activity. Second, it provides government with an incentive to provide the optimal quantity of G – that is, the quantity that maximises total surplus. Of course, in the case of autocracy, the government will then expropriate the whole of the surplus, so that citizens are left indifferent between such a government and no government at all (and no public good). This is illustrated in figure 11.1 for the case of a linear demand curve for the public good, G. The marginal cost curve (MC) indicates the constant cost of producing G, and the optimal quantity of the public good is given by L^*. The autocratic government would supply L^*, but would then capture the whole of the consumers' surplus given by the area of the triangle DEF.

Electoral control

We contrast the foregoing case with a more democratic structure in which the government is elected under a winner-takes-all electoral system, with all voters assumed to vote in a self-interested way. There will be two rival candidates (A and B) who compete for votes by offering

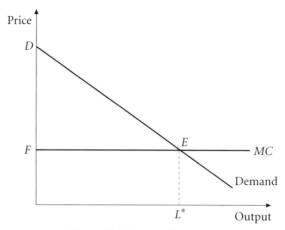

Figure 11.1 Autocratic government

policy positions which promise different levels of surplus to citizens. As before, candidates are motivated by the surplus that can be captured from the supply of *G*. Note that each candidate will still face an incentive to supply the optimal quantity of the public good. Put simply, from the point of view of a candidate, any policy platform which does not include a commitment to the optimal level of *G* will be dominated by a platform which does include such a commitment and is otherwise identical – since this will improve the candidate's probability of winning the election at no cost.

If the separation of powers is to have any chance of providing benefits to citizens we must model the electoral constraint on policy making as imperfect. If we were to adopt the standard model of winner-takes-all electoral competition, the unique equilibrium would involve each candidate offering the entire surplus associated with the optimal level of G to the citizens – any attempt to retain any part of the surplus would result in losing the election to a rival candidate who offered citizens more surplus. This is simply the standard median-voter result in which simple electoral competition fully constrains politicians to act in the public interest. In that case, there is no work for the separation of powers – or any other piece of constitutional machinery – to do. In order to make the issue of separation of powers relevant, we abandon the implausible assumption of the sharp discontinuity in the pay-offs to rival candidates. So, in our model, when candidates announce their platforms – the amount of surplus offered to citizens (S_A, S_B) – the fact that *A*'s platform offers citizens' less surplus than B's is not sufficient in itself to drive the probability of A winning the election to zero. More specifically, we will model the probability of either candidate winning the election (P_A, P_B) as a function of the difference between their platforms, so that:

$$P_i = f(S_i - S_j) \text{ for } i, \ j = A, \ B \text{ and } i \neq j,$$

where we assume only that

$$f(0) = \frac{1}{2}, \ f'(.) > 0,$$

so that if the candidates offer identical platforms, they will each win with probability $\frac{1}{2}$, and a candidate increasing the amount of surplus offered to citizens relative to the rival candidate, will always improve her chance of winning. For convenience, we will define the gradient of this function at the point where the candidates offer identical platforms, $f'(0) = \alpha$.

With this amendment to the standard model of one-dimensional electoral competition, it is still the case that the two candidates will adopt the same platform in equilibrium, but this platform will not involve all of the surplus being passed on to citizens. Specifically, if each candidate attempts to maximise the expected value of her own surplus, defined as:

$$P_i(S - S_i) \text{ for } i = A, \ B$$

where S is the fixed level of aggregate surplus associated with the optimal supply of G, subject to the specification of P_i given above, the resulting symmetric equilibrium will be one in which each candidate announces the platform S^* where:

$$S - S* = \frac{f(0)}{f'(0)} = \frac{1}{2\alpha}.$$

In equilibrium, then, the surplus captured by government ($S - S^*$) depends only on α, the sensitivity of the probability of victory function to small differences in the platforms of the two candidates. If α is large, the constraint imposed on policy by the force of electoral competition is tight, and the surplus captured by government correspondingly small. In the limit as $\alpha \to \infty$ we approach the discontinuous case of the median-voter result where electoral competition is fully constraining. If α is small, the constraint imposed on policy by the force of electoral competition is lax, and the surplus captured by government correspondingly large. In the limit, as $\alpha \to 0$, we approach the case in which the result of the election is independent of the platforms adopted, so that government will act as an unconstrained monopolist and capture the whole of the available surplus.

To summarise, in terms of figure 11.1, the introduction of the electoral constraint will not affect the quantity of the public good supplied – L^* – or the total quantity of surplus created – S is simply the area DEF. The electoral constraint will just determine the share of the surplus captured by government and the share passed on to citizens, with the shares depending on the value of α.

Separating powers

The next stage is to introduce a second branch of government so that the powers associated with the supply of G may be separated between the branches of government along functional lines. We will refer to the first branch of government – modelled above in terms of electoral competition for office – as the legislature, and add an equally stylised model of a separate executive. We conceive of the executive branch as providing the legislature with a well defined and priced menu of policy alternatives. In our simple case, where government is concerned only with the supply of a single composite public good, this amounts to the executive providing a price at which it stands ready to supply that public good in a quantity to be decided by the legislature. In a more complicated model with more than one government activity, there is a third power – a power of agenda control in delimiting which combinations of activities are to be considered as viable alternatives. That power might be allocated to the executive, the legislature or some third body (perhaps a subcommittee of the legislature). Here, in the interests of simplicity, we restrict the number of powers to two.

We will take the executive branch of government to be motivated by the prospect of the capture of surplus in a manner that is essentially identical to the legislature – so that all political agents are motivated identically. In this case, there are two possible types of constraint that might be relevant to the behaviour of the executive: a constraint imposed by means of the method of appointing or electing members, and a constraint imposed by the nature of the interaction with the legislature. We will focus on the second type of constraint since this better corresponds to the separation of powers idea.

We shall assume the following sequence of events. First, the executive announces its price of the public good G, which is then public knowledge. The two candidates for legislative power then announce their platforms. The election then determines the winner of the election who implements the announced policy. With the model set up in this way, it should be easy to see that this separation of powers between the legislature and the executive will act against the interests of citizens, and that the unification of powers would offer a Pareto improvement with both citizens and

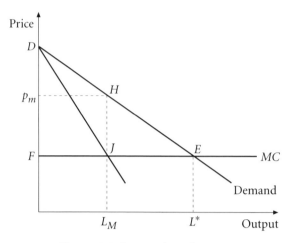

Figure 11.2 A separation of powers

politicians gaining.[6] The basic point can be explained as follows. Constrained only by the relevant demand curve for the public good and the
expected behaviour of the legislature, the executive will maximise the
surplus that it captures by setting a price above the cost of production of
G. This is illustrated in figure 11.2, which repeats the basic structure of
figure 11.1. The price announced by the executive to maximise its surplus
will be p_m, and the surplus captured by the executive is given by the area
of the rectangle p_mHJF. Given the price p_m, the rival candidates for
legislative office will set their platforms to supply the quantity L_M, so that
the surplus measured by the triangle HDp_m is realised and shared between
consumers and the legislature according to the value of α.

   The essential point here is that this separation of powers has secured a
reduction in the quantity of the public good supplied (from L^* under
either the autocratic or the simple elected government to L_M) and a
consequent reduction in the total surplus available (from the area DEF to
the area $DHJF$) as well as shifted the shares of the surplus going to
government and to citizens in favour of government (seen as the sum of
the two branches).

   Compared with the simple elected government structure, this separation of powers has introduced an externality into the system, and reduced
the surplus accruing to citizens. In this case, the fact that the executive

---

[6] Formally, this model is the same as the model of the vertical separation of
   monopoly firms, and the potential benefits of vertical integration, familiar in
   industrial economics – see, for example Tirole (1988), chapter 4.2. Brennan and
   Hamlin (1994) discussed the analogy with models of monopoly in more detail.

and the legislature act independently of each other is a problem rather than a solution. We would emphasise that this is so even though the interests of the executive and the legislature are opposed, so that the action of each acts against the interests of the other. Allowing the two branches of government to collude would allow them to increase the surplus they capture; but it would also increase the surplus available to the citizens by internalising the externality. To see this most clearly, consider the variation of the model in which the executive and the legislature are allowed to collude: that is, to make enforceable agreements which are in their mutual interests. In particular, assume that they combine in the attempt to maximise the total surplus flowing to government, given that they have two distinct powers to operate. For concreteness, consider the case in which the demand curve is given by:

$$D - sL = p,$$

and where $MC = 0$. Assume also that L is such that the electoral constraint would divide any available surplus between a simple elected legislature and the citizens equally. It is simple to show that, in this case, the complete separation of powers as described above will generate an 'executive price' of $D/2$, with the relevant surplus going to citizens of $D^2/16s$, and to government $5D^2/16s$. If the two branches of government collude, they will seek to maximise:

$$pL + \frac{(D - p)L}{4},$$

and it is easy to check that this will require the setting of an 'executive price' of $D/3$, with the relevant surplus flowing to citizens of $D^2/9s$, and to government $D^2/3s$. The move to collusion is Pareto efficient, since both government and citizens receive increased benefits. Of course, in this simple example, the citizens could be made still better off by a return to the simple elected government structure where the executive function is completely absorbed by the legislature. But our point here is that even if this outcome were not available, collusion between the branches of government might be beneficial to citizens. In this simple model, the separation of powers certainly succeeds in restricting the rents available to politicians, but it also fails to serve the interests of citizens.

A wider view

We do not claim that this simple model captures all that is important for the analysis of the strategic interaction interpretation of the separation of powers. We offer this model only as a cautionary tale – in the form of a detailed counter-example to the intuition that the strategic separation of powers will always or generally benefit citizens. While that intuition points to a class of potential benefits that may flow from the separation of powers, our example points to a class of potential costs. The precise details of our example are not crucial: similar results could be obtained whenever the separation of powers in question generates an externality between the power-holders. Persson *et al.* (1997) provide another example of this sort. Their model studies two separately elected authorities each of which has the independent power to appropriate rents, subject only to some aggregate budget constraint. They show that the imposition of this sort of separation of powers will generally harm citizens relative to the alternative in which a single elected authority has the general power to appropriate rents. They term this the 'common-pool problem' to emphasise the link with the idea of the form of externality present in the 'tragedy of the commons'. They go on to argue that the separation of powers will work in the interests of citizens only if the two powerful authorities are forced to agree to a common policy so that each has a form of veto power over the other. This interpretation of the separation of powers fits more naturally with what we have described as the division of a power and we will consider that case in the next chapter.

However, in a second paper, Persson *et al.* (1998) offer a rather different interpretation of the separation of powers – one that does not depend on veto power. In that paper, the idea of the separation of powers invokes similar issues to the 'you-cut-and-I'll-choose' example sketched above. In outline, the separation of powers is modelled in terms of the structure of agenda control: one authority decides on a level of taxation, and hence on the size of the government budget, while a second authority then allocates that budget between the supply of a public good and redistribution between sections of the population. Each authority is subject to the discipline of elections, but (as is necessary in any model of the separation of powers) that discipline is imperfect. In their particular case, the separation of powers works in the interests of citizens because of the details of the imperfection of electoral control, and the nature of the relationship between the political authorities and the various sections of the population. Effectively, each possible political authority represents a distinct section of the population – in the simple case, each politician represents a geographic constituency, where these constituencies also map out the potential patterns of redistribution. And each politician will be re-elected only if the citizens of her constituency receive at least some threshold level of utility. When the powers of tax setting and budget allocation are possessed by a single politician, that politician will set tax rates that are higher than optimal in order to raise revenues for redistribution towards her own constituents, which will in turn increase the probability of her own re-election. However, when the powers are separated in the manner described, the politician representing constituency 1 who has the primary power to set the taxation level will know that the secondary power of redistribution lies in the hands of another politician representing another constituency – so that redistribution can be expected to work against the interests of the citizens of constituency 1 and therefore diminish the probability of re-election of the incumbent politician in that constituency. The primary politician will therefore face an incentive to reduce tax rates relative to the case of unified power as a means of tying the hands of the secondary politician.

Clearly, different models produce different results. And this obvious conclusion is an important one, since it undermines any *general* claim that a separation of powers must always benefit citizens. It might be argued that no one ever really made such a sweeping claim on behalf of the separation of powers; but rereading the classic texts and more recent informal treatments of the topic suggests to us that such a claim is at least implicit. The mistake involved arises because the separation of powers does generally work to reduce the rents that political agents can extract; but it can do so as much by reducing total benefits from public activity as by reducing the share that goes to political agents. The fundamental point is that the separation of powers serves to introduce a form of externality between powers. Whether any particular separation of powers will operate in the interests of citizens will depend on exactly how the externality operates – separations that generate considerable externalities but relatively little in the way of positive strategic benefits can clearly act against the interests of citizens.

Competitive separation of powers

As already mentioned, the alternative to the strategic interaction interpretation of the separation of powers is an interpretation that draws explicitly on the idea of competition as a means of limiting monopoly power. As with the case of the strategic interaction interpretation, the intuition for the claimed benefit of the competitive separation of powers seems clear cut at first glance. Just as there is a general argument for the introduction of competition in markets for private goods based on the incentives generated by consumers' ability effectively to choose between alternative suppliers, so there seems to be a similar argument for competition within government where such competition is feasible.[7] Again, the basic source of the intuition is that arranging government in such a way that there are effective choices to be made between real alternatives – genuine exit options – will provide the suppliers of these alternatives with incentives that will serve the interests of citizens. As before, we will argue that this intuition is too quick – that it glosses over considerations that pull in the opposite direction. But before we put that argument, we wish to make two preliminary points on the competitive interpretation of the separation of powers.

The first point concerns the relationship between the competitive separation of powers and an alternative idea of competition within politics: the idea of electoral competition, which might be termed a competition *for* power. Electoral competition provides an obvious and important example of the potential advantages associated with a form of competition in politics. But the analysis of electoral competition is not an appropriate starting point for the analysis of the competitive separation of powers, for two rather different reasons. At one level, the two forms of competition might be seen as substitutes – as alternative means to the same ends. Just as in a market context we might imagine attempting to control a potentially monopolistic industry either by means of franchising the monopoly to the firm that offers the best (from the consumers' point of view) combination of price and quality commitments, or by encouraging the entry of a number of competitive firms, so in the case of politics we might attempt to control the power of government by *ex ante* competition between rival candidates for office or by structuring government so that it displays *ex post* competition between alternative government agencies. The question of whether and to what extent the second strategy is reliable as a means of serving the interests of citizens is then the key question to be addressed, and the answer to this question should be independent of our analysis of the first strategy.

At another level, however, electoral competition and the competitive separation of powers might be seen as complements – as parts of an overall institutional structure working together to deliver good government: Electoral competition, even when optimally deployed, is unlikely to deliver perfect government; the elected will generally retain some discretionary power to depart from the wishes of the electorate. It is here that the quest for further constitutional protection via the separation of powers begins. Accordingly, we need to analyse competitive separations

---

[7] Of course, the traditional economic argument for competition in private markets is not universal – there are, for example, exceptions involving increasing returns to scale, so-called 'natural' monopolies which might be thought to mirror the idea that at least some aspects of government are 'natural' monopolies.

of power in the context of structures that also incorporate electoral competition (as was also true in the case of strategic separations of power).

For this reason, care must be taken not to confuse the idea of electoral competition (or other similar competitions for power in politics, such as the use of competitive promotion policies within political hierarchies) with the idea of the competitive separation of powers within a governmental structure that may already employ such electoral competition for power. At the analytic level, electoral competition is an *ex ante*, voice-based mechanism well suited to the circumstances of the choice of a particular government – a classic example of a public good. The competitive separation of powers, by contrast, is an *ex post*, exit-based mechanism which depends on the ability of (at least some) agents to make real and effective choices between multiple suppliers. This implies that the competitive separation of powers will require a degree of 'privateness' in the service to be provided; a competitive market with multiple suppliers will not work well in the case of a pure public good.

The second preliminary point builds on the fact that the competitive separation of powers requires a degree of 'privateness'. We note that, even in principle, we cannot expect the competitive separation of governmental powers to offer a full escape from the principal–agent problem of government. The nature of government is such that elements of both monopoly and publicness are definitional. It is simply not possible to imagine the competitive provision of all aspects of government. This is a simple enough point, but it serves to underline the distinction between the idea of the competitive separation of powers and other constitutional devices such as electoral competition or the strategic interaction account of the separation of powers, either of which, in principle, could generate perfect outcomes. At best, the competitive separation of powers is of limited value – some powers simply cannot be separated in this way. Of course, this does not mean that the competitive separation of powers should be discarded as an idea – perfection is not a prerequisite of usefulness – but it does point to the importance of questions of feasibility in any particular case.

Within the framework suggested by these points, the basic question is then whether a competitive separation of powers – where such a separation is feasible – will act in the interests of citizens relative to an otherwise similar baseline case in which powers are unified. Just as in the case of the strategic interaction approach to the separation of powers, our answer is that everything will depend on the details. There are, we claim, examples where the competitive separation of powers can make citizens worse off. And the logic underlying these examples is similar to the logic of the strategic interaction case. These examples fall roughly into two groups: one group in which the problem lies in the specific nature of the particular powers that are separated, and a second group in which the problem is more structural in nature. Since federalism provides perhaps the leading example of the competitive separation of powers, capturing as it does the idea of competition between government bodies within the framework of a single constitution,[8] – we will outline in turn each kind of example in the context of a federal separation of powers.

Tax competition between state governments provides a first example in which the competitive separation of particular powers may act against the interests of citizens. In a world in which at least some resources are mobile between states, allocating the power to levy taxes to state governments will produce competition between states that will drive tax rates on mobile resources down to levels which may be below the levels required for efficiency. Tax competition, in other words, may distort the tax system by lowering taxes on mobile resources and raising taxes on immobile resources. A number of other tax inefficiencies may also arise, as state governments face incentives to export taxes and pursue a range of 'beggar-thy-neighbour' policies. And all of this is so even where each state government is assumed to be motivated to maximise social welfare within its own state. When state governments are modelled more in line with the economic model of politics – so that politicians are more self-interested, but democratically elected – then similar results can arise, but with the additional element that tax competition between states may now also limit each government's ability to capture surplus.[9] There can, however, be no guarantee that a competitive, federal separation of powers will act to the benefit of citizens in such models since, as before, the separation of powers introduces two forces pulling in opposite directions. One force acts to limit the power of government to extract surplus, but the other introduces a distorting externality between the government bodies. Either of these forces may dominate in a particular case; but note that the stronger is the discipline exerted by electoral competition, the more likely it is that the competition between state governments is damaging. In the limit, where electoral competition acts to ensure that politicians act entirely in the interests of their constituents, only the externality effect remains.

This case of tax competition points up the basic similarity between this

[8] For recent analysis and discussion of the federal case see Epple and Romer (1991), Hochman, Pines and Thisse (1995), Inman and Rubinfeld (1996), Persson and Tabellini (1996a, 1996b).
[9] See Brennan and Buchanan (1980), chapter 8, for analysis along these lines.

form of competitive separation of powers and the strategic interaction form of the separation of powers, discussed earlier. In each case, it is the deliberate introduction of an externality that defines the separation of powers; and the imposition of this externality can obviously work to the disadvantage of citizens.

The power to tax is not the only power that might feasibly be separated along competitive, federal lines: each power that might be allocated to state governments should be inspected for potentially perverse externality effects of the type outlined. Redistribution policy provides an extreme example. Epple and Romer (1991) provide a model in which redistribution policy is decentralised to the level of state governments in the face of mobility of individuals between states. Their model shows that mobility places strict limits on the extent of any redistribution that can occur in such a world, and that perfectly free mobility rules out any redistribution. The idea underlying this model is the same as that underlying the tax competition story. Any state government announcing a redistributive policy (from rich to poor, say) will encourage the in-migration of the poor and the out-migration of the rich, which will offset the state's ability to operate the policy. The more sensitive are migration flows to such policies, the less effective such policies can be. And it is worth noting that this can be true even if the intrastate redistribution is universally approved by all resident state citizens.

At the opposite extreme, certain government expenditure functions which relate to relatively immobile resources might be separated along federal lines without introducing significant externalities. We do not wish to enter into the detailed discussion of precisely which powers might usefully be separated along competitive, federal lines; the basic point we wish to emphasise, once again, is simply that not all separations of powers of this type will be beneficial.

Whereas the first group of examples concerns cases in which the competitive, federal separation of powers can have perverse effects in the case of specific powers – those which generate considerable (negative) externalities between the state governments – the second group of examples identifies a more structural aspect of the problem. The difficulty here is that not *all* governmental powers can be made subject to competitive separations. In the case of federalism, there will always be some residual role for a central, federal government: the structure of government will always include both horizontal and vertical relationships – horizontal relationships between state governments, and vertical relationships between each state government and the central, federal government. Any attempt to secure a horizontal, competitive separation of powers must also create vertical, functional separations of powers, so that, even if the horizontal separations offer benefits to citizens when considered in isolation, these benefits may be offset or even overwhelmed by the potential externalities introduced in the vertical separations.

A clear example of this type is provided by the interaction between state and federal taxes, first analysed by Flowers (1988). Consider a federal economy in which both state and federal governments have tax raising powers. Even if there are no tax competition problems in the relationships between the various state governments, there will be an externality in the relationship between each state government and the federal government since each is attempting to raise revenue from the same generalised tax base, and with the independent action imposed by full 'separation', neither will face any incentive to account for the impact of its tax policy on the revenue raising potential of the other government. As Flowers shows, both levels of government will be led to impose rates of tax such that the combined tax rate lies above the rate that a single government would impose, leaving citizens worse off *in toto*.

So, the separation of powers – whether conceived in terms of the strategic tension between monopolists or in terms of the creation of competition between government agencies – is prone to introduce unnecessary externalities and so reduce the aggregate surplus created by government activity. At the same time, the separation of powers – in either form – may be expected to reduce the ability of politicians to capture surplus. These forces offset each other when seen from the relevant normative perspective. Of course, in almost all of these cases, it is possible to internalise the externality by appropriate policy actions. In the federal examples, it will normally be possible to design revenue-sharing schemes, or systems of transfers between states that will allow of the efficient outcome. But this fact is of little interest in itself, because such schemes amount to no more than undermining the separation that is the object of analysis. Besides, the fact that it is conceptually possible to overcome the problems introduced by the separation of powers is no reason to believe that the problems will be overcome in any practical political setting. Put bluntly, we would require that the political process itself – including the relevant specification of the separation of powers – provides for the internalisation of the relevant externality, and this is far from guaranteed. As Persson and Tabellini (1996a, 1996b) and Inman and Rubinfeld (1996) point out, the operation of democratic political processes at the federal level is just as likely to amplify the problems created by political process at the state level as it is to ameliorate them. And the same is true more generally: there can be no guarantee that the ordinary democratic process will act to internalise the externalities that the separation of powers explicitly creates, and if there were it is difficult to see how the separation could do any work at all even in those cases where its effects were desirable.

The separation of powers and 'democratic desires'

So far we have been concerned to argue, contrary to the conventional intuition, that the separation of powers – taken to mean the unbundling of powers which are then placed in the hands of distinct political agents – will not necessarily benefit citizens. The entire discussion has, however, been cast in terms of the standard economic approach to politics and its motivational assumptions in particular. It has been a particular theme of the earlier part of this book that these assumptions are quite narrow – and, indeed, too narrow to form a satisfactory basis for a plausible constitutional political economy. Are we not, then, guilty of failing to practise what we preach? We offer two broad lines of argument in our defence: one of which points to the continuing relevance of the 'narrow' analysis, the other of which attempts to modify that analysis to render it still more relevant.

The first argument recalls that some of our concern regarding the 'narrow' economic approach derives from the criticism of the assumption of instrumental behaviour, particularly in the setting of democratic elections. Our account of the expressive nature of voting in large-scale elections, and the implications of such behaviour for the nature of electoral competition and the idea of representation, offers an alternative model, and alternative normative conclusions. But, despite this, we would suggest that the analysis of the separation of powers may most appropriately be carried out under the assumption of instrumental behaviour by the relevant political agents – so that, at least in this respect, the 'narrow' models of the separation of powers are still of direct relevance. This suggestion follows from the simple fact that the institutional devices that instantiate the separation of powers in modern representative democracies do so at the representative level, rather than at the popular level. And at the level of representatives, where numbers are relatively small and individual actions may be seen to be significant in determining outcomes, the assumption of instrumental behaviour is entirely reasonable. In other words, the expressive account of behaviour is directly relevant for voters in large number elections but only derivatively applicable at the level of the political agents themselves.

If we accept that representatives will typically act instrumentally – or at least that instrumental considerations will loom large in their decision making – we do not need to suppose that these representatives are produced by an instrumental process. And indeed, we explicitly deny that supposition. Specifically, we have argued that the identity and character of the representatives, elected under political institutions that encourage expressive behaviour, will differ significantly from those elected by a purely instrumental and self-interested electorate. In particular, we have argued that the electoral process will tend to select representatives who exhibit the dispositions or characters that are morally approved in society, and that this process may well be enhanced if the electoral choice is dominated by strong political parties. We have also argued that this tendency to elect representatives with relevant moral dispositions will tend to improve political outcomes for citizens. The question now is how the analysis of the separation of powers as a further institutional device will be affected by the fact that the political agents involved, though they themselves will act instrumentally, are selected by voters with an eye to candidates' dispositions and moral character.

The first point to note is simply that the more successful is the electoral process in selecting appropriate 'types' as representatives, the less work there should be for any separation of powers to do. If the electoral process is more likely to elect saints, there will be less need to constrain their behaviour. Of course, if the separation of powers were costless, it would be sensible to adopt the relevant institutions whatever the moral character of the representatives – the separation would simply offer a form of free insurance. But as we have been at pains to point out, separation is rarely costless. And when insurance is costly, you will buy less of it as the underlying risk diminishes.

However, there is a second and rather more subtle point to be made. The separation of powers, as we have modelled it, implies a sort of specialisation of political roles – political roles are increased in number and each role is more narrowly defined. And this specialisation may increase the scope for selection in the election of particular political agents. It is not difficult to imagine, for example, that the disposition most suited to the role as a legislator is rather different from the disposition most suited to the role as a judge, and that in separating the roles and powers of the legislature and the judiciary we are allowing these roles to be filled by more appropriate types. This observation opens up a line of argument in support of the separation of powers as an institutional tactic that is completely different from that studied so far. It is a line of argument that depends on motivational and dispositional heterogeneity and so fits into the category that we labelled as virtue enhancing mechanisms in the discussion of chapter 5. The separation of powers, on this account, makes room for a greater degree of selection and, therefore, a better use of the available stock of virtue in society.

This line of argument seems, at first sight, to make no reference to the need to separate the powers or roles in such a way that the powers are opposed to each other; it might seem that *any* separation of powers that creates two more specialised roles out of one existing role would offer the potential for more finely tuned selection. And this claim seems right if what we have in mind is selection for different talents or capacities. But the separation of powers specifically is designed to deal with what we have termed, somewhat loosely, the principal–agent problem in politics, and in this setting what is critical is not different talents so much as different motivations. So, for example, we may want to select as assembly members those who have a particular concern with the public interest, and as judges those who have an inordinate affection for the constitutional documents or a compulsion to follow prevailing rules and conventions. It may be that to secure these selectional ambitions, the selection mechanisms themselves should be rather different – say, popular elections for the former, and appointment of successors by incumbents in the latter case. Such differences may not only support the different roles, but also create rather different incentive structures within the 'separated' arenas. However, the point about this kind of separation is that, in so far as it is designed to ameliorate principal–agent problems, it will operate on a 'checks and balances' basis – that is, on the basis of a kind of mutual constraint that *requires* opposition between the separated powers. The object of the separation is precisely to establish a strategic interaction between the variously selected players. As in the cases examined earlier, this strategic interaction within the power structure of government may or may not be in the overall interests of citizens – and for more or less the same reasons as those earlier canvassed. Hence the continued relevance of the earlier discussion.

Note also that, unlike the arguments reviewed earlier, this argument in favour of the separation of powers is stronger the stronger is the system's ability to select appropriate agents and the finer is the ability to select for appropriate dispositions. Even if the capacity to select appropriate types is weak there may still be a case for the separation of powers. If we fill the separated roles with dispositional types entirely randomly, we might still expect that no one type will rule unchecked and hence hope to avoid extreme outcomes. However, this is a thin reed; we have to confront the prospect that the courts may be full of reckless buccaneers and the legislature full of compulsive rule followers, and that this may turn out to produce disproportionately bad outcomes. In general the strength of the case for separation on selectional grounds seems to depend on the capacity to select types accurately, and as that capacity improves so the case strengthens.

All of this points to a rather different and broader analysis of the separation of powers than in the case where agents are taken to be uniformly venal. The analysis is broader in that it incorporates the narrow analysis to the extent that political representatives are likely to be instrumental in their behaviour; but it is different in that it recognises an additional potential benefit deriving from the separation of powers acting as a virtue enhancing selection mechanism.

12

The division of power

All the powers of government, legislative, executive, and judiciary, result to the legislative body. The concentrating these in the same hands, is precisely the definition of despotic government. It will be no alleviation, that these powers will be exercised by a plurality of hands, and not by a single one. One hundred and seventy-three despots would surely be as oppressive as one.

(*Federalist* papers, 48, James Madison)

Divisions, bicameralism and coalitions

In the preceding chapter we defined a division of power in terms of spreading any particular power or bundle of powers across multiple agents rather than concentrating that power in the hands of a single agent. The division of power, so understood, is distinguished from the separation of powers, in that in the separation case a bundle of powers is disaggregated and the separate powers assigned to different agents. Both the division and separation of power involve multiple agents, but separation involves the additional feature that the domain of decision making by different agents is characteristically different. There are, in other words, two distinct dimensions in play here: the one dimension reflecting the number of agents who share any particular power; and the other dimension reflecting the extent to which the particular powers are disaggregated into their separate components. In the previous chapter we focused on the latter, separation dimension. Here we address the former, division dimension. The key idea here is captured by the shift from single-agent decision making to multiple-agent decision making, with the rules defining collective agreement (e.g. unanimity or majority) forming part of the institutional specification of any particular division of power.

The intuition that the division of power is likely to operate in the interests of citizens draws its primary force from the notion of bargaining and/or compromise. In a simple case, if any single individual is empowered to make a particular decision (subject to any constraints that may be imposed by considerations of re-election or other such devices), she will use whatever discretion is available to her to pursue her own desires. If, by contrast, the decision must be agreed by two individuals, these individuals must bargain with each other over possible outcomes so that the final result will be a compromise: neither will get exactly what she would have chosen in the single decision maker setting, but each does better than would be the case in the event of no agreement.

As in the previous chapter, we must immediately distinguish the idea of constraining politicians from the idea of benefiting citizens. While it is clear that forcing politicians to agree/compromise with each other will generally reduce the rents available to any politician below those accruing to that politician when she has undivided, dictatorial power, it is less clear that such compromise outcomes will necessarily provide significant benefits to the citizens at large. This leads directly to a second point. The nature of the compromise outcome will depend on several factors: most obviously, the desires of the parties to the compromise; the details of the process of bargaining; and the specification of the default outcome if agreement is not reached. Each of these elements is subject to institutional determination – election or appointment processes can influence the identity of the politicians and hence their desires; rules of political process can structure the bargaining game between politicians; default outcomes can be influenced by the rules for the dissolution of governments or for the calling of fresh elections; and so on. A central normative question then, is whether and how these institutional forces can be deployed to ensure that the division of power benefits citizens rather than merely serving to constrain politicians. This normative question will be in play throughout the ensuing discussion.

While compromise and bargaining are the key ideas underlying most arguments associated with the division of political power, they are not the only aspects of division that are normatively relevant. Once one allows for the wider range of motivational possibilities that we have earlier argued for, under the rubric of 'democratic desires', distinct kinds of arguments for division of power emerge quite naturally.

The idea of the division of power is already present in a number of the topics we have discussed. The account of political parties in chapter 10, for example, uses the idea of majority agreement within a party as the basis for normative comparison of a party system with a presidential system. Indeed, at the most fundamental level, the appeal of direct democracy relative to dictatorship is grounded on the idea of the division of power. However, the discussion in this chapter will focus on a specific class of institutional arrangements that implement a division of power within the structure of representative democracy. Perhaps the two leading examples of this class are bicameralism and coalitional government.[1] Bicameralism is characteristically defined in terms of the division of the legislature into two 'houses', with the requirement that any policy or proposed law must gain the support of a majority in each house in order to be approved. It is, however, clear that a similar structure is at work whenever two distinct bodies must approve a decision for that decision to be effective – even where the two bodies may not formally be defined as houses of the legislature. For example, the relationship between the US president and the Congress can be conceived as a kind of bicameralism (operating alongside other aspects of this relationship which are better thought of in terms of the functional separation of powers between the legislature and the executive). Coalitional government seems to provide another example of the same principle. Coalitions do not normally operate under a formal, constitutional requirement that decisions must be approved by a majority within each party to the coalition. Rather, the structure is one in which each party to the coalition must continually compare the relative attractions of continuing to support the coalition, at the cost of compromise on policy issues, with the cost of leaving the coalition, often with the effect of bringing down the government and precipitating an election. Coalitions, then, are concerned with preserving majority support within a house by bargaining and compromise between parties, while bicameralism is concerned with majority support in distinct houses which may each contain several parties.

The distinction between bicameralism and coalitional government should not be overdrawn. In the context of representative democracy dominated by political parties, bicameral systems may often be redescribed in coalitional terms, and vice versa. Take, for example, a political system with three political parties – R, S and T – and consider two alternative structures of the legislature. In a simple bicameral system let house 1 contain 50 party R members, 30 S members, and 10 T members; while house 2 contains 50 party S members, 30 R members and 10 T

---

[1] Recent discussions of the division of power in either the bicameral or the coalitional setting include Hammond and Miller (1987), Austen-Smith and Banks (1988), Fiorina (1992), Brennan and Hamlin (1992), Alesina and Rosenthal (1995), Persson *et al.* (1997) Tsebelis and Money (1997).

members. The requirement of bicameralism in this case is somewhat analogous to a form of coalition between R and S. Each of these parties controls an effective majority in one house and therefore has an effective veto on any policy enactment. Policies must, then, be agreed between the two parties. But the requirement of bicameralism, even in this simple case, is not equivalent to unicameral coalitional government, for if we were to combine the two houses in the example we would have a unicameral legislature with 80 members of party R, 80 members of party S and 20 members of party T. It is immediately clear that in this set up party T enjoys a much enhanced position, relative to the bicameral case, because the coalition between R and S is no longer the only possible coalition. It is, indeed, likely that the outcomes of the two political systems would differ even if the actual coalition in the unicameral case were R and S, because the shift from bicameralism to a unicameral coalition structure has changed the nature of the bargaining game between R and S, and granted T a share of the divided power.

In this way, bicameralism can often be seen as a restriction on the set of coalitions that might arise if the houses were merged – although, of course, bicameralism also allows of a division of power between parties when there are only two parties, while coalitional government is more normally concerned with cases in which the number of parties represented in the legislature is at least three. This last point is related to the point, made originally by Buchanan and Tullock (1962), that bicameralism in a legislature without political parties can be thought of as a particular restriction on the specification of the voting rule employed within the legislature. A bicameral structure in a legislature without parties will implement a sort of variable supra-majority decision-making rule, with the actual number of votes required to pass any particular legislation depending on the distribution of support across the two houses. Thus, for example, if the two houses are of equal size, it will be possible to enact legislation with a bare majority of legislators in favour, if those in favour are distributed evenly between the houses; but enaction is only guaranteed for all distributions of support across the chambers, when 75 per cent + 1 of all legislators are in favour.

Although the examples of bicameralism and coalitional government will recur in what follows, we will not organise our discussion around these two institutional forms. Rather, we will focus attention on the particular benefits that might be achieved by means of a division of power. We will then discuss some recent analyses of divided government from the literature. As in the previous chapter, this analysis of the division of power will be undertaken against the background of the standard economic model of motivation, and we will then explore the implications for the analysis of a move to the more moral motivational structure associated with democratic desires. In the last section we will offer a brief summary of our reflections on separating and dividing powers, drawing on the major themes of this chapter and the last.

The benefits of division

What sorts of benefits can the division of power provide? Although the central aim of any division of power must be to promote the public interest, it is important to recognise that the precise form the benefit takes may vary considerably from case to case. We will identify and discuss three forms of benefit: the benefit of centrism; the benefit of stability, and the benefit of insurance. We will discuss these three forms separately in what follows. However, we do not mean to imply that the forms are absolutely distinct. We offer these three labels as a convenient way of interpreting the continuum of forms that benefits might take – as providing different perspectives on the potential benefits associated with the division of powers that alert us to different ideas and different underlying mechanisms.

The centrism benefit

The basic idea involved in centrism is that while individual parties or political agents may take relatively extreme positions, the process of dividing a power between them will moderate these positions so that political outcomes will lie closer to the centre of the relevant political range. Since centrist outcomes can normally be expected to be in the *ex ante* interests of citizens – a point familiar from the normative evaluation of the median-voter result – any tendency for a division of power to generate centrist outcomes will typically count in its favour. This point is illustrated simply enough in the standard one-dimensional model of political decision making, repeated as figure 12.1. If R and S represent the policy positions adopted by the two political parties, any simple political process that grants all power to one or other of these parties must produce as its outcome either R or S (or, perhaps, an alternating pattern of R's and S's over time). However, dividing decision-making power between the two parties opens up the prospect of realising an outcome in the range between R and S. If the ideal point of the median voter (point M) lies in this range, as illustrated, it is clear that the division of power can act in the interests of citizens by shifting political outcomes towards M.

Can, but need not – several conditions must be fulfilled. First, and

Figure 12.1 One-dimensional division of power

most obviously, the parties who are to share power must be located on either side of the normatively preferred outcome. If R and S both lie on the same side of M, it is clear that the interests of the citizens will be served by granting undivided power to whichever party lies closer to M. From that reference point, any division of power will only serve to move the political outcome further from M. Divided power will however be superior to an arrangement in which R and S are equally likely or in which the outcome oscillates between R and S.

A slightly more subtle condition involves the degree of asymmetry between the parties and their relative bargaining strengths. If R and S are symmetric around M, it is clear that any policy outcome that emerges from a bargain between R and S must be closer to M than either R or S. This is just to say that any compromise between R and S will lie in the interval RS, and so will be closer to M when M is located at the midpoint of RS. But if R and S are asymmetric around M this logic fails. In particular, if RM is greater than MS – as shown in figure 12.1 – and if the bargaining power of R is great enough to ensure that the compromise outcome is close to R, then the political outcome under the division of power might be further from M than is the outcome associated with granting undivided power to S.

One might, of course, comment that it is unlikely that assigning all power to party S would be a feasible outcome if party R does indeed hold most of the bargaining power – a point the force of which we readily concede. In fact, neither bargaining strength nor party location is explained in this example. In any proper model, both would need to be derived in some fashion from a more basic set of parameters. But our object here is merely illustrative, and a more elaborate treatment seems unnecessary. One implication of the example is, however, worth underlining. This is that the benefit of centrism does presuppose that party positions are ideologically fixed: in the world of power seeking parties, the standard version of the median voter theorem would apply, with its characteristic feature of convergence of policy platforms. Only where, in equilibrium, we expect parties to differ significantly from each other can there be an argument for the division of power based on the benefit of centrism, and this occurs most obviously in models in which parties are taken to hold positions in policy space that are fixed independently of the distribution of

THE DIVISION OF POWER

citizen ideal points. In short, models in which non-convergence of political parties is a characteristic property are a necessary prerequisite of any account of the centrist benefit of the division of power.[2]

The stability benefit

A second potential benefit that might be associated with the division of power is what we will term the benefit of stability. Here the issue relates to the threat of global cycling discussed in chapter 7. Recall that, when the political issue space is multidimensional, there is the potential for global instability in the sense that there may be no policy platform that can win against all rivals. This fact gives rise to the concern over agenda control: voting behaviour can be manipulated by a strategic agenda setter to give rise to any political outcome. In this context, it is possible that a strategy of the division of powers can reduce the extent of potential cycling and, in the limit, impose stability.[3]

The nature of the argument can be best illustrated in a simple two-dimensional model of policy choice. Let figure 12.2 depict the two dimensions of policy denoted by X and Y, so that any point in the X, Y space identifies a particular policy outcome. Consider a community of six individuals labelled A–F and identified by their ideal points in the policy space (each is assumed to have simple Euclidean preferences centred on his ideal point). These six might be thought of as the members of a legislative assembly representing a larger political community. It is clear that, if these six are faced with a simple majority voting rule with no further structure placed on the process of their decision making, cycling can in general be expected.

However suppose a bicameral partition is imposed on the assembly, so that the decision making power previously enjoyed by the single house is now divided between two houses, defined in such a way that A, B and C form one house, while D, E and F form the other. Then the requirement of a simple majority in each house is sufficient to impose stability on the political outcome. To see this first construct the straight line through B and E, and consider a point on the line segment BE, such as P. The line through B and E is significant because – given this configuration of houses and ideal points – B and E are 'mutually regarding median voters' in their respective houses: that is, from the perspective of B, E appears as the

[2] Such models are discussed by Wittman (1977), Calvert (1985), Alesina (1988) and others. See Alesina and Rosenthal (1995) for more detail.
[3] See the discussion in Hammond and Miller (1987), Brennan and Hamlin (1992), Tsebelis and Money (1997).

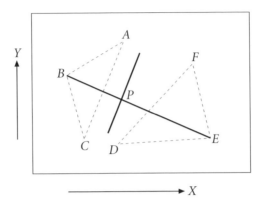

Figure 12.2 A two-dimensional division of power

median voter in the house *DEF*, while from the perspective of *E*, *B* appears as the median voter in the *ABC* house. In this illustration, the point *P* is chosen to lie on *BE* and outside of the convex hulls *ABC* and *DEF*. The claim is that *P* will be an equilibrium of the bicameral voting process.

For this claim to be true, *P* must defeat all alternatives under the bicameral voting rule, and this is indeed the case here. To see this, construct a second straight line through *P*, perpendicular to *BE*, so that four sectors are defined each including the ideal point of one representative – we will refer to these sectors by reference to the included representative. Now consider possible alternatives to *P*. If the alternative lies in the sector that includes *A* it is clear that *P* will be preferred to that alternative by at least both D and *E*: *P* will therefore command majority support against any such alternative in the *DEF* house, and so no such alternative can win in the bicameral system. Similarly, if the alternative lies in the sector that includes *D*, *P* must be preferred by at least both *A* and *B*, so that *P* will win majority support in the *ABC* house. And so on.

Of course, this illustration is very special, but similar argument shows that a bicameral division of power can always ensure the existence of an equilibrium in the two-dimensional case, for any distribution of ideal points, provided that the two houses are constructed appropriately. A sufficient condition is that the convex hulls of the sets of ideal points associated with each of the two houses are non-overlapping (as is the case in figure 12.2). Although this requirement is too strong, it does capture the importance of each house having a distinct character – only when the houses are constituted in such a way as to be clearly different from each other will bicameralism secure the existence of stable equilibria. In the limit (when the houses are completely distinct from each other, and internally homogeneous) it is almost as if each house is an individual agent, with the set of political equilibria defined as the set of points that lie on the contract curve between the two houses.

Three points of caution should be added immediately. The first is that this result does not generalise easily to the case of more than two dimensions. For bicameralism to induce the existence of equilibria in higher dimensional policy spaces, still more stringent conditions on the distributions of ideal points both within and between houses must apply. Accordingly, it is not always possible to construct bicameral partitions of the set of representatives such that the bicameral voting rule induces an equilibrium.[4] Second, it is clear from the illustrative argument outlined above that the equilibrium under any particular bicameral partition will not be unique (since there is latitude in the choice of P): there may be many different bicameral partitions each of which gives rise to a different equilibrium. For example, in figure 12.1, the six representatives might be arranged into the two houses defined by BAF and CED, in which case the relevant equilibria would lie on the line segment AD. Third, this discussion of the bicameral division of powers operates in a setting that pays no attention to political parties – and no real attention to the idea of representation. It might be thought that parties present no distinct problems: each party could be thought of as an individual voter with a well-determined position and the stability result simply extrapolated from the individual case. But there are additional complications – parties can represent different numbers of voters, and operate in both houses – and questions about precisely how the bicameral structure is devised and which parties receive a decisive voice become especially important. The issues here are related to those canvassed in chapter 9 in relation to the number of parties. We note them here but will not pursue them further at this point.

The insurance benefit

A third potential benefit that might be associated with the division of power might be termed the benefit of insurance. The idea here is that spreading a power across political agents may serve to reduce the risk associated with decision making, in the same way that spreading invest-ment across a portfolio of assets might be expected to reduce the overall risk to the capital. Of course, for any insurance benefit to arise there must

---

[4] Our earlier article, Brennan and Hamlin (1992), presented an argument on this topic. We now believe that the conditions required for equilibrium in three or more dimensions are still more stringent than we suggested there and, in particular, that symmetry in the distributions of ideal points is also required. See Tsebelis and Money (1997) for more detailed analysis.

be some risk in the political environment, but this is surely a natural assumption. The risk in question might take a number of forms. It might be that agents disagree in their beliefs about the impact of policies, and that the division of powers across such agents provides the basis for insuring against this form of uncertainty. In this case, there is a clear link between the benefit of insurance and the benefit of centrism – insurance is just a form of centrism in the dimension of uncertainty.

A slightly different interpretation of the insurance idea draws on the Condorcet jury theorems discussed in chapter 5. Recall that the jury theorems employ the idea of aggregating across essentially similar individuals each of whom is uncertain as to the correct policy to choose. The idea is similar in so far as aggregating across individuals reduces risk, but different in so far as we think of the individual agents as identical rather than holding distinct views. This link to the Condorcet jury theorems should alert us to the possibility that the division of power might be employed as a virtue enhancing mechanism as discussed in chapter 5 – a connection we will pursue below.

Related to the insurance idea is the thought that the division of power may act to reveal information. In situations where political agents have access to private information, they may exploit that informational advantage to extract rents. This is the basic structure of the principal–agent conception of politics discussed in chapter 7. If dividing power between agents can provide them with an improved incentive to reveal information then this may be expected to act in the interests of citizens by reducing their uncertainty. The connection between information revelation and insurance is simply that they are alternative ways of reducing the costs of uncertainty. One possible mechanism by which the division of power may serve to improve information revelation is the mechanism of debate. Imagine that citizens have no direct access to information on the true state of the economy, but that politicians do observe some parameters that provide at least some economic information relevant to policy making and evaluation. In the case of an undivided government power, the president can simply announce policy, and citizens will not learn anything about the true state of the economy that would enable them to evaluate that policy. In the case of a divided government power it may be that the debate and bargaining between politicians with a share in power has the effect of providing at least some information to citizens. Or it may not. There is no guarantee that the division of power and associated bargaining will improve information revelation; we merely note the possibility.[5]

---

[5] For further discussion of the possible information revelation effect of the division and separation of powers see Persson *et al.* (1997).

Divided government

With these potential benefits in mind, we now turn to two more specific models, both of which seek to incorporate the division of power within the traditional economic framework. The models differ in a number of ways – not least in the way they model political agents – but share the underlying feature of institutionally imposed compromise and bargaining. We will begin with the model presented by Persson *et al.* (1997), already mentioned in chapter 11, before going on to discuss a model developed by Alesina and Rosenthal (1995).

Recall that the baseline case in the Persson *et al.* (1997) model is that of an elected president motivated by the prospect of appropriating resources, constrained only by an imperfect electoral system. The first comparison is then with a simple institutionalisation of the separation of powers in which each of two elected agents has an independent power to appropriate resources. This gives rise to the 'common pool' case, discussed in chapter 11: the separation of powers in this case leaves citizens worse off.

Their next comparison is between the baseline case and that of a simple division of power, although Persson *et al.* do not use this particular terminology or distinguish between separations and divisions in any systematic way. The division of power introduced takes the form of a requirement that the two elected agents agree on the amounts to be appropriated – one agent proposes a policy package and hence appropriations for both agents, the other then accepts or rejects that proposal. If the proposal is rejected, a default outcome is implemented. It is not difficult to see that the outcome of this process is essentially identical to that under a single elected president. There is no longer a common pool or externality problem between the two agents, since the appropriations of the two politicians are co-ordinated. Since no externality is created, the division of power certainly does no harm to citizens. But it does no good for them either. The politician with the power to propose is limited by the need to offer the second politician sufficient to prevent her from vetoing the proposal in favour of the default option; once this constraint is met, the proposer is essentially a monopoly president as before. There is nothing in the process that benefits the taxpaying citizenry.

So far, then, the model offers a particular institutionalisation of the separation of powers that, taken by itself, acts against the interests of citizens; and a particular institutionalisation of a division of power that, taken by itself, has no impact on citizens. The authors then argue that the simultaneous adoption of both of these institutional strategies – so that powers are both separated and divided – does act in the citizens' interests.

More specifically, the two elected politicians are now set in the following context – referred to as 'two-stage budgeting'. The first agent proposes a total level of appropriation which may be accepted or rejected by the second agent (if it is rejected a default is implemented); the second agent then proposes an allocation of the total appropriation (agreed or default) across the two politicians, which may then be accepted or rejected by the first agent. If accepted, the agreed plan is implemented; if rejected, the default allocation is implemented. In this set-up, each agent has the power to propose in a different sphere (a separation of powers), while agreement is required in each sphere (a division of power). In the final move of the game, the first agent will accept any allocation that leaves her better off than the default option. Knowing this, the second agent will propose an allocation that offers the first agent the minimum amount that she will accept, and keeps the remainder for herself. But knowing this, the first agent will now set the total appropriation at a level which is just sufficient to allow both agents to gain just more than their default payments. If the total appropriation were larger than this, the first agent would not benefit since the second agent would capture all of the additional rent. In this way, the first agent is induced to act in the interests of the citizens in setting a low level of total appropriations.

This two-stage budgeting structure has much of the flavour of the 'you-cut-and-I'll-choose' type of separation of powers discussed in chapter 11; the question is, what additional role is played by the explicit division of power that requires agreement at both stages of the process? Consider a variant on the model in which no such agreement is required at either stage, so that agent one has the unilateral power to set the total appropriation and agent two has the unilateral power to determine the allocation of that appropriation. The last move of the game is now made by the second agent who will simply take the whole of the total appropriation for herself, leaving nothing for the first agent. Knowing this, the first agent would set the level of total appropriation at zero, and citizens would gain the maximum benefit possible. In this way, it seems that the role of the division of power in this model is minimal – it is the separation of powers that is doing the essential work. It might seem that our variant with no division of power actually offers citizens greater benefit since total appropriations will be zero, but this outcome simply reflects the fact that the default pay-off to each agent is zero, and in this case the model with the division of power also predicts the outcome of zero appropriation. Our claim is that – just as in the comparison between the baseline case and the simple division of power – the appropriate comparison between cases with and without the requirement of agreement reveals that this form of division of power has no impact on citizens. The contrast between the common-pool case and the two-stage budgeting case is due not to the division of powers and the need for agreement, but to the detailed differences between the form of the separation of powers in the two cases. Under two-stage budgeting, no adverse externality is introduced, and the strategic interaction between political agents works in favour of the citizens.

So, just as in the case of separations of powers, the division of power is by no means guaranteed to operate in the interests of citizens. The simple move from decision making by a single individual to decision making by a committee is not sufficient in itself to protect citizens. And this is most notably the case when political agents are modelled as essentially identical, as is the case in Persson *et al.* (1997). The second model we wish to discuss – presented by Alesina and Rosenthal (1995) – takes a very different perspective on the division of powers, one that is based on fundamental differences between political agents, and the possibility of strategic action by voters.

In outline the Alesina and Rosenthal model has the following structure. There are two disciplined political parties who adopt fixed ideological positions, such that if either party were elected to a position of absolute power it would adopt its own ideologically ideal policy package. These parties are labelled R and D, and their ideal policies θ_R and θ_D respectively. There are two separate elections: one for the presidency organised on a simple majority voting basis within the national electorate, and one for the legislature organised on a perfectly proportional representation basis, so that the two parties share the seats in exactly the proportions that they share the popular vote. The policy actually implemented, x, is then decided by bargaining between the president and the legislature, with the composition of the legislature (rather than just the identity of the majority party) playing a role. More specifically:

$$x = \alpha \theta p + (1 - \alpha)[V_R \theta_R + V_D \theta_D]$$

where θ_P is the ideal policy of the elected president, V_R and V_D are the vote shares of the parties in the legislature election, and $0 \leq \alpha \leq 1$ represents the weight or bargaining power of the president in policy formation. The term in the square bracket represents the policy position of the legislature and is simply the vote share-weighted average of the ideal policies of the two parties.[6]

Alesina and Rosenthal focus on the comparison between this structure and the simple case of a single elected president and, in particular, on the

---

[6] See Alesina and Rosenthal (1995), pp. 45–72. The equation given in the text combines their equations 3.1 and 3.2.

instrumentally rational voting behaviour of citizens (all of whom are assumed to vote, so that $V_R + V_D = 1$). In sharp contrast to the standard Downsian model of electoral competition in which parties or candidates are strategic in their choice of policy positions and voters relatively straightforward in their choice of which candidate to support, the Alesina and Rosenthal model involves non-strategic parties and offers voters a relatively rich set of strategic options. Specifically, many individual voters may have incentives to split their votes, voting for different parties in different elections in order to achieve outcomes that are closer to their personal ideals. And this possibility will be further encouraged if the elections are staggered so that, for example, the party affiliation of the president is already known at the time of the election of the legislature.

This line of argument leads to the identification of equilibrium strategies for voters which, in turn, imply equilibrium political outcomes. Broadly the conclusion is that, for a range of parameter values, the party winning the presidency does not obtain a majority of the votes (and therefore seats) in the legislature. Citizens optimally split their votes so as to ensure that the legislature acts as a counterbalance to the president and vice versa. When the party positions are roughly symmetric around the median voter's position, there are normally two equilibria, with either party winning the presidency and the other party holding the larger share of power in the legislature, while in the more asymmetric case there is just one equilibrium in which the party closer to the median voter's position wins the presidency and the other party typically holds more seats in the legislature. Of course there are also parameter values where equilibrium implies undivided government in the sense that the presidency and the majority in the legislature are in the hands of the same party; but even here the legislature moderates political outcomes. Indeed, all equilibria in this model produce outcomes that are identical to the ideal point of the median citizen, because assumptions about the sophistication of the voters ensure that this is so. Essentially, voters 'see through' the institutional structure of politics, including the ideological stands taken by parties, and focus on the real choice of policy. Because they vote strictly on the basis of policy, no outcome other than the median citizen's ideal point can be an equilibrium. The role of the political institutions in this type of model is to offer sophisticated voters enough degrees of freedom to exercise full control over political outcomes despite the involvement of imperfect political agents.

All of this may be seen as a detailed and extensive elaboration of the very simple model sketched earlier in outlining the idea of the benefit of centrism. But there are two points that we wish to take up. The first point concerns the detail of the model and the identification of the real institutional source of the benefit of centrism, and may be thought of as an attempt to clarify an aspect of the Alesina and Rosenthal model. To make the point, we shift attention from the comparison with simple presidential rule to the comparison with a structure of proportional representation in an elected legislature and without the role of a president. Given the notation outlined above, the policy outcome in the proportional representation case would just be:

$$x = [V_R\theta_R + V_D\theta_D]$$

and, depending on the sophistication of the voters, the outcome would again be at the median citizen's ideal point. The addition of the president to this model provides voters with an additional instrument but one that is inessential, since it does not change the fundamental ability of the electorate to gain the benefit of centrism in the presence of two ideologically fixed parties. Given sophisticated voters, this model of proportional representation is sufficient to achieve the benefits claimed of the division of powers between the president and the legislature. But notice that this model of proportional representation is a very special one – it identifies policy outcomes as the vote share-weighted average of the policy positions of parties and so invokes proportionality at the level of a policy determination rule. This model involves a conception of proportional representation that is a long way from more standard conceptions, which concern themselves only with the determination of the composition of the representative assembly. Proportional representation in this standard sense carries no implications at all about which policies will be implemented by the assembly. For example, if the decision rule within the assembly is simple majority voting, whichever party wins a majority of the popular vote in the election for the legislature will control the legislature and implement its own ideal policy. That form of proportional representation would not offer the benefit of centrism in the two-party case.

Thus, we would suggest that the Alesina and Rosenthal model contains two elements which should be distinguished. The particular characterisation of proportional representation as a policy determination rule is sufficient in itself to offer sophisticated voters the benefit of centrism. On the other hand, if the legislature were to be modelled as being controlled by the dominant party (whether dominance is achieved via a proportional representation voting rule or otherwise), then the division of power between the legislature and the president offers sophisticated voters an alternative means of achieving the benefit of centrism. Both the particular model of proportional representation and the division of power between legislature and president allow voters to see policy outcomes as weighted averages of the two party positions. Since there are only two parties, having two steps to the process of weighting, adds complexity without changing anything of fundamental significance.

In fact, proportional representation as a policy determination rule can itself be thought of as a form of the division of powers. To see this, think how such a policy determination rule could be institutionalised. We have already argued that the use of proportional representation as the method of electing representatives to the legislature is insufficient (and even unnecessary) to institutionalise proportional representation as a policy determination rule. It is the detailed structure and decision-making process within the legislature that is crucial. The point is that any institutionalisation of such a policy determination rule must itself involve a division of powers between political parties – perhaps by invoking a bicameral structure and ensuring that each party has control over one house. Whatever the institutional details, the aim would be to achieve a situation in which the institutional framework granted each party bargaining power that reflected its vote share.

The idea of sophisticated voters also leads us to our second point – which is more critical of the Alesina and Rosenthal approach. The Alesina and Rosenthal model of divided government places considerable stress on the instrumental nature of voting; citizens are modelled as 'seeing through' politicians and the political structure and as voting not for candidates or their policy platforms, but by reference to the ultimate impact that their vote will have on the policy outcome. But, as with most instrumental voting models, it is clear that any single citizen can expect to exert only a negligible impact on the final policy outcome. Even conceiving proportional representation as a policy determination rule in the way Alesina and Rosenthal do, the impact of a single vote on the relevant vote shares, and hence on policy outcomes, will be below the threshold of significance. We will not repeat our arguments against the instrumental account of voting – or our more positive arguments for an expressive account of voting. We simply point to the fact that arguments for the division of powers that are based on sophisticated instrumental voting make especially heavy demands on the instrumental account of voting; so that, to the extent that the instrumental model is flawed, so will be the derived account of the division of powers. And this fact seems to us to be important and to have implications well beyond the particular Alesina and Rosenthal model. We have argued that the benefits associated with the division of powers – and particularly the benefit of centrism – are most strikingly relevant in models, like the Alesina and Rosenthal model, in which parties adopt ideological positions. But within the standard economic motivational framework, this assumption itself is decidedly problematic. In that sense the assumptions of the model seem to negate the feasibility of the proffered solution. Of course, once parties are modelled in this way, it is natural to look to other mechanisms including specifically sophisticated voting as a means of generating outcomes that are more responsive to the interests of citizens. The basic role of the design of institutions in that context must be to give citizens the flexibility to counteract the fixity of the parties. But if sophisticated instrumental voting is problematic in its own terms – as we have argued – there seems to be relatively little scope for the strategy of the division of power.

Division of power and 'democratic desires'

Our discussion of models of the division of power constructed under standard economic assumptions suggest that while the division of power can offer benefits to citizens these benefits will often depend on sophisticated instrumental behaviour by citizen-voters. The obvious further question is whether there are alternative prospects for the division of power to work to the advantage of citizens under the more moral motivational assumptions that we have labelled 'democratic desires'? The answer to this question lies in the political mechanisms of screening, virtue production and virtue enhancing that were identified and discussed in chapter 5, since these are the additional mechanisms that are brought into play by the shift from standard economic motivations to democratic desires.

We have already suggested one possible case in which the division of power might act as a virtue enhancing mechanism. This possibility uses the division of power across political agents to increase the likelihood that at least some of the political agents are virtuous. Now, without any reliable screening effect, such a virtue enhancing effect can only operate successfully either if virtue is relatively common, or if the political process grants considerable power to individual politicians or small groups of politicians.

If virtue is common (say, the majority of representatives are virtuous in the relevant sense) dividing power to increase the number of representatives involved in policy decision making will act in the interests of citizens. This is a straightforward application of the Condorcet jury theorem. Consider a simple numerical example. Let 60 per cent of the relevant population of representatives (or potential representatives) be virtuous, understood in terms both of the desire and the capacity to promote the public interest. If a single representative is given discretionary decision-making power under these assumptions, the probability of a public-interested outcome is just 60 per cent. However if the power is divided even across a group of just three representatives, with decisions being made by simple majority voting within this group, the probability of obtaining a public-interested outcome rises to approximately 65 per cent, with the probability of a public-interested outcome rising further as the size of the committee grows.

If virtue is sufficiently scarce that only a minority of representatives are virtuous in the relevant sense, the logic of the Condorcet theorem operates in reverse. A public-interested outcome is more likely to emerge the smaller is the relevant committee, and hence there is a presumption against the division of power. This presumption may not, however, be decisive. Only if the non-virtuous majority is relatively homogeneous in terms of interests will the non-virtuous majority translate directly into policy outcomes that depart from the public-interested benchmark. If the non-virtuous majority differ significantly among themselves, the virtuous minority may still exert considerable influence over the outcome. In the simple case of a one-dimensional policy issue, for example, a sufficient condition for a public-interested outcome is that the median member of the group is virtuous.

Other decision-making procedures may also serve to enhance the effect of a virtuous minority. We gave a relatively detailed example in the context of enforcement in chapter 5. The most obvious decision-making processes which enhance the strength of minorities are more inclusive voting rules. Of course, such supra-majoritarian voting rules have been a key theme in traditional public choice scholarship since Buchanan and Tullock (1962), but the argument on which they are defended is essentially an argument about the reduction of the possibilities for inefficient exploitation of minority interests by majority interests. The difference here is that the recognition of a virtuous group improves the performance of any supra-majority voting rule by allying the virtuous group with the minority interest group.

In addition to supra-majoritarian voting, we would identify a further type of process that we would associate with the property of enhancing the effects of a virtuous minority within a structure of divided power – what might be termed 'whistle-blower' processes. The intuitive idea here is simple enough. In many settings, a minority – even a single individual – has the power to overturn or delay a decision by invoking some special procedure. Think of this invocation as 'whistle-blowing'. In practice it might take the form of mounting a legal challenge, or simply making public a previously private debate. The point is that whistle-blowing shifts the domain of the decision; new procedures become relevant – legal procedures perhaps. Now, if this were all that were at stake, whistle-blowing (and the threat of whistle-blowing) might be recognised as an activity that increased the power of the individual or minority group without necessarily favouring the virtuous: self-interested whistle-blowers might be just as effective against virtuous majorities as virtuous whistle-blowers were against interested majorities. But we believe that there is a further step to the argument that advantages the virtuous in the process of whistle-blowing. This step is simply that the process of whistle-blowing itself is (or can be) designed to favour certain types of argument over other types of argument. It is not possible to 'blow the whistle' on some activity or decision simply because you do not like that activity – simply because the decision operates against your private interests. In shifting from the normal domain of decision making to the exceptional domain, the argument must be presented in more disinterested terms if it is to be effective. After all, the normal domain is precisely the appropriate domain for the discourse of interests. And if whistle-blowing is more likely to succeed the more disinterested and public the argument, then whistle-blowing will indeed serve to enhance virtue.

If the strategy of dividing power can operate as a virtue enhancing mechanism – whether virtue is restricted to a minority or not – it is also plausible to argue that it can operate as a virtue producing mechanism. In other words, at least in some circumstances the division of power may operate to encourage a more virtuous choice of disposition. This is so because, as we argued in a more general context in chapters 4 and 6, anything that raises the return to virtue – that is, any institutional device that operates to generate public-interested outcomes from virtuous dispositions – will tend to encourage virtue in production.

The strategies of dividing power that seem to be recommended by these considerations may appear to be remote from the standard forms of bicameralism and coalitional government discussed at the outset of this chapter. The ideas here seem much more to do with voting rules, the design of committee procedure and the relationship between these. But, as we have tried to suggest, the distance between these areas may be more apparent than real. Bicameralism can be thought of as a particular structure of supra-majoritarian voting rule, and also as a form of coalitional government. The design of committee procedures influences the bargaining power of representatives and parties in the legislature. The design of a system of parliamentary committees, for example, may involve many aspects of the division of power: aspects of bicameralism – with the committee acting as a further 'house'; the provision of a whistle-blowing option to reinforce and enhance virtue; the creation of a further round of selection as parliamentarians are chosen by some process to sit on committees, and so on. Our point is just that many of these aspects are simply overlooked if the appropriate motivations and mechanisms – desires and devices – are ruled out by assumption.

Overview of separations and divisions of power

Our discussion of the separation and division of powers has ranged over considerable material. In summary, we have been critical of traditional lines of argument in at least two general senses. First, we have been insistent that not all separations and divisions of powers operate in the interests of citizens – in some cases the separation/division may be effectively useless and in others it may actually harm the citizenry. Second, we have argued that standard economic models of both separations and divisions of power miss out many of the potentially relevant aspects of these institutional devices in focusing almost exclusively on their incentive-related properties. The study of the structuring of power is both more open, and richer, than the existing literature might suggest.

The strategies of the separation and division of powers need to be set in the context of some of our other discussions of the key institutions of representative democracy. In particular we must confront the tension between the ideas of separation and division, on the one hand, and the idea of strong representative party government developed particularly in chapters 9 and 10. This tension is most clearly displayed by returning to a traditional example of the division of powers – bicameralism – and of the separation of powers – the separation of the executive and the legislature. In each of these examples, it is clear that the relevant separation or division can only be effective if the identified bodies are truly independent political agents. If the bodies are under the control of a single political party, there is no real separation or division. But, to make the same point in reverse, if the bodies are not under the control of a single party, any division or separation must involve some dilution of the clear political responsibility that we identify in our discussion of the merits of party organisation as critically important. If political policies are seen as compromises between parties – or as the outcome of strategic games between rival power centres – it is more difficult to recognise a particular government as principled, more difficult to hold politicians to account, more difficult to see politics as a vehicle for expressive activity and so on.

Of course, we do not mean to suggest that any move toward genuine separation or division of powers destroys the prospect of responsible and trustworthy politics – indeed, as we have been at pains to point out, some separations and divisions of powers may actually serve to reinforce and enhance the operation of virtue in politics. But we do recognise a trade off – a need to balance the sorts of benefits offered by strategies of separation and division against the sorts of benefits offered by strong and responsible party representation – the two are not fully compatible. This trade off, and the major theme of this book, might be (over)dramatised by contrasting three caricatures: the first a caricature of the orthodox rational actor model in the general style of the Alesina and Rosenthal model discussed earlier in this chapter; the second a caricature of a naive model of politics as an exercise in applied ethics – what we have termed the compliance view of politics; and the third a caricature of our own position developed throughout this book.

In the first case we have a view in which individual citizens are well informed, self-interested, sophisticated, instrumental voters, and political parties are ideological entities seen as vehicles for the interests of politicians. In this extreme context, there is no possibility of any idea of virtuous representation, no possibility of real responsibility, and the only relevant means of improving political outcomes is to design institutions that effectively wrest power back from parties and politicians and place it in the hands of the voters. Representative democracy is seen as an indirect means of implementing direct democracy.

In the second case, and at the opposite extreme, individual citizens are essentially moral and compliant so that political institutions are concerned chiefly with structuring the society in such a way as to encourage democratic deliberation, and avoid co-ordination and other collective action problems. Questions of the control of power do not arise.

To caricature our own position: individual citizens are both rational and moral, with considerable heterogeneity in motivations; most individuals are poorly informed on detailed political issues and voting is largely expressive in nature; representation operates as a selection mechanism, and parties reinforce that selection mechanism and enhance reliability. In this context, the design of democratic political institutions is preoccupied not only with limiting governmental or party power, but also with directing that power, with realising the potential of representative democracy rather than insisting on direct democracy as the appropriate benchmark.

These three caricatures clearly place our own approach in the middle ground between the two extremes – as we intended from the outset. But this position in the middle ground comes at the cost of additional conceptual and analytic complexity; the task of institutional design is inherently more difficult because the range of relevant considerations, and of the trade offs between them, is greater than at either extreme. For our own part, naturally, we see this extra complexity as essential if we are to use rational choice models to address the central issues of political theory in a manner that does not reduce those issues to shadows of their true selves. We hope that this book has both made an argument for the movement to this middle ground and provided some steps in that direction, though we concede readily enough that there is still a long way to go.

Bibliography

Aldrich, J. (1993), Rational Choice and Turnout, *American Journal of Political Science*, 37, 246–78.

(1995), *Why Parties?*, Chicago: University of Chicago Press.

Alesina, A. (1988), Credibility and Policy Convergence in a Two-party System with Rational Voters, *American Economic Review*, 78, 796–806.

Alesina, A. and Rosenthal, H. (1995), *Partisan Politics, Divided Government, and the Economy*, Cambridge: Cambridge University Press.

Anscombe, G. (1958), Modern Moral Philosophy, *Philosophy*, 1–19.

Arrow, K. (1963), *Social Choice and Individual Values* (2nd Edition), New York: Wiley.

(1974), *The Limits of Organisations*, New York: Norton.

Austen-Smith, D. and Banks, J. (1988), Elections, Coalitions and Legislative Outcomes, *American Political Science Review*, 82, 407–22.

Baker, K. (ed.) (1975), *Condorcet: Selected Writings*, Indianapolis: Bobbs-Merrill.

Baier, A. (1986), Trust and Antitrust, *Ethics*, 96, 231–60.

Barro, R. (1973), The Control of Politicians: an Economic Model, *Public Choice*, 14, 19–42.

Barry, B. (1980), Is it Better to be Powerful or Lucky? (parts I and II), *Political Studies*, 28, 183–94 and 338–52.

Becker, L. (1996), Trust as Noncognitive Security about Motives, *Ethics*, 107, 43–61.

Bell, D. (1976), *The Cultural Contradictions of Capitalism*, New York: Basic Books.

Besley, T. and Case, A. (1995), Does Electoral Accountability Affect Economic Policy Choices? Evidence from Gubernatorial Term Limits, *Quarterly Journal of Economics*, 110, 769–98.

Besley, T. and Coate, S. (1997), An Economic Model of Representative
    Democracy, *Quarterly Journal of Economics*, 112, 85–114.
Birch, A. H. (1972), *Representation*, London: Pall Mall.
Black, D. (1958), *The Theory of Committees and Elections*, Cambridge:
    Cambridge University Press.
Bohman, J. (1998), The Coming of Age of Deliberative Democracy, *Journal
    of Political Philosophy*, 6, 400–25.
Brams, S. and Fishburn, P. (1995), When is Size a Liability? Bargaining
    Power in Minimal Winning Coalitions, *Journal of Theoretical Politics*, 7,
    301–16.
Brennan, G. (1993), Economics, in Goodin, R. and Pettit, P. (eds.) *A
    Companion to Contemporary Political Theory*, Oxford: Basil Blackwell.
Brennan, G. and Buchanan, J. M. (1980a), Predictive Power and the Choice
    among Regimes, *Economic Journal*, 83, 89–105.
    (1980b), *The Power to Tax*, Cambridge: Cambridge University Press.
    (1985), *The Reason of Rules*, Cambridge: Cambridge University Press.
Brennan, G. and Hamlin, A. (1992), Bicameralism and Majoritarian
    Equilibrium, *Public Choice*, 74, 169–79.
    (1993), Rationalizing Parliamentary Systems, *Australian Journal of
    Political Science*, 28, 443–57.
    (1994), A Revisionist View of the Separation of Powers, *Journal of
    Theoretical Politics*, 6, 345–68.
    (1995a), Constitutional Political Economy: The Political Philosophy of
    homo economicus?, *Journal of Political Philosophy*, 3, 280–303.
    (1995b), Economising on Virtue, *Constitutional Political Economy*, 6,
    35–56.
    (1998), Expressive Voting and Electoral Equilibrium, *Public Choice*, 95,
    149–75.
    (1998), Fiscal Federalism, in Newman, P. (ed.) *The New Palgrave
    Dictionary of Economics and the Law*, London: Macmillan.
    (1999), On Political Representation, *British Journal of Political Science*, 29,
    109–27.
    (forthcoming), Nationalism and Federalism: the Political Constitution of
    Peace, in Galeotti, G., Salmon, P. and Wintrobe, R. (eds.) *Competition
    and Structure: The Political Economy of Collective Decisions. Essays in
    Honor of Albert Breton*, Cambridge: Cambridge University Press.
Brennan, G. and Kliemt, H. (1994), Finite Lives and Social Institutions,
    Kyklos, 47, 551–72.
Brennan, G. and Lomasky, L. (1985), The Impartial Spectator goes to
    Washington, *Economics and Philosophy*, 1, 189–212.
    (1993), *Democracy and Decision*, Cambridge: Cambridge University Press.
    (1997), Is There a Duty to Vote?, *mimeo*.
Brennan, G. and Pettit, P. (1990), Unveiling the Vote, *British Journal of
    Political Science*, 20, 311–33.

Buchanan, J. M. (1954), Social Choice, Democracy and Free Markets, *Journal of Political Economy*, 62, 114–23.

(1964) What Should Economists Do?, *Southern Economic Journal*, 30, 213–22.

(1979) *What Should Economists Do?*, Indianapolis: Liberty Press.

(1984), Politics without Romance, in Buchanan, J. M. and Tollison, R. (eds.) *The Theory of Public Choice II*, Ann Arbor: University of Michigan Press.

(1990) The Domain of Constitutional Economics, *Constitutional Political Economy*, 1, 1–18.

Buchanan, J. M. and Congleton, R. (1998), *Politics by Principle*, Cambridge: Cambridge University Press.

Buchanan, J. M. and Tullock, G. (1962), *The Calculus of Consent*, Ann Arbor: University of Michigan Press.

Buchanan, J. M., Tollison, R. and Tullock, G. (eds.) (1980) *Towards a Theory of the Rent Seeking Society*, College Station: Texas A&M University Press.

Burke, E. (1975), *Edmund Burke on Government, Politics and Society* (ed. B. W. Hill), London: Fontana.

Calvert, R. (1985), Robustness of the Multidimensional Voting Model: Candidates' Motivations, Uncertainty and Convergence, *American Journal of Political Science*, 29, 69–95.

Coase, R. (1937), The Nature of the Firm, *Economica*, 4, 386–405.

(1988a), The Nature of the Firm: Origins, *Journal of Law, Economics and Organisation*, 4, 1–18.

(1988b), The Nature of the Firm: Meaning, *Journal of Law, Economics and Organisation*, 4, 19–32.

(1988c), The Nature of the Firm: Influence, *Journal of Law, Economics and Organisation*, 4, 33–47.

Cohen, J. (1989), Deliberation and Democratic Legitimacy, in Hamlin, A. and Pettit, P. (eds.) *The Good Polity*, Oxford: Basil Blackwell.

Cohen, J. and Rogers, J. (1983), *On Democracy*, Harmondsworth: Penguin.

Comanor, W. (1976), The Median Voter Rule and the Theory of Political Choice, *Journal of Public Economics*, 5, 169–77.

Coughlin, P. (1982), Pareto Optimality of Policy Proposals with Probabilistic Voting, *Public Choice*, 39, 427–34.

(1990), Majority Rule and Election Models, *Journal of Economic Surveys*, 3, 157–88.

Dixit, A. (1996), *The Making of Economic Policy: a Transactions Cost Approach*, Cambridge, Mass.: MIT Press.

Downs, A. (1957), *An Economic Theory of Democracy*, New York: Harper and Row.

Dummett, M. (1997), *Principles of Electoral Reform*, Oxford: Oxford University Press.

Elkin, S. (1996), Madison and After: the American Model of Political Constitution, *Political Studies*, 44, 592–604.

Elkin, S. and Soltan, K. (eds.) (1993), *A New Constitutionalism*, Chicago: University of Chicago Press.

Ellison, G. (1994), Cooperation in the Prisoner's Dilemma with Anonymous Random Matching, *Review of Economic Studies*, 61, 567–88.

Elster, J. (1979), *Ulysses and the Sirens*, Cambridge: Cambridge University Press.

(1983), *Sour Grapes*, Cambridge: Cambridge University Press.

(1986), The Market and the Forum: Three Varieties of Political Theory, in Elster, J. and Hylland, A. (eds.) *The Foundations of Social Choice Theory*, Cambridge: Cambridge University Press.

Enelow, J. and Hinich, M. (1990), *Advances in the Spatial Theory of Voting*, Cambridge: Cambridge University Press.

Epple, D. and Romer, T. (1991), Mobility and Redistribution, *Journal of Political Economy*, 99, 828–58.

Feddersen, T. and Pesendorfer, W. (1998), Convicting the Innocent: the Inferiority of Unanimous Jury Verdicts under Strategic Voting, *American Political Science Review*, 92, 23–35.

Fiorina, M. (1992), *Divided Government*, New York: Macmillan.

Fishkin, J. (1991), *Democracy and Deliberation*, New Haven, Conn.: Yale University Press.

Flowers, M. (1988), Shared Tax Sources in a Leviathan Model of Federalism, *Public Finance Quarterly*, 16, 67–77.

Foot, P. (1978), *Virtues and Vices*, Oxford: Basil Blackwell.

Frank, R. (1988), *Passions within Reason*, New York: Norton.

Frankfurt, H. (1971), Freedom of the Will and the Concept of a Person, *Journal of Philosophy*, 68, 5–20.

Frey, B. (1997a), A Constitution for Knaves Crowds out Civic Virtues, *Economic Journal*, 107, 1043–53.

(1997b), *Not Just for the Money*, Cheltenham: Edward Elgar.

Gambetta, D. (ed.) (1988), *Trust: Making and Breaking Co-operative Relations*, Oxford: Basil Blackwell.

Gauthier, D. (1986), *Morals by Agreement*, Oxford: Oxford University Press.

Geach, P. (1977), *The Virtues*, Cambridge: Cambridge University Press.

Goodin, R. (1986), Laundering Preferences, in Elster, J. and Hylland, A. (eds.) *The Foundations of Social Choice Theory*, Cambridge: Cambridge University Press.

Griffin, J. (1996), *Value Judgements: Improving our Ethical Beliefs*, Oxford: Oxford University Press.

Hamlin, A. (ed.) (1996), *Ethics and Economics* (2 vols.), Cheltenham: Edward Elgar.

Hamlin, A. (1996), Promoting Integrity and Virtue: the Institutional Dimension, *The Good Society*, 6, 35–40.

Hamlin, A. and Hjortlund, M. (1999), Proportional Representation with Citizen Candidates, *Public Choice*, in press.

Hamlin, A. and Pettit, P. (1989), The Normative Analysis of the State, in Hamlin, A. and Pettit, P. (eds.) *The Good Polity*, Oxford: Basil Blackwell.

Hammond, T. and Miller, G. (1987), The Core of the Constitution, *American Political Science Review*, 81, 1155–74.

Hampton, J. (1997), The Wisdom of the Egoist: the Moral and Political Implications of Valuing the Self, *Social Philosophy and Policy*, 14, 21–51.

Hardin, R. (1996), Trustworthiness, *Ethics*, 107, 26–42.

Harrington, J. E. and Hess, G. D. (1996), A Spatial Theory of Positive and Negative Campaigning, *Games and Economic Behaviour*, 17, 209–29.

Hausman, D. and McPherson, M. (1996), *Economic Analysis and Moral Philosophy*, Cambridge: Cambridge University Press.

Hayek, F. (1945), The Use of Knowledge in Society, *American Economic Review*, 35, 519–30.

Hirsch, F. (1976), *Social Limits to Growth*, Cambridge, Mass.: Harvard University Press.

Hirschman, A. (1971), *Exit, Voice and Loyalty*, Cambridge, Mass.: Harvard University Press.

(1982), *Shifting Involvements*, Oxford: Blackwell.

(1985), Against Parsimony, *Economics and Philosophy*, 1, 7–21.

Hobbes, T. (1651/1968), *Leviathan* (ed. C. B. McPherson), Harmondsworth: Penguin

Hochman, O., Pines, D. and Thisse, J.-F. (1995), On the Optimal Structure of Local Governments, *American Economic Review*, 85, 1224–40.

Holler, M. (1982), Forming Coalitions and Measuring Voting Power, *Political Studies*, 30, 262–71.

(1983), Power, Luck and the Right Index, *Journal of Economics*, 43, 21–9.

(1998), Two Stories, One Power Index, *Journal of Theoretical Politics*, 10, 179–90.

Hollis, M. (1998), *Trust within Reason*, Cambridge: Cambridge University Press.

Hume, D. (1985), *Essays Moral, Political and Literary* (ed. E. Miller), Indianapolis: Liberty Classics.

Ingberman, D. and Rosenthal, H. (1995), Median Voter Theorems for Divisible Government, *Mimeo*, Department of Politics, Princeton University.

Inman, R. and Rubinfeld, D. (1996), Designing Tax Policy in Federalist Economies: an Overview, *Journal of Public Economics*, 60, 307–34.

Jones, K. (1996), Trust as an Affective Attitude, *Ethics*, 107, 4–25.

Jones, P. and Hudson, J. (1998), The Role of Political Parties: an Analysis based on Transactions Costs, *Public Choice*, 94, 175–89.

Kandori, M. (1992), Social Norms and Community Enforcement, *Review of Economic Studies*, 59, 63–80.

Kelman, S. (1987), Public Choice and Public Spirit, *Public Interest*, 87, 80–94.

Kolm, S.-C. (1996), Moral Public Choice, *Public Choice*, 87, 117–41.

Ledyard, J. (1984), The Pure Theory of Large Two-Candidate Elections, (1995), Public Goods: a Survey of Experimental Research, in Kagel, J. and Roth, A. (eds.) *Handbook of Experimental Economics*, Amsterdam: North Holland.

Levin, J. and Nalebuff, B. (1995), An Introduction to Vote-Counting Schemes, *Journal of Economic Perspectives*, 9, 3–26.

Lewis, D. (1989), Dispositional Theories of Value, *Proceedings of the Aristotelian Society*, 63, 113–37.

MacIntyre, A. (1981), *After Virtue*, London: Duckworth.

Manin, B. (1997), *The Principles of Representative Government*, Cambridge: Cambridge University Press.

Mansbridge, J. (1990), *Beyond Self-interest*, Chicago: University of Chicago Press.

Marlow, M. (1992), Intergovernmental Competition: Voice and Exit Options and the Design of Fiscal Structures, *Constitutional Political Economy*, 3, 73–88.

McGuire, M. and Olson, M. (1996), The Economics of Autocracy and Majority Rule, *Journal of Economic Literature*, 34, 72–96.

McKelvey, R. (1976) Intransitivities in Multidimensional Voting Models and some Implications for Agenda Control, *Journal of Economic Theory*, 12, 472–82.

(1979), General Conditions for Global Intransitivities in Formal Voting Models, *Econometrica*, 47, 1085–1110.

McLean, I. and Hewitt, F. (1994), *Condorcet: Foundations of Social Choice and Political Theory*, Cheltenham: Edward Elgar.

McLean, I. and Poulton, J. (1987), Good Blood, Bad Blood and the Market: the Gift Relationship Revisited, *Journal of Public Policy*, 6, 431–45.

Mill, J. S. (1861/1946), *Considerations on Representative Government* (ed. R. McCallum), Oxford: Basil Blackwell.

Mueller, D. (1989), *Public Choice II*, Cambridge: Cambridge University Press. (1996), *Constitutional Democracy*, Oxford: Oxford University Press.

Myerson, R. (1995), Analysis of Democratic Institutions: Structure Conduct and Performance, *Journal of Economic Perspectives*, 9, 77–89.

Myerson, R. and Weber, R. (1993), A Theory of Voting Equilibria, *American Political Science Review*, 87, 102–14.

Olson, M. (1965), *The Logic of Collective Action*, Cambridge, Mass.: Harvard University Press.

Ortuno-Ortin, I. (1997), A Spatial Model of Political Competition and Proportional Representation, *Social Choice and Welfare*, 14, 427–38.

Osborne, M. and Slivinski, A. (1996), A Model of Political Competition with Citizen-Candidates, *Quarterly Journal of Economics*, 111, 65–96.

Palfrey, T. (1984), Spatial Equilibrium with Entry, *Review of Economic Studies*, 51, 139–56.

Parfit, D. (1984), *Reasons and Persons*, Oxford: Oxford University Press.

Persson, T. and Tabellini, G. (1996a), Federal Fiscal Constitutions: Risk Sharing and Moral Hazard, *Econometrica*, 64, 623–46.

(1996b), Federal Fiscal Constitutions: Risk Sharing and Redistribution, *Journal of Political Economy*, 104, 979–1009.

Persson, T., Roland, G. and Tabellini, G. (1997), Separation of Powers and Political Accountability, *Quarterly Journal of Economics* 112, 1163–1202.

(1998), Comparative Politics and Public Finance, *mimeo*.

Pettit, P. and Brennan, G. (1986), Restrictive Consequentialism, *Australasian Journal of Philosophy*, 64, 438–55.

Pitkin, H. F. (1967), *The Concept of Representation*, Los Angeles: University of California Press.

Pomper, G. (1992), Concepts of Political Parties, *Journal of Theoretical Politics*, 4, 13–59.

Rawls, J. (1993), *Political Liberalism*, New York: Columbia University Press.

Robertson, D. (1956), *Economic Commentaries*, London: Staples Press.

Rowley, C. (ed.) (1993), *Social Choice Theory* (3 Volumes), Cheltenham: Edward Elgar.

Sabine, G. H. (1973), *A History of Political Theory* (3rd edn.), London: Harrap.

Sally, D. (1995), Conversation and Cooperation in Social Dilemmas, *Rationality and Society*, 7, 58–92.

Samuelson, P. (1954) The Pure Theory of Public Expenditure, *Review of Economics and Statistics*, 36, 387–89.

(1955) Diagrammatic Exposition of a Theory of Public Expenditure, *Review of Economics and Statistics*, 37, 350–56.

(1958) Aspects of Public Expenditure Theories, *Review of Economics and Statistics*, 40, 332–38.

Schmidtz, D. (1995), *Rational Choice and Moral Agency*, Princeton: Princeton University Press.

Schultz, C. (1996), Polarization and Inefficient Policies, *Review of Economic Studies*, 63, 331–43.

Schumpeter, J. (1950), *Capitalism, Socialism and Democracy* (3rd edn.), New York: Harper and Row.

Segal, J. (1997), Separation of Powers Games in the Positive Theory of Congress and Courts, *American Political Science Review*, 91, 28–44.

Sen, A. (1970), *Collective Choice and Social Welfare*, San Fransisco: Holden-Day.

Shepsle, K. (1986), The Positive Theory of Legislative Institutions, *Public Choice*, 50, 135–78.

Shepsle, K. and Weingast, B. (1981), Structure Induced Equilibrium and Legislative Choice, *Public Choice*, 37, 503–19.

Slote, M. (1997), The Virtue in Self-Interest, *Social Philosophy and Policy*, 14, 264–85.

Slutsky, S. (1975), Abstentions and Majority Equilibrium, *Journal of Economic Theory*, 11, 292–304.

Smith, M. (1994), *The Moral Problem*, Oxford: Basil Blackwell.

Stigler, G. (1981), Economics or Ethics?, in McMurrin, S. (ed.) *Tanner Lectures on Human Values* (vol. II), Cambridge: Cambridge University Press.

Stiglitz, J. (1989) *The Economic Role of the State*, Oxford: Basil Blackwell.

Taylor, G. (1985), *Pride, Shame and Guilt*, Oxford: Clarendon Press.

Tideman, N. (1995), The Single Transferable Vote, *Journal of Economic Perspectives*, 9, 27–38.

Tiebout, C. (1956), A Pure Theory of Local Expenditures, *Journal of Political Economy*, 64, 416–24.

Tirole, J. (1988), *The Theory of Industrial Organisation*, Cambridge, Mass.: MIT Press.

　(1996), A Theory of Collective Reputations, *Review of Economic Studies*, 63, 1–22.

Titmuss, R. (1970), *The Gift Relationship*, London: Allen & Unwin.

Tsebelis, G. and Money, J. (1997) *Bicameralism*, Cambridge: Cambridge University Press.

Tullock, G. (1971), The Charity of the Uncharitable, *Western Economic Journal*, 9, 379–92.

　(1981), Why So Much Stability?, *Public Choice*, 37, 189–202.

Vile, M. D. C. (1967), *Constitutionalism and the Separation of Powers*, Oxford: Oxford University Press.

Ware, A. (1979), *The Logic of Party Democracy*, New York: St Martin's Press.

Weber, S. (1992), On Hierarchical Spatial Competition, *Review of Economic Studies*, 59, 407–25.

Weingast, B. (1984), The Congressional-Bureaucratic System: a Principal–Agent Perspective, *Public Choice*, 44, 147–92.

Williams, B. (1973), *Problems of the Self*, Cambridge: Cambridge University Press.

　(1978), Politics and Moral Character, in S. Hampshire (ed.) *Public and Private Morality*, Cambridge: Cambridge University Press.

Williamson, O. (1964), *The Economics of Discretionary Behavior*, Englewood Cliffs, New Jersey: Prentice Hall.

　(1985), *The Economic Institutions of Capitalism*, New York: Free Press.

Wilson, J. (1973), *Political Organisations*, New York: Basic Books.

Wittman, D. (1977), Candidates with Policy Preferences: a Dynamic Model, *Journal of Economic Theory*, 14, 180–9.

(1995), *The Myth of Democratic Failure*, Chicago: University of Chicago Press.

Young, P. (1995), Optimal Voting Rules, *Journal of Economic Perspectives*, 9, 51–64.

Index